# USING

## microsoft®
# publisher
## 2010

Brien Posey

WITHDRAWN

**que®**

800 East 96th Street, Indianapolis, Indiana 46240 USA

# Using Microsoft® Publisher 2010

## Copyright © 2011 by Pearson Education, Inc.

ISBN-13: 978-0-7897-4296-4
ISBN-10: 0-7897-4296-9
The Library of Congress Cataloging-in-Publication Data is on file.
Printed in the United States of America
First Printing: August 2010

## Trademarks

## Warning and Disclaimer

## Bulk Sales

Que Publishing offers excellent discounts on this book when ordered in quantity for bulk purchases or special sales. For more information, please contact

**U.S. Corporate and Government Sales**
**1-800-382-3419**
**corpsales@pearsontechgroup.com**

For sales outside of the U.S., please contact

**International Sales**
**international@pearson.com**

**Associate Publisher**
Greg Wiegand

**Senior Acquisitions Editor**
Loretta Yates

**Development Editor**
Mark Cierzniak

**Managing Editor**
Sandra Schroeder

**Senior Project Editor**
Tonya Simpson

**Copy Editor**
Water Crest Publishing

**Indexer**
Brad Herriman

**Proofreader**
Language Logistics

**Technical Editor**
JoAnn Paules

**Publishing Coordinator**
Cindy Teeters

**Cover Designer**
Anna Stingley

**Designer**
Anne Jones

**Compositor**
Mark Shirar

# Contents at a Glance

Introduction

1     An Introduction to Publisher 2010

2     Getting Started with Publisher 2010

3     Working with Visual Elements

4     Designs and Layouts

5     Working with Longer Documents

6     Tables

7     Finalizing Your Publisher Document

8     Printing Your Documents

9     Publishing Online

10    Bulk Mailing Techniques

Index

# Media Table of Contents

To register this product and gain access to the Free Web Edition and the audio and video files, go to quepublishing.com/using.

Chapter 1:     **An Introduction to Publisher 2010**

Show Me  **Media 1.1**—Installing Microsoft Office 2010 ....................14
Show Me  **Media 1.2**—Uninstalling Microsoft Office 2010 ..............16
Tell Me More  **Media 1.3**—How Different Is Publisher 2010 from
Publisher 2007? ....................20

Chapter 2:     **Getting Started with Publisher 2010**

Show Me  **Media 2.1**—Creating a New Document ....................22
Show Me  **Media 2.2**—Grid Guides ....................27
Show Me  **Media 2.3**—Using Ruler Guides ....................31
Show Me  **Media 2.4**—Creating a Document from a Template ..........44
Show Me  **Media 2.5**—Saving Your Document ....................49
Tell Me More  **Media 2.6**—Do You Really Need Guides and Rulers? ......50

Chapter 3:     **Working with Visual Elements**

Show Me  **Media 3.1**—Creating a Text Box ....................54
Show Me  **Media 3.2**—Working with Fonts ....................59
Show Me  **Media 3.3**—Picture Styles and Shapes ....................62
Show Me  **Media 3.4**—Fill Effects ....................70
Show Me  **Media 3.5**—Creating 3-D Shapes ....................75
Tell Me More  **Media 3.6**—Avoiding Visual Element Overkill ............83

Chapter 4:     **Designs and Layouts**

Show Me  **Media 4.1**—Creating a Calendar ....................88
Show Me  **Media 4.2**—Creating a Postcard ....................91
Show Me  **Media 4.3**—Creating a Custom Color Scheme ............95
Show Me  **Media 4.4**—Using WordArt ....................100
Tell Me More  **Media 4.5**—More Design Ideas ....................107

Chapter 5:     **Working with Longer Documents**

Show Me  **Media 5.1**—Linking Text Boxes ....................112
Show Me  **Media 5.2**—Creating Master Pages ....................116
Show Me  **Media 5.3**—Importing Word Documents ..............120
Show Me  **Media 5.4**—Text Wrapping ....................128
Tell Me More  **Media 5.5**—Keeping Large Documents Reasonable ....137

Chapter 6:     **Tables**

Show Me  **Media 6.1**—Creating a Table ....................143
Show Me  **Media 6.2**—Formatting Tables and Cells ....................155
Show Me  **Media 6.3**—Importing Spreadsheets ....................159
Show Me  **Media 6.4**—Creating a Chart ....................165
Tell Me More  **Media 6.5**—The Practicality of Using Spreadsheet
Data in Publisher ....................165

Chapter 7:     **Finalizing Your Publisher Document**

Show Me  **Media 7.1**—Adjusting Design Elements ....................176

Show Me  **Media 7.2**—Adding Metadata ............................179
Show Me  **Media 7.3**—Adding Business Information ....................180
Show Me  **Media 7.4**—Design Checking ............................185
Tell Me More  **Media 7.5**—Final Thoughts on the Design Checker ......185

Chapter 8:   **Printing Your Documents**

Show Me  **Media 8.1**—Choosing a Color Model .........................197
Show Me  **Media 8.2**—Using Spot Color ............................200
Show Me  **Media 8.3**—Using the Pack and Go Wizard ..................204
Tell Me More  **Media 8.4**—Considerations for Commercial Printing ....206

Chapter 9:   **Publishing Online**

Show Me  **Media 9.1**—Creating a Simple Website ......................210
Show Me  **Media 9.2**—Adding Elements to a Web Page ..................218
Show Me  **Media 9.3**—Creating a Full-Blown Website ..................222
Tell Me More  **Media 9.4**—Your Options for Web Development ..........231

Chapter 10:   **Bulk Mailing Techniques**

Show Me  **Media 10.1**—Filtering ................................239
Show Me  **Media 10.2**—A Basic Mail Merge .........................245
Show Me  **Media 10.3**—E-mail Merge ............................251
Tell Me More  **Media 10.4**—The Importance of Reviewing Your
Documents Before Merging Business Data ............................256

# Table of Contents

Introduction ........................................................................1

1   **An Introduction to Publisher 2010** .................**5**

What Is Microsoft Publisher? ...........................................7

Getting Started ...................................................................8

System Requirements .........................................................8

   Minimum Hardware Requirements for Office 2010 ..............9

   System Requirements for Publisher 2010 .........................10

   Operating System Requirements .........................................10

   My Recommendations ...........................................................10

   Verifying Your System's Hardware .....................................11

Installing Office 2010 .......................................................12

What's New in Publisher 2010 ........................................16

   The Ribbon ..............................................................................16

   How Documents Are Displayed ...........................................18

   Going Backstage ....................................................................18

   Printing ....................................................................................18

   PDF and XPS Support ............................................................18

   Image Controls .......................................................................19

   Minor Improvements .............................................................20

   What's Up with Web Mode? .................................................20

2   **Getting Started with Publisher 2010** .............**21**

Using Publisher for the First Time .................................21

Creating a New Document ...............................................21

Page Margins .....................................................................22

   Custom Margins .....................................................................23

Grid Guides .......................................................................25

   Built-In Guides .......................................................................27

Ruler Guides ......................................................................27

   High-Precision Guides ...........................................................29

   Using Multiple Ruler Guides ................................................30

   Enabling and Disabling Rulers .............................................32

   Enlarging Rulers .....................................................................32

   Changing the Units of Measurement ..................................33

   Moving Rulers .........................................................................33

   Moving the Zero Mark ...........................................................35

Page Orientation ..............................................................37

Page Sizes ..........................................................................38

Page Backgrounds . . . . . . . . . . . . . . . . . . . . . . . . . . . . . . . . . . . . . . . . . . . . . 40

Templates . . . . . . . . . . . . . . . . . . . . . . . . . . . . . . . . . . . . . . . . . . . . . . . . . . . . . 40
    Web-Based Templates . . . . . . . . . . . . . . . . . . . . . . . . . . . . . . . . . . . . 41
    Locally Installed Templates . . . . . . . . . . . . . . . . . . . . . . . . . . . . . . . . 43
    The Anatomy of a Template-Based Document . . . . . . . . . . . . . 44
    Changing Templates . . . . . . . . . . . . . . . . . . . . . . . . . . . . . . . . . . . . . . 45
    Creating a Custom Template . . . . . . . . . . . . . . . . . . . . . . . . . . . . . . 45

Saving Your Documents . . . . . . . . . . . . . . . . . . . . . . . . . . . . . . . . . . . . . . 47
    Alternative Document Types . . . . . . . . . . . . . . . . . . . . . . . . . . . . . . 47

Creating a New Document . . . . . . . . . . . . . . . . . . . . . . . . . . . . . . . . . . . 49

Opening a Publisher Document . . . . . . . . . . . . . . . . . . . . . . . . . . . . . . 50

**3   Working with Visual Elements** . . . . . . . . . . . . . . . . . . . . . . . . **51**

Text Boxes . . . . . . . . . . . . . . . . . . . . . . . . . . . . . . . . . . . . . . . . . . . . . . . . . . . 51
    Creating a New Text Box . . . . . . . . . . . . . . . . . . . . . . . . . . . . . . . . . . 52
    Entering Text into a Text Box . . . . . . . . . . . . . . . . . . . . . . . . . . . . . . 53

Fonts . . . . . . . . . . . . . . . . . . . . . . . . . . . . . . . . . . . . . . . . . . . . . . . . . . . . . . . . . 54
    Purchasing Fonts . . . . . . . . . . . . . . . . . . . . . . . . . . . . . . . . . . . . . . . . . 54
    Typography . . . . . . . . . . . . . . . . . . . . . . . . . . . . . . . . . . . . . . . . . . . . . . 56
    Installing a Font . . . . . . . . . . . . . . . . . . . . . . . . . . . . . . . . . . . . . . . . . . 56
    Previewing a Font . . . . . . . . . . . . . . . . . . . . . . . . . . . . . . . . . . . . . . . . 57
    Formatting Pictures . . . . . . . . . . . . . . . . . . . . . . . . . . . . . . . . . . . . . . 60
    Transparency . . . . . . . . . . . . . . . . . . . . . . . . . . . . . . . . . . . . . . . . . . . . 60
    Picture Styles and Shapes . . . . . . . . . . . . . . . . . . . . . . . . . . . . . . . . 62
    Changing a Picture . . . . . . . . . . . . . . . . . . . . . . . . . . . . . . . . . . . . . . . 62
    Picture Captions . . . . . . . . . . . . . . . . . . . . . . . . . . . . . . . . . . . . . . . . . 63
    Changing a Caption's Color . . . . . . . . . . . . . . . . . . . . . . . . . . . . . . . 64
    Going Beyond Simple Colors . . . . . . . . . . . . . . . . . . . . . . . . . . . . . 65
    Gradients . . . . . . . . . . . . . . . . . . . . . . . . . . . . . . . . . . . . . . . . . . . . . . . 66
    The Texture Tab . . . . . . . . . . . . . . . . . . . . . . . . . . . . . . . . . . . . . . . . . 67
    Patterns . . . . . . . . . . . . . . . . . . . . . . . . . . . . . . . . . . . . . . . . . . . . . . . . 68
    Photos . . . . . . . . . . . . . . . . . . . . . . . . . . . . . . . . . . . . . . . . . . . . . . . . . . 68
    Tint . . . . . . . . . . . . . . . . . . . . . . . . . . . . . . . . . . . . . . . . . . . . . . . . . . . . . 70

Clip Art . . . . . . . . . . . . . . . . . . . . . . . . . . . . . . . . . . . . . . . . . . . . . . . . . . . . . . 71

Clip Art Key Words . . . . . . . . . . . . . . . . . . . . . . . . . . . . . . . . . . . . . . . . . . 72

Copyright Issues . . . . . . . . . . . . . . . . . . . . . . . . . . . . . . . . . . . . . . . . . . . . 73

Shapes . . . . . . . . . . . . . . . . . . . . . . . . . . . . . . . . . . . . . . . . . . . . . . . . . . . . . . 74
    Adding a 3-D Effect . . . . . . . . . . . . . . . . . . . . . . . . . . . . . . . . . . . . . . 75
    Coloring a Shape . . . . . . . . . . . . . . . . . . . . . . . . . . . . . . . . . . . . . . . . 76

Layering . . . . . . . . . . . . . . . . . . . . . . . . . . . . . . . . . . . . . . . . . . . . . . . . . . . . 77

Other Objects . . . . . . . . . . . . . . . . . . . . . . . . . . . . . . . . . . . . . . . . . . . . . . . 79

Drawings . . . . . . . . . . . . . . . . . . . . . . . . . . . . . . . . . . . . . . . . . . . . . 80

Equations . . . . . . . . . . . . . . . . . . . . . . . . . . . . . . . . . . . . . . . . . . . . 82

**4    Designs and Layouts** . . . . . . . . . . . . . . . . . . . . . . . . . . . . . **85**

Calendars . . . . . . . . . . . . . . . . . . . . . . . . . . . . . . . . . . . . . . . . . . . . 85

    Additional Customizations . . . . . . . . . . . . . . . . . . . . . . . . . 87

Postcards . . . . . . . . . . . . . . . . . . . . . . . . . . . . . . . . . . . . . . . . . . . . . 90

Greeting Cards . . . . . . . . . . . . . . . . . . . . . . . . . . . . . . . . . . . . . . . . 92

Additional Visual Elements . . . . . . . . . . . . . . . . . . . . . . . . . . . . 92

    Color Schemes . . . . . . . . . . . . . . . . . . . . . . . . . . . . . . . . . . . 93

    Word Art . . . . . . . . . . . . . . . . . . . . . . . . . . . . . . . . . . . . . . . 96

Creating Building Blocks . . . . . . . . . . . . . . . . . . . . . . . . . . . . . 105

**5    Working with Longer Documents** . . . . . . . . . . . . . . . . **109**

Text Boxes Revisited . . . . . . . . . . . . . . . . . . . . . . . . . . . . . . . . . 110

    Formatting . . . . . . . . . . . . . . . . . . . . . . . . . . . . . . . . . . . . . 110

    Linking Text Boxes . . . . . . . . . . . . . . . . . . . . . . . . . . . . . . . 111

    Navigating Text Boxes . . . . . . . . . . . . . . . . . . . . . . . . . . . . 112

    Layout Strategies . . . . . . . . . . . . . . . . . . . . . . . . . . . . . . . . 113

Master Pages . . . . . . . . . . . . . . . . . . . . . . . . . . . . . . . . . . . . . . . 113

    Additional Master Page Options . . . . . . . . . . . . . . . . . . . . 117

Importing Microsoft Word Documents . . . . . . . . . . . . . . . . . . 118

    Adding Images to the Document . . . . . . . . . . . . . . . . . . . . 120

    Word Documents with Images . . . . . . . . . . . . . . . . . . . . . . 125

Wrapping Text Around Images . . . . . . . . . . . . . . . . . . . . . . . . 125

    Irregularly Shaped Images . . . . . . . . . . . . . . . . . . . . . . . . 129

Formatting Text Boxes . . . . . . . . . . . . . . . . . . . . . . . . . . . . . . . 132

    Text Fitting . . . . . . . . . . . . . . . . . . . . . . . . . . . . . . . . . . . . . 132

    Text Direction . . . . . . . . . . . . . . . . . . . . . . . . . . . . . . . . . . 133

    Hyphenation . . . . . . . . . . . . . . . . . . . . . . . . . . . . . . . . . . . 134

    Alignment . . . . . . . . . . . . . . . . . . . . . . . . . . . . . . . . . . . . . 134

    Columns . . . . . . . . . . . . . . . . . . . . . . . . . . . . . . . . . . . . . . 134

    Word Art Lite . . . . . . . . . . . . . . . . . . . . . . . . . . . . . . . . . . 135

    Drop Cap . . . . . . . . . . . . . . . . . . . . . . . . . . . . . . . . . . . . . 135

    Number Styles . . . . . . . . . . . . . . . . . . . . . . . . . . . . . . . . . 137

**6    Tables** . . . . . . . . . . . . . . . . . . . . . . . . . . . . . . . . . . . . . . . . . **139**

What Are Tables? . . . . . . . . . . . . . . . . . . . . . . . . . . . . . . . . . . . . 139

Creating Tables . . . . . . . . . . . . . . . . . . . . . . . . . . . . . . . . . . . . . 140

Formatting Tables . . . . . . . . . . . . . . . . . . . . . . . . . . . . . . . . . . . 141

    Resizing a Table . . . . . . . . . . . . . . . . . . . . . . . . . . . . . . . . 141

Fill Effects ............................................. 143
Borders ................................................ 143
Table Rotation ........................................ 146
Text Wrapping ........................................ 147
Cell Alignments and Margins ........................ 148

Table Design ............................................. 151
Table Formats ......................................... 151

Table Layout ............................................. 151
Inserting Rows and Columns ......................... 152
Deleting Rows and Columns ......................... 153
Diagonals ............................................. 153
Merging and Splitting Cells .......................... 153

Importing Excel Spreadsheets ........................ 155
Importing a Spreadsheet ............................. 156

Importing Excel Charts ................................ 160
Importing an Existing Chart ......................... 165

**7 Finalizing Your Publisher Document** ............. **167**

A Visual Inspection .................................... 167
Proofreading Techniques ............................. 168

Adjusting Document Spacing .......................... 169
Use a Compact Font ................................... 169
Text Boxes ............................................ 170
Overlapping Frames .................................. 171
Coming Up Short ...................................... 172

Test Printing the Document ........................... 176

Document Metadata .................................... 177
Working with Metadata ............................... 178

The Design Checker .................................... 181

Creating PDF and XPS Files ........................... 185

**8 Printing Your Documents** ...................... **187**

Design Checking Your Document ..................... 187

Printing Documents Yourself .......................... 188
Basic Printing ......................................... 188

Professional Printing .................................. 190
What Will the Job Cost? ............................. 191
How Long Will It Take? .............................. 192
How Long Will It Take to Correct Printing Mistakes? .. 192
Is There Anything That You Won't Print? ........... 192
In What Format Should Materials Be Submitted? ... 193

Color Models ................................................ 193
    Grayscale ............................................... 194
    RGB ..................................................... 194
    HSL ..................................................... 195
    CMYK .................................................... 195
    PANTONE ................................................. 195

Choosing a Color Model ..................................... 196
    Offset Printing ......................................... 196

What a Printing Company Expects ............................ 201
    Packaging Your Print Job ................................ 202

How to Save on Printing Costs .............................. 204
    Stock ................................................... 204
    File Preparation ........................................ 205
    Quantity ................................................ 205
    Ink Colors .............................................. 205
    Deadlines ............................................... 205
    Use the Correct Printing Device ......................... 206

**9    Publishing Online** ................................. **207**

Creating a Website ......................................... 208

The Anatomy of a Web Page .................................. 210

Enhancing a Web Page ....................................... 212
    More Hyperlinking Techniques ............................ 214
    Bookmarks ............................................... 217
    Editing Hyperlinks ...................................... 219
    Changing a Hyperlink's Appearance ....................... 219

Using a Web Template ....................................... 220
    Working with the Template ............................... 221

Previewing Your Website .................................... 221

The Web Tab ................................................ 222
    Hot Spot ................................................ 222
    Navigation Bar .......................................... 223
    Form Controls ........................................... 225
    HTML Code Fragment ...................................... 226
    Web Page Options ........................................ 226

Publishing Your Website .................................... 228
    Acquiring a Domain Name ................................. 229
    Choosing a Hosting Company .............................. 229
    DNS Entries ............................................. 230
    Uploading Your Website .................................. 231

**10    Bulk Mailing Techniques** ..........................**233**

   Mail Merge .......................................................233

      Creating the Recipient List ...............................235

      Adding Merge Fields to Your Document ...............241

      Performing the Mail Merge ..............................243

      Alternative Data Sources ................................245

   Email Merge ...................................................248

      The Recipient Experience ................................251

   Snail Mail ......................................................251

      Index ..........................................................257

# About the Author

**Brien Posey** is a seven-time Microsoft MVP who is best known for writing about topics related to enterprise networking. In his nearly two decades of IT work, Posey has published thousands of technical articles and written or contributed to over three dozen books on a variety of subjects.

In addition to writing, Brien routinely speaks at IT conferences and engages in various consulting projects.

Prior to going freelance, Posey was a CIO for a national chain of hospitals and healthcare facilities. He has also previously served as a network engineer for the United States Department of Defense at Fort Knox.

When Brien isn't writing, he enjoys traveling to exotic destinations with his wife, shredding waves in his Cigarette boat, and scuba diving.

You can visit Posey's personal website at www.BrienPosey.com.

# Dedication

I would like to dedicate this book to my wife, Taz, for her continued love and support throughout my writing career. Writing even a short book is a time-consuming process, but the extremely short deadlines involved in creating this book meant a month of barely even seeing Taz. I am incredibly grateful to be married to someone who is so understanding of my crazy schedule.

# Acknowledgments

I would like to thank the following people:

Laura Taylor and Troy Thompson of Relevant Technologies (www.RelevantTechnologies.com)

Shamir Dasgupta, Jeremy Broyles, and Billy Brown at Xpressions Interactive (www.xpressions.com)

I would also like to thank Loretta Yates from Pearson Education for making this project as easy on me as possible.

Finally, I want to thank Taz, Junior, Melinda, Shawn, and Kelly for taking me to the beach last weekend, and helping me to clear my head so that I could finish this book. Watching Junior chase sand crabs in the dark was a hoot!

# We Want to Hear from You!

As the reader of this book, *you* are our most important critic and commentator. We value your opinion and want to know what we're doing right, what we could do better, what areas you'd like to see us publish in, and any other words of wisdom you're willing to pass our way.

As an associate publisher for Que Publishing, I welcome your comments. You can email or write me directly to let me know what you did or didn't like about this book—as well as what we can do to make our books better.

*Please note that I cannot help you with technical problems related to the topic of this book. We do have a User Services group, however, where I will forward specific technical questions related to the book.*

When you write, please be sure to include this book's title and author as well as your name, email address, and phone number. I will carefully review your comments and share them with the author and editors who worked on the book.

Email:    feedback@quepublishing.com

Mail:     Greg Wiegand
          Associate Publisher
          Que Publishing
          800 East 96th Street
          Indianapolis, IN 46240 USA

# Reader Services

Visit our website and register this book at quepublishing.com/register for convenient access to any updates, downloads, or errata that might be available for this book.

# Introduction

Those of you who know me (or my work) know that I am best known for the books and articles that I have written about enterprise networking products, such as Exchange Server and Office Communications Server. Even so, I decided to take a break from the norm and write a book on Microsoft Publisher 2010.

The reason why I decided to write this book is because I have always thought that Publisher was, without a doubt, the most underrated of all the products in the Microsoft Office Suite. Publisher has been around since 1991, and yet relatively few people seem to use it. In fact, when I was in college, I was required to take a class on using Microsoft Office, but the instructor didn't even acknowledge the existence of Publisher. I have always thought that the seeming lack of interest was odd, because you can do some really cool things with Publisher.

I have to confess that Publisher is the only Microsoft Office products that I can really say that I enjoy using. Don't get me wrong—Word, Excel, Outlook, and the other Office applications are great tools. I couldn't do my job without them. The thing is that when I am working with Word, Excel, or Outlook, the task at hand feels like work. Let's face it: Most of the Microsoft Office products are really geared toward producing business documents, and really, how much fun is that?

Publisher, on the other hand, allows for a much higher degree of creativity and expression than the other Microsoft Office products do. I have found creating Publisher documents to be a rather enjoyable process, and the end result is always highly satisfying. Needless to say, I jumped at the chance to write a book on Publisher 2010.

Before I get started, I want to take this opportunity to put your fears at rest. I realize that some of you might have panicked when you realized that you bought a book that was written by someone who normally writes hard-core technical material. I'll let you in on a little secret....

As someone who writes about numerous different subjects, I am constantly having to educate myself on various products and technologies. As such, I read pretty much anything that I can get my hands on. What I have found is that many technology authors like to impress their readers by using a lot of big words, complex acronyms, and convoluted diagrams. This doesn't really help me, though. My fast-paced production schedule demands that I learn new material quickly. As such, I greatly prefer reading a simple explanation of a technology to one that is overly complex.

Over time, I have discovered that many of my readers are in the same boat I am. They need to learn about something new but don't have the time or the desire to dissect a complex explanation. Therefore, I have always tried to break down complex material and present it in as simple of a manner as possible, and I will use this same approach in writing about Publisher 2010.

Yes, Publisher does have a bit of a learning curve, but I promise to make it as painless as I possibly can. Please understand that I don't use this approach because I think that my readers are stupid, or as a way of insulting anyone's intelligence. It's just that I know that most people are busy, so I try to keep things simple as a way of respecting my reader's time. With that said, I hope you enjoy the book.

# How This Book Is Organized

This book introduces you to Microsoft Publisher 2010, and shows you how to use it to do everything from creating simple documents to creating highly customized documents that are based on your business data. Additionally, you will learn numerous best practices for working with Publisher 2010, and you will learn about when it is appropriate to use Publisher as opposed to one of the other Microsoft Office applications. *Using Microsoft Publisher 2010 offers you the following:*

- It discusses the overlap between Publisher and Microsoft Word, and when it is appropriate to use each application.

- It discusses both the benefits and limitations associated with using Publisher 2010.

- It discusses the interaction between Publisher 2010 and other Microsoft products.

- It explains key concepts in detail for novice users, but also covers topics of interest to those who already have experience in using Publisher.

- It offers real-world examples that you can relate to.

# Using This Book

This book enables you to customize your own learning experience. The step-by-step instructions in the book give you a solid foundation in using Publisher 2010, while rich and varied online content, including video tutorials and audio sidebars, provide the following:

- Demonstrations of step-by-step tasks covered in the book

- Additional tips or information on a topic

- Practical advice and suggestions
- Direction for more advanced tasks not covered in the book

### LET ME TRY IT

Let Me Try It tasks are presented in a step-by-step sequence so you can easily follow along.

### SHOW ME   Media—This Is the Title of a Show Me Video

*Show Me videos walk through tasks you've just got to see—including bonus advanced techniques.*

### TELL ME MORE   Media—This Is the Title of a Tell Me More Recording

*Tell Me More audio delivers practical insights straight from the experts.*

## Special Features

More than just a book, your Using product integrates step-by-step video tutorials and valuable audio sidebars delivered through the **Free Web Edition** that comes with every Using book. For the price of the book, you get online access anywhere with a web connection—there are no books to carry, content is updated as the technology changes, and you receive the benefit of video and audio learning.

## About the Using Web Edition

The Web Edition of every Using book is powered by **Safari Books Online**, allowing you to access the video tutorials and valuable audio sidebars. Plus, you can search the contents of the book, highlight text and attach a note to that text, print your notes and highlights in a custom summary, and cut and paste directly from Safari Books Online.

To register this product and gain access to the Free Web Edition and the audio and video files, go to **quepublishing.com/using**.

**Installing Microsoft Publisher 2010 is a breeze. Once installed, you can begin exploring all the new features.**

1

# An Introduction to Publisher 2010

Microsoft Office 2010 is the latest version of their flagship productivity suite. Among the applications included in the Microsoft Office Suite is Publisher 2010.

Although Microsoft Publisher 2010 is brand new, the Microsoft Publisher franchise has been around for a long time. The first version of Publisher was released in 1991. Computer-based desktop publishing has been around for even longer, though.

I will never forget the first time that I was exposed to desktop publishing. When I was a kid back in the 1980's (wow, I feel old!), I saved up the cash that I made mowing lawns and bought a Radio Shack TRS-80 Color Computer 2.

I always thought that the software that was available for the Color Computer (better known as the CoCo) did the machine a big disservice. Although the CoCo was just as well equipped as the Commodore 64 and the PCs of the time, there wasn't very much software available for it. What little software you could buy really wasn't very good. Amateur CoCo enthusiasts routinely created freeware that was far better than most of the commercial applications that were available.

One afternoon, I was killing time at Radio Shack when a new application caught my attention. I can't seem to recall the name of the application, but it was a desktop publisher.

One thing that you have to understand about the CoCo is that although it had plenty of processing power, word processing wasn't exactly its strong point. In fact, the word processing software that I had would not even display lowercase letters (although it could print them). Capital letters were displayed as black characters against a green background. Lowercase letters were displayed onscreen as green capital letters on a black background (a negative image of a capital letter). You can see what this effect looked like in Figure 1.1.

The desktop publishing software that I held in my hand offered all kinds of features that were absolutely unheard of for the CoCo. Not only did it support true lowercase text (onscreen, no less), but it also included multiple fonts, all of which could be scaled to different sizes. The fact that the software could also format text into columns and that you could add images to your documents was the icing on the cake. I absolutely had to buy the application right then and there.

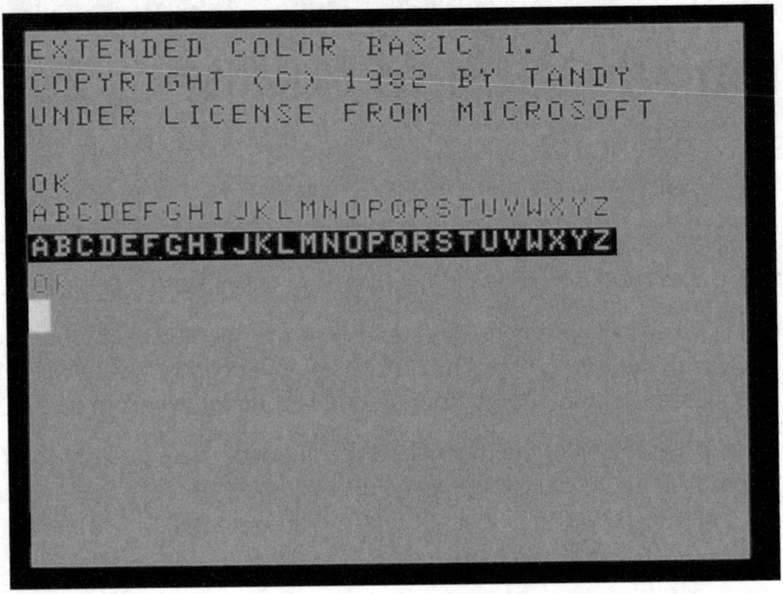

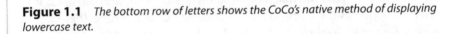

**Figure 1.1** *The bottom row of letters shows the CoCo's native method of displaying lowercase text.*

As soon as I got home from the store, I popped the disk into my computer and loaded the program. I had no idea how to use a desktop publisher, so I decided to load the sample document that the program came with, just so that I could see if the program could really produce documents like the ones shown on the box.

To make a long story short, the document that was displayed onscreen did indeed match the one that was shown on the box. Unfortunately, though, it took the computer half an hour to even load the document.

As I began to get my feet wet, it became painfully obvious that desktop publishing wasn't quite ready for prime time (at least not on the CoCo). Even the simplest actions, such as switching fonts, incurred wait times of several minutes. It didn't take me long to discover that creating rich documents on my CoCo just wasn't practical.

A few months later, I had all but forgotten about my desktop publishing software. Eventually, though, a friend asked me if I could help to put together a newsletter for a computer user group that he was starting. Being that the group would be filled with geeks who could truly appreciate what the desktop publishing software could deliver, I decided to give my software another try.

Creating the newsletter was a grueling process, but when I was done, I was extremely satisfied with the results of my hard work. There was just one teensy problem that I hadn't counted on—the desktop publishing software wasn't compatible with my printer. Because a new printer wasn't in my budget, I had to throw in the towel.

It's absolutely amazing how much things can change in the span of 20 years or so. Microsoft Publisher 2010 is infinitely more powerful than the desktop publishing software that I ran on my CoCo so long ago. More importantly, though, Publisher makes creating and printing high-quality documents absolutely painless. Any reasonably equipped PC is more than adequate for running Microsoft Publisher.

## What Is Microsoft Publisher?

If you read the preceding section, you know that Microsoft Publisher is a desktop publishing application. As was the case with the desktop publishing software that I ran on my CoCo back in the '80s, Microsoft Publisher enables you to create rich documents that use a variety of visual elements, such as fonts and images.

If you have never worked with any of the previous versions of Publisher before, you might be wondering what makes Publisher so special. After all, Microsoft Word also enables you to create elaborate documents that contain a variety of visual elements. So what makes Publisher different from Word?

I will be the first to admit that there is a lot of overlap between the two applications. If you need to create a simple document containing text and a few images, then you could use either program. The similarities end there, though.

Microsoft Word is a word processor. Its main job is to enable you to create text-based documents. You can include images or other visual elements in a Word document if you like, but these types of functions are not Microsoft Word's primary focus.

In contrast, Microsoft Publisher focuses more on page layout and visual appeal than it does on providing the best possible environment for composing or editing text. Yes, you can compose and edit text in Publisher, but Publisher isn't exactly the tool of choice for writing long, text-based documents.

To put things a little bit more into prospective for you, consider this: I am using Microsoft Word to write this book. As I write these words, I really don't care what page of the book they will end up being printed on, nor do I care about this paragraph's position on the printed page. My goal is only to write the words that you are reading right now (and to capture a few screenshots along the way), and Microsoft Word is by far the best tool for the job.

Once I finish my work, though, I have to send my manuscript and my screen captures to the book's publisher. It is their job to lay out the book's pages in a meaningful way. In doing so, they will use either Microsoft Publisher or a similar application to take the raw text and graphics that I have sent to them and turn it into the book that you are reading right now. Although Microsoft Word could technically be used to lay out a book, a desktop publishing application is a better tool for the job because it provides much better control over the page layout and the publication's final appearance than what is possible using Microsoft Word.

## Getting Started

If the entire concept of desktop publishing seems foreign to you, don't worry. As I explained earlier, there was a time when I didn't know how to use a desktop publisher either!

My plan for this book is to use this chapter to show you how to install Publisher 2010. The next few chapters are designed to get you up and running quickly. I show you simple techniques that you can use to create professional-looking documents. Toward the end of the book, I discuss some of the more advanced techniques, such as mail merge. I also discuss professional printing and show you how to use Publisher as a tool for creating websites.

## System Requirements

For as long as I can remember, Microsoft has always provided a list of both minimum and recommended hardware requirements for their products. In many cases, a computer that was equipped with the minimum hardware requirements just wasn't practical for actually using the application in an efficient manner.

Microsoft has taken a completely different approach to defining the hardware requirements for Office 2010. According to a Microsoft blog post (http://blogs.technet.com/office2010/archive/2010/01/22/office-2010-system-requirements.aspx), many of Microsoft's customers found having two separate lists of hardware requirements to be confusing. For example, if an application has a stated minimum requirement of 1 GB of memory but a recommended requirement of 2 GB, when do you really need 1 GB or 2 GB?

That being the case, Microsoft is providing only a list of the minimum hardware requirements for running Office 2010. According to Microsoft, the stated minimums should provide adequate performance to users who are using Microsoft Office 2010 to complete a small job. As always, though, higher performance hardware will generally provide a better experience.

# Minimum Hardware Requirements for Office 2010

The stated minimum hardware requirements vary slightly depending on the edition of Microsoft Office 2010 that you are running.

I have chosen to list the minimum hardware requirements for Microsoft Office Professional Plus 2010. I chose this particular edition because it has the most stringent set of requirements (although not by much). Here are the minimum hardware requirements:

- CPU: 500 MHz

- Memory: 256 MB

- Hard Disk: 1.5 GB of available space

- Display: 1024 × 768

- A DirectX 9.0c-compliant video card with 64 MB of video memory

In addition to these general requirements, there are a number of other feature specific requirements and recommendations that do not directly affect Publisher. Here are the additional requirements:

- If you are going to use the inking feature, you will need Windows XP Tablet PC Edition (or later).

- Speech recognition requires a close talk microphone and a sound card.

- Instant Search requires Windows Desktop Search 3.0.

- Some of Outlook's features are available only when connected to an Exchange mailbox.

- Many of the collaboration features require connectivity to a SharePoint server.

- Internet Explorer 6 or higher is required for Internet-related features.

- Outlook's instant search feature requires a minimum of 1 GB of memory.

- Word 2010 will not enable grammar and contextual spelling checks unless the computer is equipped with at least 1 GB of memory.

- The Silverlight plug-in is required for some web features.

You can find Microsoft's full list of hardware requirements at http://technet.microsoft.com/en-us/library/ee624351(office.14).aspx.

# System Requirements for Publisher 2010

Interestingly, Microsoft publishes an entirely separate list of system requirements for each of the Office 2010 applications. That way, if you only want to install a single application rather than the entire Office suite, you will know what hardware is required.

Microsoft also lists some other requirements that come into play if you use only certain features. These requirements include the following:

- A sound card and a close talk microphone (for speech recognition)
- Windows XP Tablet PC Edition (for inking)
- Internet Explorer 6 (for web-based features)
- Internet connectivity and a Windows Live ID (to share templates and building blocks)

# Operating System Requirements

Now that I have talked about the hardware that is required to run Office 2010, I want to talk about the operating system requirements. Office 2010 is the first version of Microsoft Office to offer native 64-bit support. Don't get me wrong.... It was possible to run Office 2007 on a 64-bit system, but Office 2007 was a 32-bit application and was unable to take advantage of the 64-bit architecture. Microsoft will be offering both 32-bit and 64-bit versions of Office 2010. The 32-bit version will run on both 32-bit and 64-bit versions of Windows. The 64-bit version requires a 64-bit Windows operating system, though.

Microsoft Office 2010 is officially supported on the following operating systems:

- Windows 7
- Windows Vista (with SP1 or higher)
- Windows Server 2008
- Windows Server 2008 R2
- Windows XP with SP3 (32-bit only)
- Windows Server 2003 R2 with MSXML 6.0 (32-bit only)

# My Recommendations

In spite of Microsoft's best efforts to clarify the system requirements for Office 2010, they can still be a bit confusing. This is especially true when you take all the optional requirements into account. That being the case, I wanted to give you my take on the system requirements.

If you are running Office 2007 on your PC right now, you probably will have no trouble running Office 2010. The CPU and memory requirements are identical for both Office 2007 and Office 2010. You will just have to make sure that your computer has enough free hard disk space to load Office 2010 and that you have a decent graphics card. If your computer is running Windows Vista or Windows 7 and the Aero interface is enabled, you probably have the graphics card requirement covered.

So what if you aren't running Office 2007 right now? If your computer is less than five years old, it will probably be sufficient to run Office 2010, but you do need to take the time to check its hardware capabilities.

Regardless of whether your system is old or new, and in spite of Microsoft's stated minimum requirements, I would recommend that your PC be equipped with a minimum of 1 GB of memory. Today, memory is cheap, and almost every new PC comes with more than 1 GB of memory. Having at least 1 GB of memory will enable you to get the maximum benefit from Office 2010, and adding extra memory goes a long way toward improving a computer's performance.

## Verifying Your System's Hardware

There are lots of different ways that you can check the hardware that is installed in your computer. Probably the easiest way is to use the DirectX Diagnostic Tool, which is built into Windows. You can access this tool by entering the DXDIAG command at the computer's Run prompt.

As you can see in Figure 1.2, the System tab provides you with information about your computer's CPU and the amount of memory that is installed. You can also verify your DirectX version from this tab.

The DirectX Diagnostic Tool's Display tab tells you the system's current display resolution. It also provides you with an estimate of the total amount of video memory that is installed in the system.

Checking the amount of hard disk space that is available in the system is simply a matter of choosing the Computer option (or the My Computer option, depending on what version of Windows you are running) from the Windows Start menu. The resulting screen will show you how much space is available on your C: drive. The computer in Figure 1.3, for example, has 113 GB of free disk space, which is more than enough to install Office 2010.

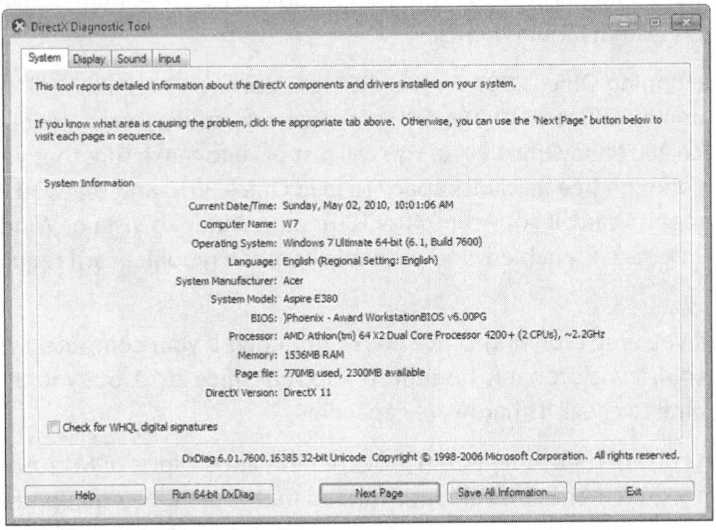

**Figure 1.2**   *The DirectX Diagnostic Tool is handy for verifying system hardware.*

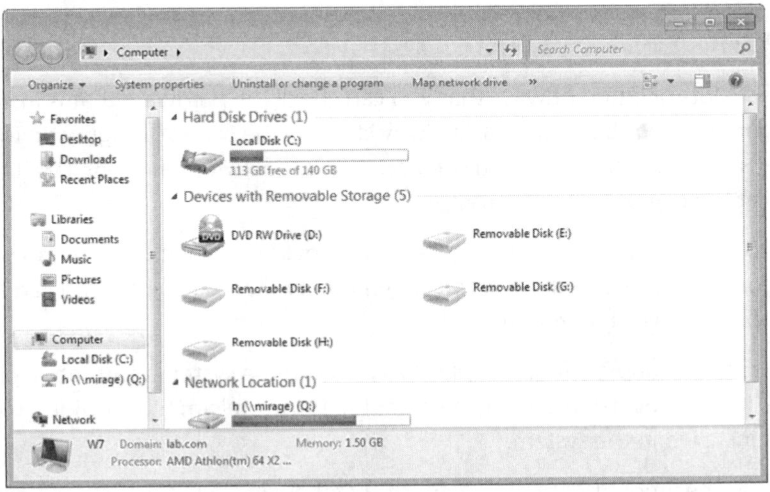

**Figure 1.3**   *The Computer window shows how much disk space is available.*

## Installing Office 2010

Now that I have shown you how to verify your computer's hardware, let's go ahead and install Office 2010. Office 2010 enables you to perform either a clean installation or an in-place upgrade from Office 2007. I will show you how to perform a clean installation first. If you happen to have Office 2007 currently installed, you can still perform a clean installation, but I recommend upgrading instead because doing so will preserve your customizations.

 **LET ME TRY IT**

## Performing a Clean Installation

Performing a clean installation of Office 2010 is simple. To do so, follow these steps:

1. Insert your Microsoft Office 2010 installation DVD and run Setup.exe if necessary.

2. Click the I Accept the Terms of This Agreement check box.

3. Click Continue.

4. At this point, Setup will ask you if you want to go ahead and install Office 2010, or if you want to customize the installation. You don't have to make any customizations unless you want to, but go ahead and click the Customize button so that you can see what options are available to you.

5. The customization screen, shown in Figure 1.4, enables you to choose the components that you want to install, and to provide a custom file location. If you want to make any customizations, do so now.

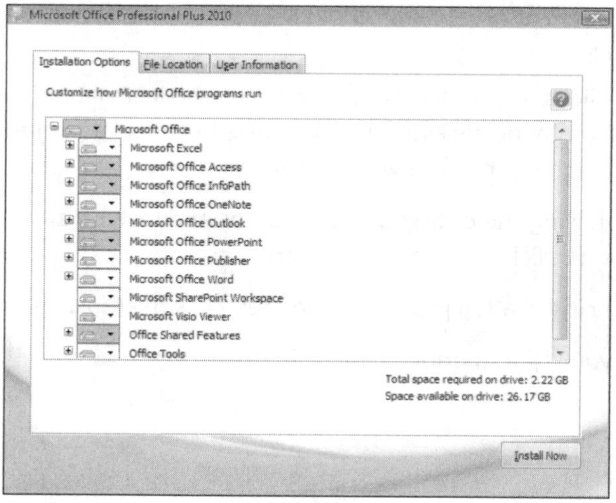

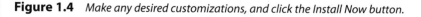

**Figure 1.4**   *Make any desired customizations, and click the Install Now button.*

6. When you are done making any desired customizations, click the Install Now button.

7. When the installation process completes, click Close.

**LET ME TRY IT**

# Upgrading from Office 2007

**SHOW ME**   Media 1.1—Installing Microsoft Office 2010
*Access this video file through your registered Web edition at*
***my.safaribooksonline.com/9780132182591/media***

The process of upgrading from Office 2007 to Office 2010 is similar to performing a clean installation. To upgrade, follow these steps:

1. Insert the installation DVD.

2. Run Setup.exe if necessary

3. When prompted, select the I Accept the Terms of This Agreement check box.

4. Click Continue.

5. If Windows contains a previous version of Microsoft Office, you will receive a prompt asking you if you want to upgrade or customize, as shown in Figure 1.5.

6. You can click the Upgrade button to begin the installation process. However, I recommend clicking the Customize button instead just to see if there is anything that you want to change.

7. After reviewing the customization options and making any desired customizations, click the Upgrade button.

8. When the installation process completes, click the Close button.

9. Reboot your system prior to using Office 2010.

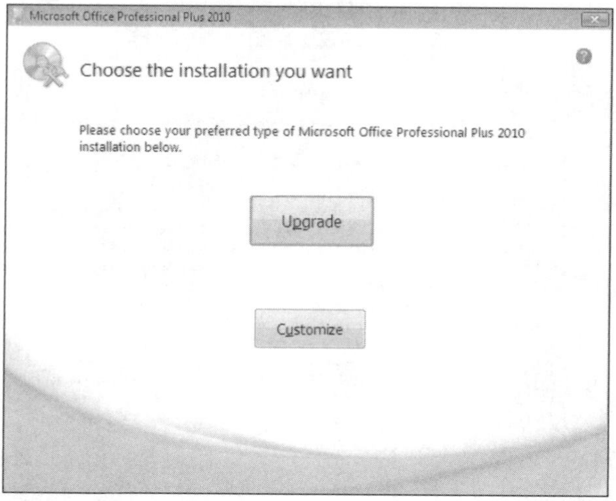

**Figure 1.5**   *You have the option of performing an upgrade or a custom installation.*

### LET ME TRY IT

## Uninstalling Office 2010

Because I just showed you how to install Office 2010, it probably seems a bit odd to be talking about uninstalling it so soon. Occasionally, though, the need may arise to uninstall Office 2010, so I wanted to go ahead and show you how to do so.

The actual method that you must use to uninstall Office varies depending on the version of Windows that you are using. The following procedure is based on Windows 7. This procedure works slightly differently in Windows XP and Vista.

To remove Office 2010, follow these steps:

1. Click the Windows Start button and choose the Control Panel option.

2. When the Control Panel opens, click the Uninstall a Program link.

3. Select Microsoft Office from the list of installed programs, as shown in Figure 1.6.

4. Click the Uninstall button.

5. When asked if you want to remove Microsoft Office 2010, click Yes.

6. When the process completes, click Close.

7. When prompted, reboot your system.

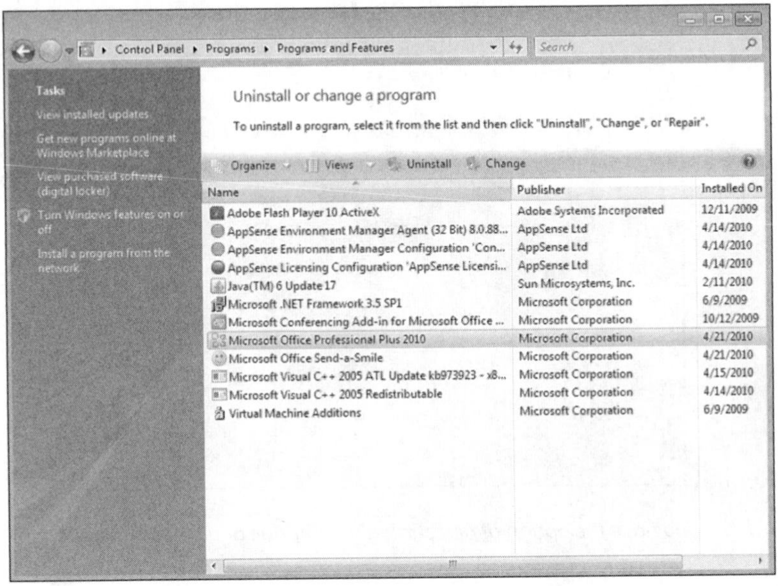

**Figure 1.6**    *Select the option for Microsoft Office 2010 and click the Uninstall button.*

**SHOW ME**    Media 1.2—Uninstalling Microsoft Office 2010
*Access this video file through your registered Web edition at*
*my.safaribooksonline.com/9780132182591/media*

## What's New in Publisher 2010

Now that you have Office 2010 up and running, you are probably curious as to how Publisher has changed since the previous version. Although there are some things that have changed, Publisher 2010 isn't vastly different from its predecessor.

## The Ribbon

When Microsoft created Office 2007, it introduced a new ribbon design for some, but not all, of the Office applications. Publisher was one of the applications that did not end up getting a facelift. However, Microsoft has decided to incorporate the ribbon design into Publisher 2010.

To see how Publisher 2010 compares to Publisher 2007, take a look at Figures 1.7 and 1.8. Figure 1.7 shows what Publisher 2007 looked like. When compared to this image, Publisher 2010's new ribbon really stands out in Figure 1.8.

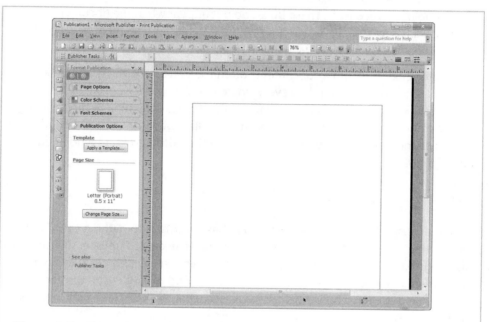

**Figure 1.7**  *This is what Publisher 2007 looked like.*

**Figure 1.8**  *Publisher 2010 uses the ribbon design.*

# How Documents Are Displayed

In Microsoft Publisher, every visual element exists within a box. Text is placed within a text box, and there is also a box that surrounds every image that you include in your Publisher document. These boxes do not appear when the document is printed; they are necessary when working with the Publisher document because they provide control over individual visual elements.

In Publisher 2007, complex documents often took on a very messy appearance because the boxes surrounding every single visual element were all displayed onscreen. In Publisher 2010, Microsoft decided to clean up things a bit by hiding most of these boxes. Now, the only box that is displayed is the one surrounding the visual element that is currently selected. All of the other boxes are hidden until you need them.

# Going Backstage

Another cosmetic feature that is new to Publisher 2010 is something called backstage view. The backstage is merely an area that is linked to Publisher's File menu. It is designed to provide access to things like opening, saving, printing, and sharing documents. The backstage is also where you will find various customization options and access to online help. You can see what the backstage area looks like in Figure 1.9.

# Printing

Another area where Microsoft has made a lot of improvements is in printing Publisher documents. Now when you get ready to print a document like the one shown in Figure 1.10, Publisher shows you a large preview of what the document will look like when printed.

As you can see in the figure, there are a number of print options located just to the left of the preview. As you select a different set of print options, the preview will change to reflect the options that you have chosen.

# PDF and XPS Support

After the release of Microsoft Office 2007, Microsoft began offering an add-in that would allow documents to be saved as PDF or XPS files. This functionality is natively included in Publisher 2010 without the need for an add-in. Furthermore, Publisher even supports password-protecting PDF documents.

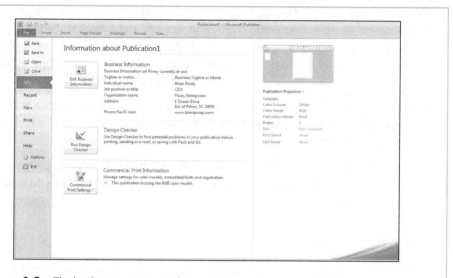

**Figure 1.9**   *The backstage area provides access to common document functions.*

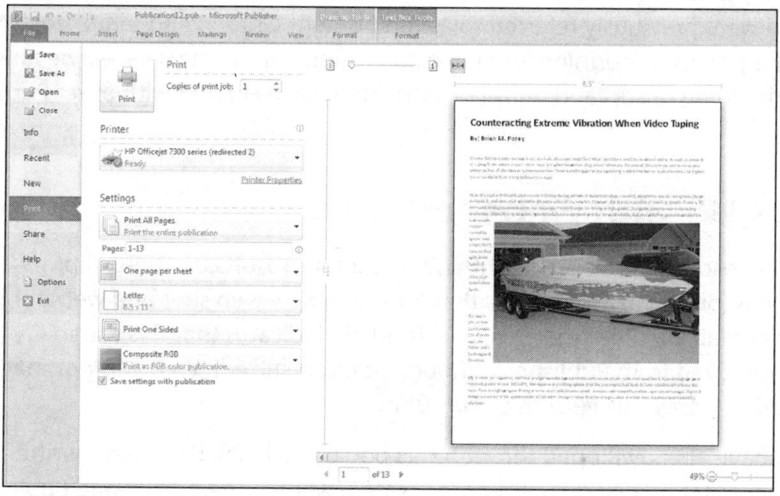

**Figure 1.10**   *The backstage area provides access to common document functions.*

# Image Controls

Publisher has always enabled you to include graphic images in your documents and to perform some degree of editing on those images. Microsoft has made several improvements to Publisher's capability to work with shapes and images.

My favorite of these new image controls is the capability to replace one picture with another, while still retaining the image size and the overall document layout. Similarly, you can now create picture placeholders as a way of reserving a place in a document for an image that will be inserted later. Once the image is added to the document, it will take on the size and shape of the placeholder.

Publisher 2010 enables you to crop images into nonrectangular shapes. You also can now add captions to images. In fact, Publisher provides an entire gallery of captions that you can choose from.

Finally, Publisher 2010 enables you to hide objects that are in the scratch area. Some of the other new features include Smart Guides, Live Preview, and improved page navigation.

## Minor Improvements

Besides the improvements I have already mentioned, Microsoft has made a few minor improvements to the merge process in an effort to make it easier to merge business data into Publisher documents.

Another minor improvement worth mentioning has to do with building blocks (which were previously referred to as the Content Library) and templates. Microsoft is in the process of forming an online community in which users will be able to share building blocks and templates that they have created with other Publisher users.

## What's Up with Web Mode?

One Microsoft TechNet article (http://technet.microsoft.com/en-us/library/ ee694636(office.14).aspx) states that "Creating new web sites and web publications is not available in Publisher 2010." This article indicates that this capability has been removed from Publisher, although you can still edit Web content that was created in a previous version of Publisher.

If you have already flipped through this book, you know that I have written an entire chapter on using Publisher to create a website. As it turns out, Publisher 2010 contains some fairly rich web development capabilities. I will say, however, that most of the web development options are not accessible unless you create your web page from a web template.

 **TELL ME MORE**    Media 1.3—How Different Is Publisher 2010 from Publisher 2007?
*To listen to a free audio recording about how Publisher 2010 differs from Publisher 2007, log on to **my.safaribooksonline.com/9780132182591/media**.*

# Getting Started with Publisher 2010

Now that you have installed Microsoft Office 2010, I will show you how to use Publisher. In this chapter, I create a new Publisher document and show you how to lay out your document. We won't actually add any visual elements to the document until the next chapter.

## Using Publisher for the First Time

Upon opening Microsoft Publisher, you are taken to the screen shown in Figure 2.1. Publisher's initial screen enables you to choose from numerous templates. The built-in templates make it easier to create specific types of documents. For example, there are templates for creating brochures, business cards, calendars, and more.

Although templates are one of Microsoft Publisher's most useful features, I won't cover them in detail right now. A template lays the groundwork for creating various types of documents. In doing so, templates use some elements that may be unfamiliar to you. So I want to start by showing you how some of these elements work within a blank document. After I do, I'll return and discuss templates in more detail later in this chapter.

## Creating a New Document

As mentioned in the previous section, a template expedites the document creation process. Let's create a new document by using one of the blank templates.

Double-click on the blank 8.5 x 11-inch template. When you do, you will be taken to the Main Publisher interface, as shown in Figure 2.2. The Publisher interface is similar to Microsoft Office applications.

The big white area in the middle of the screen represents a single page of the document that you are creating. Notice a smaller white rectangle in the upper-left portion of the screen. This rectangle displays a preview of the page. Right now, the preview is less than impressive because our document is only one page in length. If a document spans multiple pages, though, the preview area makes it easier to locate an individual page within the document.

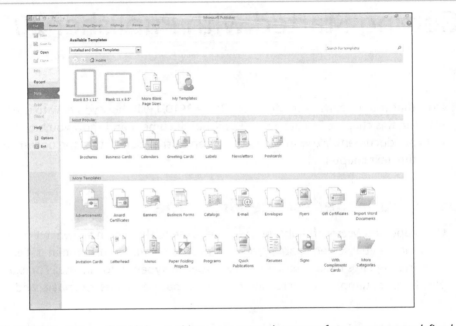

**Figure 2.1**     *Microsoft Publisher enables you to create documents from numerous predefined templates.*

**SHOW ME**     **Media 2.1—Creating a New Document**
*Access this video file through your registered Web edition at*
***my.safaribooksonline.com/9780132182591/media.***

# Page Margins

If you look at Figure 2.2, notice the blue rectangle that appears on the page. This rectangle represents the page margins. By default, Publisher sets the margins to half an inch.

Note that the margins exist only for your guidance. In Microsoft Word, any of the text that you type is placed within the margins. This isn't always the case with Publisher. It is possible to place text, graphics, or other objects outside the document margins.

**Figure 2.2**    *Main Publisher interface. Note the menu commands at the top.*

You might wonder why Microsoft displays the margins at all if it's so easy to ignore them. Margins exist because many printers are not capable of printing all the way to the edge of the page. Even if your printer can print on page edges, most printed documents don't look right without margins. Therefore, Microsoft Publisher displays the margins on the screen in an effort to help you create an aesthetically pleasing (and fully printable) document.

## Custom Margins

In most cases, the default half-inch margins are acceptable. If you need to adjust the margin size, though, select the Page Design tab, and then choose the Margins option from the toolbar. Publisher then displays several different margins that you can choose from. This menu also gives you the option of creating custom margins.

If you choose the Custom Margins option, the dialog box shown in Figure 2.3 appears. This dialog box provides you with the option of setting the left, right, top, and bottom margins to any size you want.

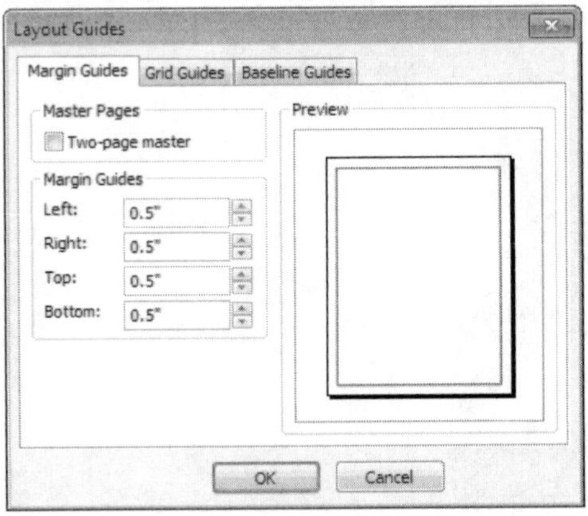

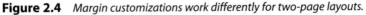

**Figure 2.3**    *The Layout Guides dialog box enables you to create custom margins.*

Notice the check box labeled Two-Page Master. Selecting this check box changes the page layout to display two separate pages, as shown in Figure 2.4. The references to the right and left margins have been replaced by inside and outside margins.

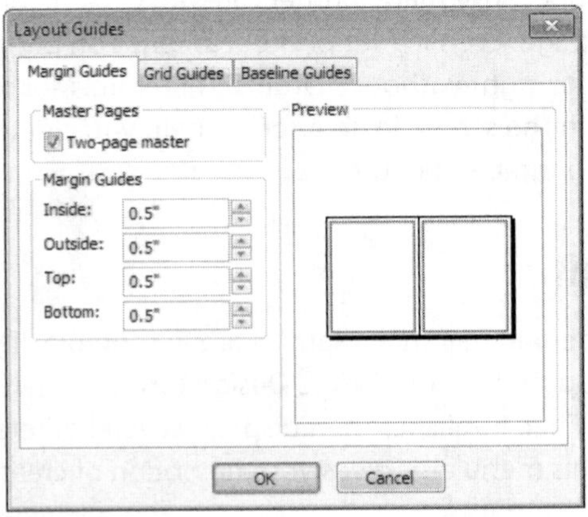

**Figure 2.4**    *Margin customizations work differently for two-page layouts.*

# Grid Guides

As you begin laying out your new Publisher document, you might find that it is tough to place the various design elements on the screen in the exact location. One solution to this problem is to divide the page into a grid.

 **LET ME TRY IT**

## Dividing a Page Into a Grid

To divide a page into a grid, follow these steps:

1. Go to Publisher's Page Design tab.

2. Click the Margins icon.

3. Choose the Custom Margins option from the Margins menu.

4. When the Layout Guides dialog box appears, select the Grid Guides tab.

In Figure 2.5, the Grid Guides tab divides the page into a series of rows and columns. Although similar to the blue lines that represent the page margins, the grid guides only exist as document reference points, and do not show up when you print the document.

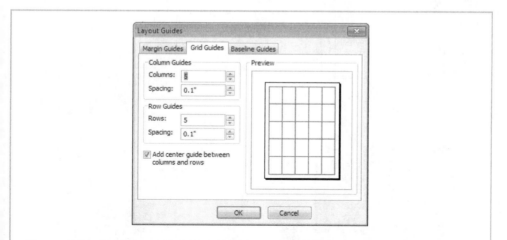

**Figure 2.5**   *Grid lines can make it easier to lay out a Publisher document.*

As you can see in the figure, Publisher gives you the option of specifying the number of rows and the number of columns that you want to display on the page. Publisher is quirky about setting up rows and columns, as it creates twice as many rows or columns as you specify. Publisher uses two separate lines to separate the row or column from the one next to it. By default, the lines that publisher creates are a 10th of an inch apart from each other. To rectify this quirk, notice in Figure 2.5 the option to set the spacing for rows and columns. You can increase the spacing to make the lines that separate rows and columns much farther apart. There is also a check box that you can use to add a centerline between the lines that separate rows and columns.

In a default layout, it can be difficult to see that the line separating rows and columns are double lines with spacing between them. As you increase the spacing, though, the double lines become more obvious.

To show you what I am talking about, I have configured Publisher to divide the page into two columns and two rows. I have also increased the spacing to 1 inch and added a centerline between the columns and rows. The results, which are shown in Figure 2.6, clearly display the spacing between the lines as well as the optional centerline.

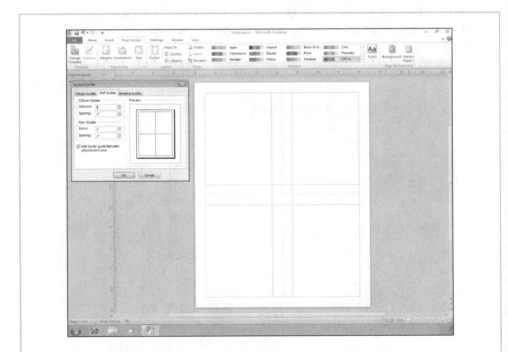

**Figure 2.6**  *You have the option of increasing line spacing.*

# Built-In Guides

Having an onscreen grid is handy when placing various design elements within your document. Sometimes, though, you may already have an idea of what your finished document should look like, and a generic grid can only get in the way.

Sometimes, onscreen grids can be counterproductive for another reason. As you begin learning the basics of creating Publisher documents, you will see that the screen becomes cluttered with design elements. That isn't to say that your finished document will be cluttered, though. Each design element that you add to your document exists within a box. If you put enough of these boxes on the screen at the same time, things start to look too busy. If you throw in a grid too, then you have a mess.

As you have already seen, Microsoft makes the use of grid guides optional. Although it's nice to turn off the grid guides when you aren't using them, you may occasionally find that you do need the grid guides but you don't want the entire document page cluttered with them. For example, you might only need a grid guide on a certain portion of the page. You can accomplish this by using one of the built-in grid guides.

 **LET ME TRY IT**

## Choosing a Grid Guide

To access the alternative sets of grid guides, follow these steps:

1. Select Publisher's Page Design tab.

2. Click on the Guides icon, found on the toolbar.

3. Select the grid guide that you want to use. You can see the available grid guides in Figure 2.7.

 **SHOW ME**    Media 2.2—Grid Guides
*Access this video file through your registered Web edition at*
***my.safaribooksonline.com/9780132182591/media.***

# Ruler Guides

So far, I have shown you how to divide a document page by using various types of grid guides. These grid guides help you precisely position various design elements.

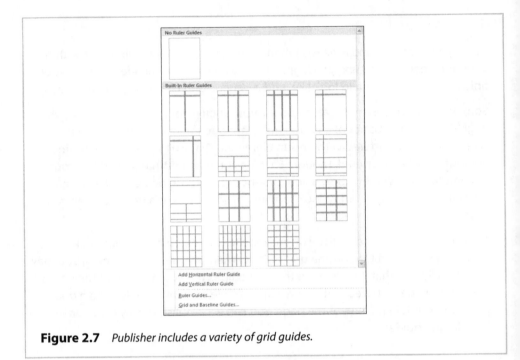

**Figure 2.7**    *Publisher includes a variety of grid guides.*

Sometimes, though, you might find that design element placement requires a higher degree of precision than what any of the grid guides can provide. In these situations, use a ruler guide.

A ruler guide is similar to the grid guides that I have already talked about, but with one major difference. Ruler guides are linked to rulers that border the page. As such, you can move a ruler guide to any spot on the page, with a high degree of precision.

 **LET ME TRY IT**

## Enabling Ruler Guides

To enable ruler guides, follow these steps:

1. Go to Publisher's Page Design tab.

2. Click the Guides icon.

3. Choose the Add Horizontal Ruler Guide command from the Guides menu.

4. Click the Guides icon.

5. Choose the Add Vertical Ruler Guide command from the Guides menu.

The page is now divided into four segments, as shown in Figure 2.8. Although the lines shown in the figure look the same as the grid guides that I have already shown you, they are instead linked to the rulers that appear above and to the left of the document. Click the lines and drag them into the desired position by using markers that will appear on the rulers as you begin moving the guide lines.

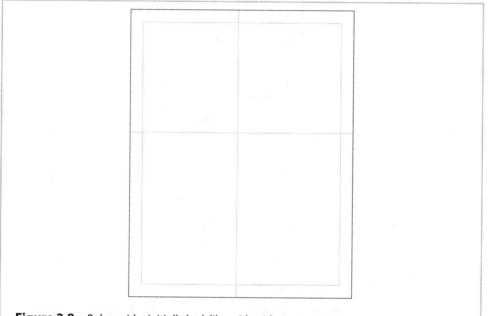

**Figure 2.8**   *Ruler guides initially look like grid guides.*

# High-Precision Guides

Even though dragging and dropping ruler guides works pretty well, drag and drop isn't exactly a high-precision operation.

 **LET ME TRY IT**

## Setting High-Precision Guides

If you need to set the ruler guides with a higher degree of accuracy, you can do so by completing the following steps:

1. Select Publisher's Page Design tab.

2. Click the Guides icon found on the toolbar.

3. Choose the Ruler Guides command from the Guides menu.

4. When the Ruler Guides dialog box appears, select either the Horizontal or the Vertical tab, depending on which ruler guide you want to position.

5. Enter the desired ruler guide position, as shown in Figure 2.9.

6. Click OK.

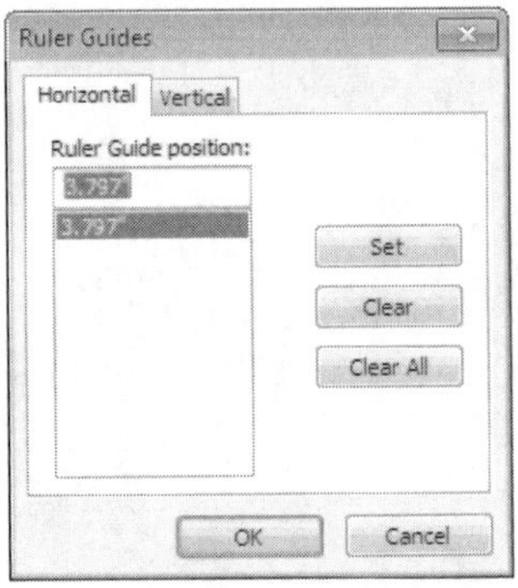

**Figure 2.9**   *Enter the desired location for your ruler guide.*

## Using Multiple Ruler Guides

Having a horizontal and a vertical ruler guide can be very handy, but when it comes to creating more advanced documents, you might need to do a lot more measuring. Fortunately, you can create additional ruler guides on an as-needed basis using the same steps that we already performed.

**LET ME TRY IT**

### Creating Additional Ruler Guides

If you want to create an additional horizontal ruler guide, you can do so by completing these steps:

1. Select Publisher's Page Design tab.

2. Click the Guides icon, located on the toolbar.

3. Choose the Add Horizontal Ruler Guide option from the Guides menu.

Earlier, I showed you how to use the Ruler Guides dialog box to precisely position a ruler guide. You can use this same technique, even after creating multiple ruler guides.

In Figure 2.10, there is a page containing two horizontal ruler guides. The Ruler Guides dialog box displays the current position of each of the ruler guides. To move a ruler guide, select the listing for the guide's current position, enter a new position, and click the Set button. If you want to completely remove a ruler guide, simply select the listing that displays the guide's current position, and then click the Clear button. As you would expect, you can use the Clear All button to remove all the ruler guides from the page.

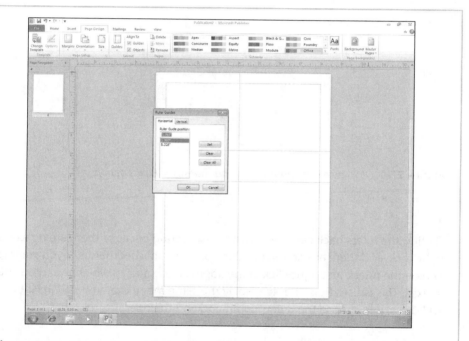

**Figure 2.10**   *You can control the location of multiple ruler guides.*

 **SHOW ME**   **Media 2.3—Using Ruler Guides**
*Access this video file through your registered Web edition at*
***my.safaribooksonline.com/9780132182591/media.***

# Enabling and Disabling Rulers

The rulers should be enabled by default when you use Publisher, but it is always possible that for whatever reason, the rulers might not appear on the screen (especially if you are borrowing someone else's computer). Likewise, I have known of at least one person who found the rulers to be a distraction and wanted them gone. That being the case, I want to take a moment and show you how to turn the rulers on and off.

You can hide the rulers by right-clicking on a ruler, and then choosing the Rulers command from the resulting shortcut menu, which you can see in Figure 2.11. Upon doing so, the rulers will immediately disappear.

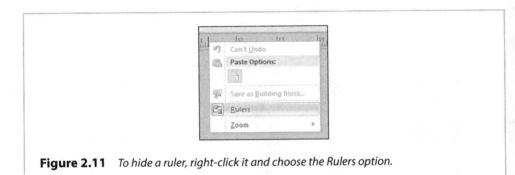

**Figure 2.11**   *To hide a ruler, right-click it and choose the Rulers option.*

Getting the rulers back can seem a little bewildering because there are no rulers to right-click, and there are no ruler options on the Publisher menus. If you want to unhide the rulers, just right-click in the approximate area in which the rulers used to exist. This causes Publisher to display the same menu that you saw in Figure 2.11. Now, just choose the Rulers command and the ruler returns.

# Enlarging Rulers

You have probably noticed in the screen captures that the rulers can be small. This isn't usually a problem if you have a large monitor, but if you have bad vision, a small monitor, or both, you might be looking for a way to enlarge the rulers.

Publisher does not enable you to enlarge the rulers directly. However, you can enlarge your view of the document, which has the effect of enlarging the rulers in the process. There is a slide bar in the lower-right corner of the screen that you can use to adjust the document size.

# Changing the Units of Measurement

By default, Publisher's rulers measure documents in inches. This is fine for many of you, but you might want to measure your documents in centimeters. Similarly, if you are using Publisher to create web content, you might want to measure the document in pixels.

To change the way that Publisher measures your documents, choose the Options command from the File menu. When the Publisher Options dialog box appears, click the Advanced link. When you do, you will find an option to change the units of measurement within the Display section, as shown in Figure 2.12. As you can see in the figure, you can set the ruler to display Inches, Centimeters, Picas, Points, or Pixels.

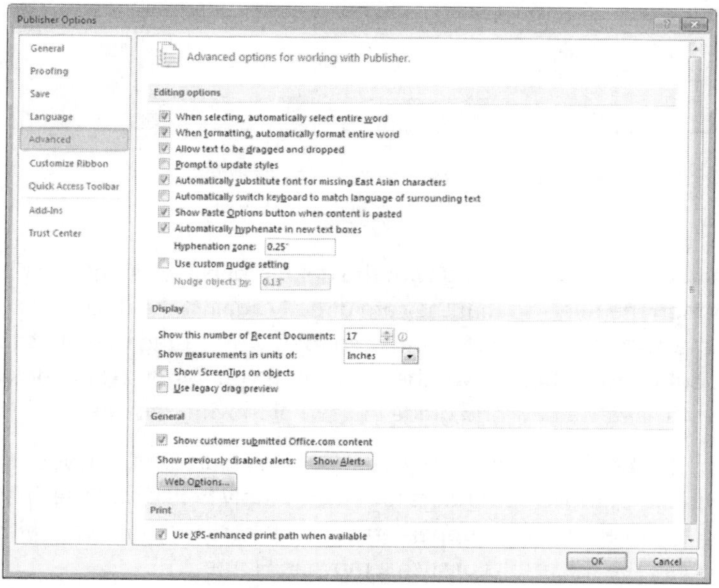

**Figure 2.12**    *You might want to change the unit of measurement.*

# Moving Rulers

When you initially begin creating a new document, the rulers are positioned as shown in Figure 2.13. As you can see, the rulers are kind of far away from the document. This might not be a problem because as you move your mouse, markers on the ruler reflect the mouse's current position.

**Figure 2.13**    *This is how the rulers are positioned by default.*

Although there is nothing wrong with the default behavior, some people may prefer to position the rulers so that they are directly against the document page (or even on the document page). Publisher enables you to drag the rulers to a new position, but to do so, hold down the Shift key. If you forget to hold down Shift, Publisher will create a new grid guide instead of moving the ruler.

You can move the rulers individually, as shown in Figure 2.14, but you don't have to. If you prefer to move both rulers together, simply hold down the Shift key and then drag the rulers from the upper-left corner where they intersect with each other. You can see the results of such a move in Figure 2.15.

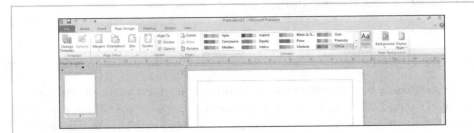

**Figure 2.14**    *You can move the rulers independently of each other.*

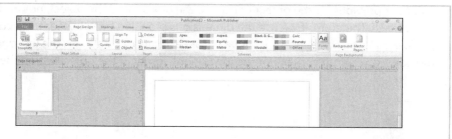

**Figure 2.15**  *The rulers can be moved together.*

# Moving the Zero Mark

In all the previous screen captures, both rulers have placed the zero mark in the upper-left corner of the page. This is easiest to see in Figure 2.15 because the rulers are placed against the edge of the page. In the earlier screen captures, the zero mark is located in the same position, but the fact that the ruler displays negative numbers to the left of the zero mark can be distracting.

In most cases, placing the zero mark at the upper-left corner of the page makes a lot of sense. By doing so, it becomes very easy to measure any point on the entire page. When you get into some of the more advanced document designs, though, you may find yourself doing a lot of math.

To give you an idea of what I am talking about, take a look at Figure 2.16. In this figure, I have drawn an arrow on the page. If you look at the banner along the bottom of the Publisher window, you can see that the top-left corner of this object is at 2.63 inches horizontally by 1.78 inches vertically. Additionally, you can see that the object itself (the box containing the arrow) is 0.55 inches wide by 0.88 inches tall. Now here comes the tricky part....

Imagine that our design required another object to be placed EXACTLY 1.38 horizontal inches to the right and 4.27 vertical inches from the existing object. Although it would take some work, you could calculate the new object's location based on the previous object's location and on the new object's required proximity to the existing object. In some cases, however, using math won't help you.

To see why, imagine that one of the requirements in the situation that I just described is that the second object's location must use the existing object's lower-right corner as the frame of reference. Well, that complicates things a little bit, but you might still be able to work out the new location mathematically because Publisher provides you with the selected object's dimensions. In this case, though, the object that we are using as a point of reference is an arrow. This means that the top of the object (the arrow head) is wider than the bottom. The dimensions that

Publisher provides for the object pertain to the box around the object, not to the object itself. Therefore, if we use the dimensions provided by Publisher to calculate the lower-right corner's position, what we are actually calculating is the location of the box's lower-right corner, not the lower-right corner of the object within the box.

**Figure 2.16**    *The banner along the bottom of the Publisher window tells you the currently selected object's size and position.*

The easiest way to deal with this problem is to move the ruler, and then set the lower-right corner of the arrow as our zero mark. After doing so, it becomes simple to locate the position for the next object that we want to create because all the measurements are based on a common frame of reference.

Begin the process by holding down the Shift button, and then dragging the rulers to the location that you want to use as a frame of reference. As you can see in Figure 2.17, even though we have moved the rulers, the zero mark remains in the upper-left corner of the page.

Now, move your mouse pointer to the point at which the two rulers intersect. Hold down the Shift key, but this time click your right mouse button. When you do, the location where the two rulers intersect will become the new zero mark, as shown in Figure 2.18. We can now find the required position on the page with ease.

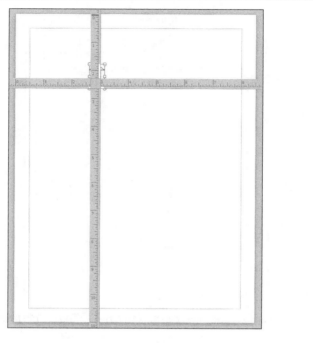

**Figure 2.17**  *Move the ruler to your new point of reference.*

# Page Orientation

Everything so far has been geared toward showing you how to lay out a page so that you can create a document. Sometimes, though, you might find that you have to make some changes to the page itself.

 **LET ME TRY IT**

## Changing the Page Orientation

One such change involves switching the page orientation. So far we have been working with a blank document in portrait format, but we can easily switch to landscape mode. To do so, follow these steps:

1. Select Publisher's Page Design tab.

2. Click the Orientation icon, found on the toolbar.

3. Choose the Landscape option, as shown in Figure 2.19.

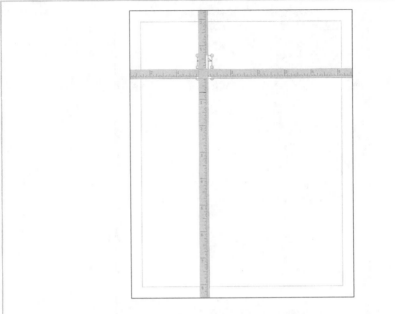

**Figure 2.18**    *Re-zeroing the rulers can make it easier to find certain points within a document.*

**Figure 2.19**    *Use the Orientation option to switch between portrait and landscape mode.*

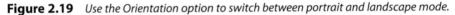

# Page Sizes

The blank document we are creating is presently formatted to fit on an 8.5 × 11 sheet of paper. Even though this is a standard document size, it is far from being the only page size that Publisher supports. Depending on the type of document you are creating, you may occasionally have to set a different page size before you begin creating your document.

 **LET ME TRY IT**

## Changing Page Sizes

To do so, follow these steps:

1. Select Publisher's Page Design tab.

2. Click the Size icon, found on the toolbar.

3. Choose the desired page size from the Size menu.

As you can see in Figure 2.20, Publisher supports several common page sizes. The most common page sizes are displayed directly on the Sizes menu, but there is also a More Preset Page Sizes option that you can select if you can't locate the page size that you need. Publisher contains presets for most standard paper sizes, but if you need something unusual, you can use the Create New Page Size option to set up a custom page size.

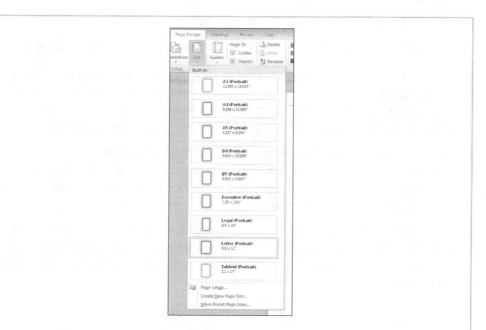

**Figure 2.20**  *Publisher supports several common page sizes.*

It is important to choose your page size carefully, because Publisher does not allow you to mix page sizes and orientations within a single document. If you must use multiple page sizes or orientations, you will have to create separate documents.

# Page Backgrounds

So far, all the screen captures that I have included in this chapter have shown Publisher documents in which the page is displayed as a white piece of paper. Keep in mind, though, that the page background isn't really white. The white background simply represents an absence of color. This means that if you put a piece of blue paper into the printer and print a Publisher document, Publisher isn't going to turn the blue paper white.

 **LET ME TRY IT**

## Changing Page Backgrounds

You aren't stuck using an empty background, though. Publisher will enable you to fill in a document's background. To do so, follow these steps:

1.  Go to Publisher's Page Design tab.

2.  Click the Background icon, located in the toolbar.

3.  Choose the background that you want to use from the Background menu.

If you look at Figure 2.21, you can see that Publisher really doesn't initially give you very many choices when it comes to page backgrounds. You can opt for a solid background, a gradient background, or no background. It might also initially appear that you are limited to using red, blue, and gray as background colors.

All is not what it seems, though. The bottom of the Backgrounds menu contains an option labeled More Backgrounds. Choosing this option enables you to fill the background with any color you choose, a gradient color, a gradient made of multiple colors, patterns, pictures, and more.

I'm not going to go into all the individual fill options right now because I will be covering each option in detail in the next chapter when I talk about shapes and captions. For right now, I at least wanted to make you aware of the fact that these options exist.

# Templates

At the beginning of this chapter, I showed you that when you open Publisher, you are presented with a screen similar to the one shown in Figure 2.22, asking you what type of template you want to use. As you can see in the figure, some of the more popular templates are designed for things such as brochures, business cards, and calendars. Although the template names are pretty self explanatory, you might be wondering what the templates really do.

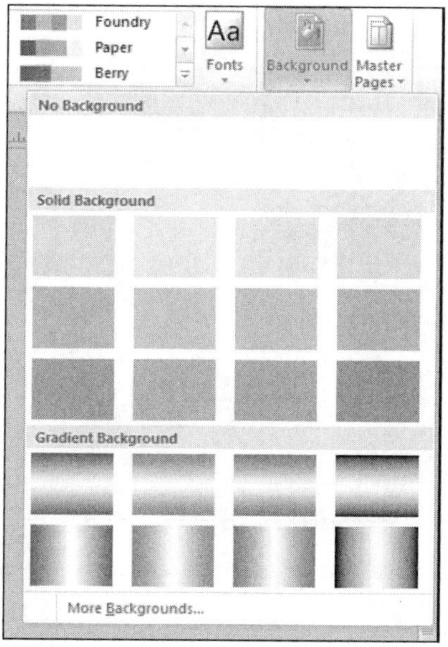

**Figure 2.21**   *You can choose a page background from the Backgrounds menu.*

The first thing that you need to understand about the templates shown in Figure 2.22 is that aside from the blank templates you have already been using, most of the templates that are shown in the figure aren't really templates, but rather template categories. To see what I mean, choose the Brochures template. When you do, you will be taken to the screen shown in Figure 2.23.

# Web-Based Templates

The Brochure template isn't really a template at all, but rather a collection of templates for creating various types of brochures. Also notice in the figure that some of these templates are installed locally, whereas others are available on Office.com. If you select an Internet-based template, the column on the far right displays a preview of the template and provides you with a bit of summary information about it. If you like what you see, you can click the Download button located just beneath the preview.

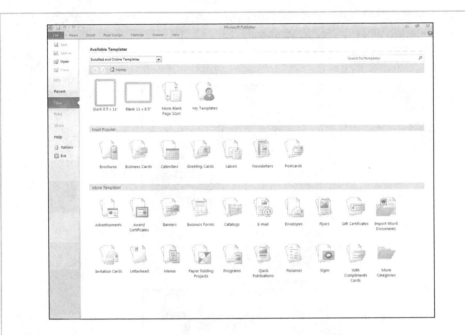

**Figure 2.22**   *Templates make it easier to create certain types of documents.*

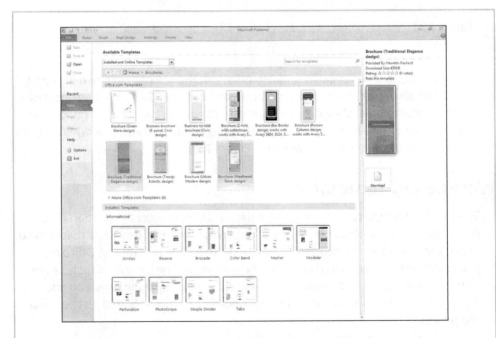

**Figure 2.23**   *The Brochures template is actually a collection of brochure templates.*

# Locally Installed Templates

As was the case with web-based templates, clicking on a locally installed template causes a preview of the template to be displayed in the column on the far right. As you can see in Figure 2.24, Publisher gives you a few more options for locally installed templates than you have for web-based templates.

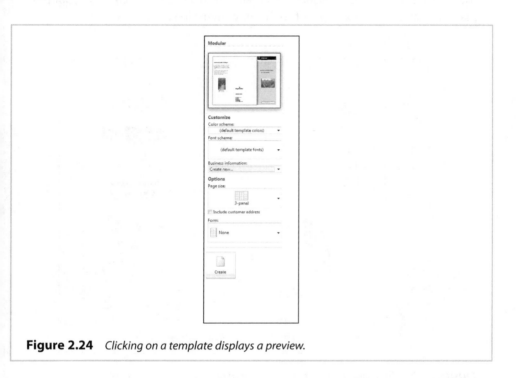

**Figure 2.24** *Clicking on a template displays a preview.*

This figure shows that Publisher gives you the option of selecting a different color scheme for use with the template. You also have the option of selecting a different font scheme. A font scheme is a collection of three different fonts that will be used within the document that you are creating from the template.

The Business Information section enables you to automatically insert information about your business. I talk about this feature in more detail in a later chapter.

The Options section enables you to customize the template's layout. In the case of a brochure, your options include creating a three-panel or four-panel layout. Typically, you would use a three-panel layout if you are going to print the brochure on standard letter-size paper, whereas a four-panel layout would be more appropriate if you are going to print the brochure to legal paper.

The Form section enables you to optionally include a form within the document that you are creating. Publisher offers several different predefined forms. In the case of a brochure, you can include an order form, a response form, or a sign-up form.

When you have selected the options that you want to use with the template, click the Create button, and Publisher will create a new document based on your template. You can see an example of such a document in Figure 2.25.

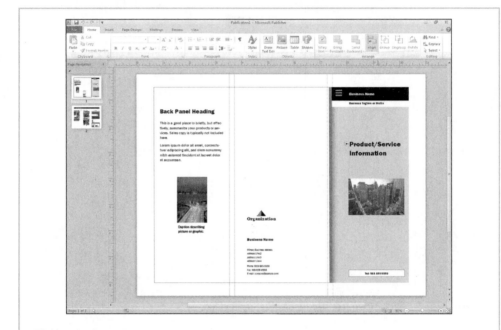

**Figure 2.25** *Publisher creates documents based on templates.*

**SHOW ME**    Media 2.4—Creating a Document from a Template
*Access this video file through your registered Web edition at*
***my.safaribooksonline.com/9780132182591/media.***

## The Anatomy of a Template-Based Document

The document shown in Figure 2.25 is an actual Publisher document. You can view it, print it, and edit it, just as if you had created the document from scratch.

As you look at this document, there are a few things that should look familiar to you. For starters, notice that our template-based document contains a margin offset just like our blank document did. There are also four vertical ruler guides present on the document. These ruler guides help to point out where the brochure will eventually be folded.

Besides the margins and ruler guides, the document contains a variety of text and graphic elements, all of which I discuss in the next chapter. Finally, if you look at the document preview, you can see that the document consists of two pages. You can navigate between document pages by clicking on a page within the preview.

# Changing Templates

Sometimes when you create a document from a template, you might discover that you really don't care for the template after all. When this happens, you don't always have to start completely over from scratch. It is possible to change templates.

 **LET ME TRY IT**

## Switching Templates

To switch to a different template, follow these steps:

1. Go to Publisher's Page Design tab.

2. Click the Change Template icon, found on the toolbar.

3. Choose the new template that you want to use from the list of available templates.

4. Make any necessary customizations to the template, and click OK.

# Creating a Custom Template

Earlier you saw that a template is really nothing more than a Publisher document that has been constructed in such a way that you can just fill in the blanks to create a finished document. You aren't limited to using the templates that Microsoft provides, though—you can create your own. This is useful if you want to create documents in a standardized way.

To give you a better example of what I am talking about, I own the domain name poker-run-boats.com. Before the economy went belly up, I was in the process of creating a website to sell parts for customizing high-performance boats. Although the site has not yet come to fruition, I had an artist design a logo for the site. Eventually, when I do open the site for business, it would probably be useful to have some corporate letterhead. So let's make some.

**LET ME TRY IT**

## Using a Template to Create Letterhead

If you look at Figure 2.26, you can see a document on which I have inserted the poker-run-boats.com logo. We will pretend that this is the final design that I want to use for my company's letterhead. As such, the next step is to turn the document into a template. To do so, complete these steps:

1. Choose the Save As command from the File menu.

2. When the Save As dialog box opens, set the Save As Type option to Publisher Template.

3. By default, the template's category is set to General, but you can change it by clicking the Change button, shown in Figure 2.27.

4. Click the Save button to complete the process.

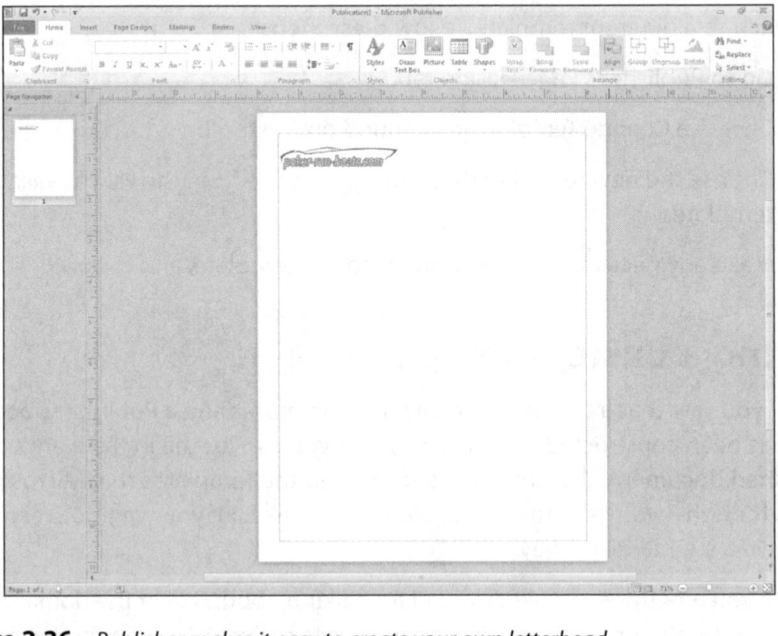

**Figure 2.26** *Publisher makes it easy to create your own letterhead.*

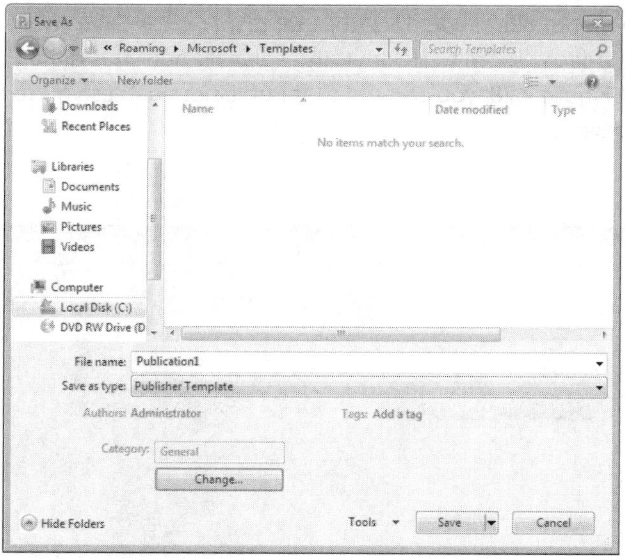

**Figure 2.27**   *You can save your document as a Publisher template.*

If you refer to Figure 2.22, you will notice that the last template on the top row was listed as My Templates. Choosing this option reveals templates that you have created. Simply select your custom template and click the Create button to create a document based on your custom template.

## Saving Your Documents

If you have ever used any of the other Microsoft Office applications, you know that saving an Office document isn't exactly rocket science. Like other Microsoft Office applications, Publisher makes the saving process very painless. To save a document, just click the disk icon in the upper-left portion of the window. When you do, Publisher will prompt you to enter the name of the document that you are saving. You also have the option of entering an optional path.

As an alternative, you can also save a Publisher document by clicking the Save command, found on the File menu.

## Alternative Document Types

Normally when you save a Publisher document, Publisher saves the document in its own proprietary format. However, you can save your documents in some other formats. That way, you can open your Publisher document using other applications.

To save a Publisher document in a nonnative format, choose the Save As command from the File menu. When you do, Publisher displays the Save As dialog box. At first glance, there doesn't seem to be anything special about this dialog box. However, if you look at Figure 2.28, you can see that Publisher enables you to choose from a variety of file types.

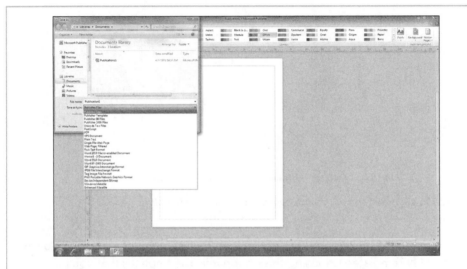

**Figure 2.28**   *Publisher enables you to save documents in a number of different formats.*

It is important to realize that the only option on the entire list that does not impose limitations on your document is the Publisher Files option. This is Publisher's native file format. Some of the file formats impose minor limitations. For example, the Publisher 98 and Publisher 2000 Files options will allow your document to be backward compatible with older versions of Publisher. These options are great if you are going to have to do additional editing and will be limited to using a legacy version of Publisher. The downside to using these file formats is that the older file formats do not support Publisher's newer features. As such, you might see some document elements converted in ways that you do not expect, in an effort to retain backward compatibility.

The Publisher 98 and Publisher 2000 file formats are examples of formats that impose minor limitations. Some of the other file formats are extremely limiting. For instance, Publisher enables you to save documents as a JPEG file. When you do, your document will essentially be converted into a picture. You can still print the document or view it on the screen, but you will no longer be able to edit the document using Publisher. Furthermore, depending on the resolution of the JPEG file, you might find that a hard copy does not look as good as a printout made from the original Publisher document.

Some of the other formats involve similar limitations. For example, Publisher allows you to save a document as a PDF file. PDF documents can be viewed onscreen or printed. If you happen to have a copy of Acrobat (or a competing product), you may do some light editing. However, once a document has been saved as a PDF file, you will not be able to do the degree of editing that is possible natively through Publisher.

You might have noticed in the screen capture that Publisher gives you the option of saving documents as a Microsoft Word file. I discuss conversions between Word and Publisher documents in detail in Chapter 5, "Working with Longer Documents." Likewise, Publisher offers an option to save documents as a web page. I engage in an in-depth discussion of this option in Chapter 9, "Publishing Online."

As you have seen, there are limitations associated with all the file formats except for the one that Publisher uses natively. Even so, there is nothing wrong with saving a Publisher document to an alternative format. However, I would caution you to save your documents in the native format first, and then save to your alternative format. That way, if you decide that you need to make a change to your document, you can do so without having to start from scratch.

 **SHOW ME**   Media 2.5—Saving Your Document
*Access this video file through your registered Web edition at*
**my.safaribooksonline.com/9780132182591/media.**

## Creating a New Document

At the beginning of this chapter, I showed you how you could create a brand-new document simply by opening Publisher and double-clicking the type of document you want to create. Occasionally though, you might decide that you need to create a new document while you are working with Publisher.

You don't have to close and re-open Publisher to create a new document. Instead, simply choose the New command from the File menu. If you presently have a document open, Publisher will ask you whether you want to save your work prior to creating a new document.

You will receive the prompt shown in Figure 2.29, because before Publisher can create a new document, it must close the current document. If you happen to click the New command accidentally, you can always click the Cancel button to return to your work.

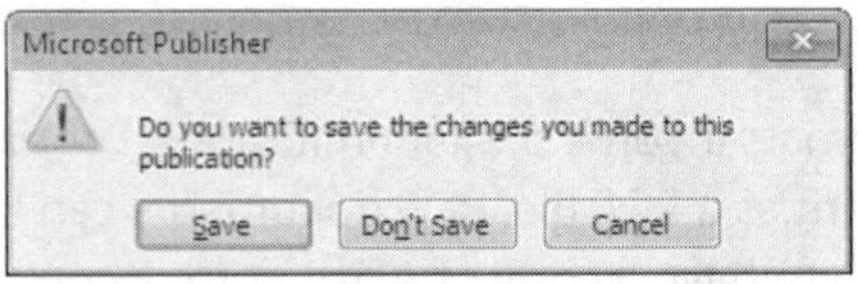

> Microsoft Publisher                                    ✕
>
> ⚠  Do you want to save the changes you made to this
>     publication?
>
>     [ _S_ave ]    [ Do_n_'t Save ]    [ Cancel ]

**Figure 2.29**   *Clicking the New button causes the current document to be closed.*

Clicking the New button isn't the only way to close the document on which you are working. Other options include choosing the Close command from the File menu or simply closing Publisher.

## Opening a Publisher Document

Opening an existing Publisher document is just as easy as saving a document. To do so, choose the Open command from Publisher's File menu. When the Open Publication dialog box appears, navigate to the location in which the document is located, click on the document that you want to open, and then click the Open button.

**TELL ME MORE**    Media 2.6—Do You Really Need Guides and Rulers?
*To listen to a free audio recording about guides and rulers, log on to*
*my.safaribooksonline.com/9780132182591/media.*

**3**

# Working with Visual Elements

In Chapter 2, I showed you some basic techniques for laying out a document page. Now that you have performed the initial setup for your document, it is time to begin adding design elements to the page. I show you how to add text to your document, and then we make things more interesting by adding various types of graphics.

## Text Boxes

In this section, I teach you about text boxes. Before I do, you need to understand how Publisher differs from a word processor, such as Microsoft Word. Although Microsoft Word is capable of incorporating many of the same design elements as Publisher, the two applications are very different.

Microsoft Word is primarily geared toward producing text documents, whereas Publisher mixes text, graphics, and other design elements. As such, when you want to produce a text document in Microsoft Word, you start typing. Publisher will also enable you to type text into a new document, but the process works a bit differently than it does in Word.

In the previous chapter, I mentioned that any design elements that you use in a Publisher document must exist within a box. This goes for text too. If you try to create a new Publisher document, and then you just start typing text, Publisher will automatically create a full-page text box to accommodate your text.

When you create a text box, Publisher places a large rectangle just outside the page margins. This rectangle is the text box that holds the text you type. You can use the small circles and squares that are incorporated into the rectangle to resize the text box. Simply click on one of these markers and drag it into the desired position to resize the text box.

If you move your mouse over the text box anywhere other than above one of the resize markers, the cursor will take the shape of four arrows. This is Publisher's move icon. When the cursor takes this shape, hold down the mouse button, and then move the text box to another location on the page.

Any time you create a text box, Publisher places a green circle just above it. This circle can be used to rotate the text box. To do so, just click on the green circle, and then move your mouse to the left or to the right to rotate the text box, as shown in Figure 3.1.

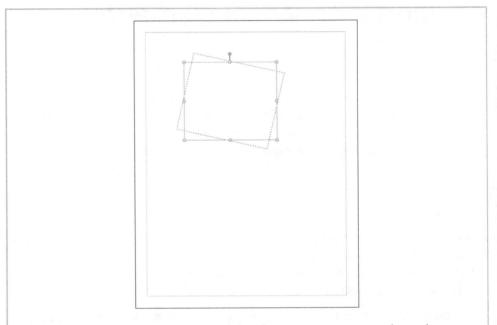

**Figure 3.1**    *Click on the green circle, and then drag your mouse to rotate the text box.*

As we progress through the various lessons, it is important to keep in mind that every visual element that we will be working with is placed in a box. As such, you will be able to resize, reposition, or rotate any design element using exactly the same methods that you used for the text boxes.

## Creating a New Text Box

From the previous section, if you simply start typing text onto a blank page, Publisher creates a text box for you. As you might have already guessed, though, this isn't the preferred way of doing things. In Chapter 2, "Getting Started with Publisher 2010," I showed you how to use grid guides to lay out your document, and I did that for a reason.

There is nothing wrong with letting Publisher automatically create a text box, and then sizing and positioning the text box to meet your needs. However, as you will eventually discover, most Publisher documents require the use of multiple text boxes. As such, it is important for you to know how to create additional text boxes on demand.

 **LET ME TRY IT**

## Creating a New Text Box

Publisher enables you to create a new text box by drawing it in the shape and location that you want. To create a text box, complete these steps:

1. Click Publisher's Home tab.

2. Click the Draw Text Box icon, located on the toolbar.

3. Move the cursor to the area where you want to place the new text box's upper-left corner.

4. Hold the left mouse button, and move the cursor into the position where you want to place the text box's lower-right corner.

5. Release the mouse button, and the text box will be created. You can adjust the text box's size and position by using the techniques that I showed you earlier.

# Entering Text into a Text Box

The concept of entering text into a text box probably sounds like a no brainer. Just click on a text box before you enter text into it. It's that easy.

Note that when you are working on other design elements, text boxes you have previously created might seem to vanish. If this happens to you, all you have to do is click on the area where the text box should be, and it will reappear.

If you have already entered text into the text box, locating the text box is easy because the text itself won't usually disappear. You might have to hunt around a bit if you need to locate an empty text box. That being the case, if you create a text box but aren't ready to populate it yet, I would put a few words of placeholder text into the text box just to make the box easy to find.

Normally, if a text box contains text, the text box may disappear while you are working with other visual elements but the words within the text box will remain onscreen. This isn't always the case, though. Publisher makes it possible for visual elements to overlap one another. When this happens, you might see a text box's contents disappear. I show you how to deal with this problem later in this chapter.

**SHOW ME    Media 3.1—Creating a Text Box**
*Access this video file through your registered Web edition at*
**my.safaribooksonline.com/9780132182591/media.**

# Fonts

Just like every other Microsoft Office application, Publisher 2010 enables you to choose from a variety of different fonts. You also can change a font's point size and color, and can make a number of additional customizations that I talk about in Chapter 4, "Designs and Layouts."

Because fonts are used heavily within Publisher, I wanted to take the opportunity to give you a crash course on the fonts that Windows supports.

Windows 7 supports two types of fonts: TrueType and OpenType. Unlike the bitmap font files that were used by some of the older versions of Windows, TrueType fonts are designed to scale cleanly. If you increase the size of a bitmap font, eventually it will become blocky. TrueType fonts do not have this problem. Furthermore, TrueType fonts work with any printer that Windows supports.

OpenType fonts are similar to TrueType fonts, except they are Unicode based. The Unicode support allows OpenType fonts to support a greater range of character sets than what is possible with TrueType fonts. In addition to the basic character set, an OpenType font might also include a small capitalization set or a condensed set.

# Purchasing Fonts

Windows ships with a fairly decent collection of built-in fonts; in fact, Windows 7 contains about 40 new fonts. In addition, Publisher includes many additional fonts. Even so, you may find that the built-in font set simply doesn't contain a font that conveys the desired look and feel for your project.

To give you a more concrete example of such a situation, a few years ago I bought a new Cigarette boat. For those of you who are not familiar with marine culture, it is traditional to give a boat a name and to display the boat's home port (the city where you keep the boat) in a smaller type size beneath the boat's name.

When it comes to higher-end boats, the name is almost never displayed in plain text. It is usually more like a logo. That being the case, I decided that Publisher would be the perfect tool for creating the lettering for my boat.

Laying out the text for the home port and for the boat's registration numbers was no big deal. I just used a standard font in the boat's color scheme and added a drop shadow. Designing the boat's name was much more challenging, though. For one thing, the fonts that were included with Windows all seemed either too businesslike, too childish, or too overused. I wanted something unique. Thankfully, there are numerous fonts available on the Internet. Many of these fonts are free, but if you can't find exactly what you are looking for, there are also fonts available for purchase.

To make a long story short, I ended up purchasing a TrueType font for use in my boat's logo. I got the font for a decent price, but it is worth noting that font prices can vary widely.

Since it has been about five years since I created the logo for my boat, I can't remember exactly how much the font cost me, but if memory serves me, I think that I paid around $10 for it. As I said, though, the price of fonts varies widely. I have seen fonts sell for as low as a buck, or as high as about $400.

So why the big difference in cost? Typically, the higher-priced fonts give you a little bit more bang for the buck. For example, a high-priced commercial font may provide you with many different variations of that font (light, bold, ultra black, light italic, bold condensed, and so on). Free and low-priced fonts, on the other hand, typically include fewer (if any) variations.

For example, I recently downloaded the font that the band Iron Maiden uses on all their album covers. Because this was a free font, it included only a single TTF file, with no variations. I'm not saying that you can't make it bold or italic or change the point size—you can. It's just that the free font didn't include variations, such as black condensed or ultra bold.

Obviously, these days everyone is on a budget, and paying big bucks for a single font might not be an option. Fortunately, there are some alternatives to purchasing expensive commercial fonts.

One option is to do an Internet search on the font name. Sometimes a font will be available from multiple websites, and the pricing is not always consistent from one site to another. It pays to shop around.

Another option is to see whether you can find the font included as a part of a font family. A font family is a collection of fonts that have a similar appearance. Using fonts that are vastly different from one another can sometimes give the document a feeling of disarray. Designers create font families as a way of grouping fonts that do a good job of complementing each other. I have found that font families can be less expensive than a single font, but may lack the style variations found in a high-priced commercial font.

# Typography

In the previous section, I talked about how I used Microsoft Publisher to create the logo for my Cigarette boat. In retrospect, Publisher was the perfect tool for the job. I was able to give the font a color that matched my boat, add a drop shadow, and insert a graphic to go along with it. More importantly, though, the rulers that I talked about in the previous chapter allowed me to ensure that my design would fit within the allotted space on the boat, but without being too small. Incidentally, this also required me to work with the printing company to ensure that my vinyl graphics would be printed in the correct dimensions. I talk all about the printing process in Chapter 8, "Printing." For right now, though, I want to show you how to install and preview a font.

# Installing a Font

Because fonts are a Windows-level component, the method for installing them differs from one version of Windows to the next. In Windows 7, you can install a font by copying the font file to the C:\Windows\Fonts folder.

 **LET ME TRY IT**

# Enabling ClearType

ClearType is a technology used by Windows to make fonts easier to read. It works by applying shading to certain parts of the characters, to make the characters appear smoother. You can enable ClearType in Windows 7 by following these steps:

1. Open Windows Explorer and navigate to C:\Windows\Fonts.

2. Click the Adjust ClearType Text link.

3. Select the Turn On ClearType check box.

4. Click Next.

5. Windows shows you two text previews. Select the preview that looks the best to you, and click Next.

6. Windows displays three more screens, each requiring you to select the text that looks the best to you. When the process completes, click Finish.

As an alternative to using Windows Explorer, you can open the Start menu and enter the phrase Adjust ClearType Text: into the Search box. When the result appears, click on it.

# Previewing a Font

As you prepare to add text to your document, one of the first decisions that you will have to make involves choosing the font that you want to use. Publisher contains a dropdown list on the Home tab that you can use to select the font of choice. This dropdown list provides a short preview of what the various fonts look like, as shown in Figure 3.2, but it usually isn't the best option for deciding on a font.

**Figure 3.2**  *You can select a font from Publisher's Home tab.*

**LET ME TRY IT**

# Previewing Fonts

In my opinion, you are better off using Windows as a mechanism for previewing fonts. The exact method for doing so varies from one version of Windows to another. In Windows 7, you can preview fonts by performing the following steps:

1. Click the Start button.

2. Open the Control Panel.

3. Click the Appearance and Personalization link.

4. Click the Fonts link.

The resulting screen shows you a list of each available font, as shown in Figure 3.3. Although you can get somewhat of an idea of what each font looks like from this screen, you can do better. Simply right-click on a font and choose the Preview option to see a full-blown preview. Windows even gives you the option of printing the preview.

**Figure 3.3**   *The Windows Control Panel displays each font that is installed on the system.*

If you want to see how a font will appear in your document, select it and then hover over the font you are considering using in the list of fonts. The text dynamically changes to show you a preview of what the font would look like if it were applied.

**SHOW ME**    Media 3.2—Working with Fonts
*Access this video file through your registered Web edition at*
***my.safaribooksonline.com/9780132182591/media.***

**LET ME TRY IT**

# Inserting Pictures

Inserting a picture is easy. To do so, follow these steps:

1.  Go to Publisher's Insert tab.

2.  Click the Picture icon, located on the toolbar.

3.  Select the picture that you want to insert into your document.

4.  Click the Insert button.

As you can see in Figure 3.4, Publisher inserts the picture between the document's margins. Like all visual elements, the picture exists within a box, and you can use the markers on the box to rotate, move, or resize the picture.

**Figure 3.4**   *Pictures can be inserted directly into Publisher documents.*

# Formatting Pictures

As you look at Figure 3.4, notice that the toolbar icons have changed to reflect the fact that I currently have a picture selected. As you can see in the screen capture, Publisher displays icons that can be used for adjusting the picture's brightness and contrast.

Another cool option is the Recolor option. By clicking the Recolor icon, shown in Figure 3.5, you are given the opportunity to recolor the image using a variety of effects. For example, you can make a color image black and white or turn the whole image sepia.

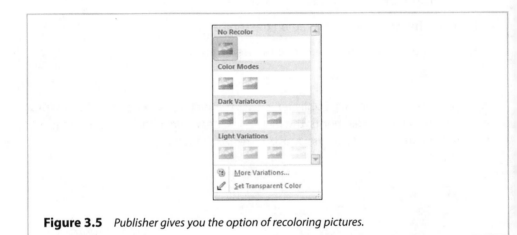

**Figure 3.5**  *Publisher gives you the option of recoloring pictures.*

If the color variations that are presented on the recolor menu don't fit your needs, you can always use the More Variations option. This option enables you to tint your picture to match any color in the rainbow.

# Transparency

Another fun thing that you can do with colors is to make a portion of an image transparent. To do so, you must designate a color within the image to become transparent. When you do, the background (or underlying layers of the image) will be displayed in place of the color that you have removed.

 **LET ME TRY IT**

## Make an Image Transparent

To make a portion of an image transparent, complete these steps:

1. Go to Publisher's Format tab.

2. Click on the image that you want to work with.

3. Click the Recolor icon, found on the toolbar.

4. Choose the Set Transparent Color option from the Recolor menu.

5. Move the cursor to the color that you want to render transparent, and click the left mouse button.

It is worth noting that making a color transparent tends to work much better if your picture is a diagram rather than a photograph. Photographs tend to use millions of colors. As such, an object within a photograph may appear to be a solid color, but in reality it is commonly made up of numerous different shades of that color. Publisher does not always pick up on all of the varying shades. Experience has shown that sometimes transparency is also applied to unexpected areas of a photograph.

 **LET ME TRY IT**

## Resetting a Picture's Color

Sometimes you may recolor all or part of an image, only to decide that you don't like the change. If you make this decision immediately, you can use the Undo button to undo your changes. Sometimes, though, you might not decide that you want a change until much later in the design process, when it is far too late to click Undo.

To reset a picture to its original color, complete these steps:

1. Go to Publisher's Format tab.

2. Click on the image that you want to modify.

3. Click the Recolor icon.

4. Choose the No Recolor option from the Recolor menu.

This process will not remove a transparent color. The only way to do so is to right-click on the picture and choose the Change Picture | Reset Picture commands from the shortcut menus. Keep in mind, though, that this resets everything about the image, including positioning and scaling.

## Picture Styles and Shapes

You can achieve some rather dramatic effects by applying styles or shapes to the photographs that you include in your Publisher documents. In Figure 3.5, you might have noticed the Picture Styles section on the toolbar. You can choose from any one of these styles, and Publisher will change the shape of the image to match the style that you have chosen. Although only four styles are initially shown, additional styles are available by clicking the down arrow in the lower-right corner of the Picture Styles section. You can see an example of some of the styles that are available to you in Figure 3.6.

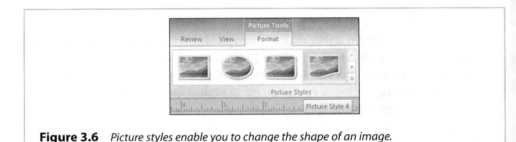

**Figure 3.6**   *Picture styles enable you to change the shape of an image.*

As you look at Figure 3.6, you might have noticed that although numerous picture styles are available, they all conform to the same basic shapes. Publisher doesn't limit you quite as much as you might think, though. If you want to mold a picture into a shape other than what is available through the Picture Style section, you can do so by clicking the Picture Shapes icon located on the toolbar. As you can see in Figure 3.7, there are a wide variety of shapes that you can apply to your picture.

 **SHOW ME**   Media 3.3—Picture Styles and Shapes
*Access this video file through your registered Web edition at*
**my.safaribooksonline.com/9780132182591/media.**

## Changing a Picture

The picture toolbar, displayed on the Format tab, contains an icon labeled Change Picture. You can use this icon if you want to reset the picture to its original state or replace it with a new picture. Using this icon removes the picture but leaves the picture object behind. Because the picture object retains its shape and position, it is easy to place the replacement picture in exactly the same position.

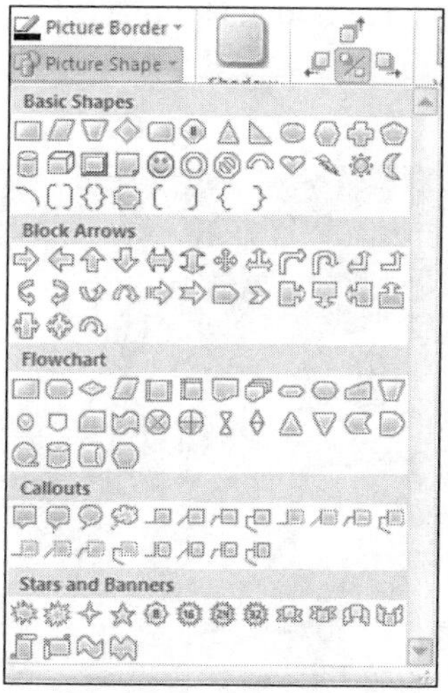

**Figure 3.7**    *Numerous shapes are available.*

# Picture Captions

If you are including photographs in your Publisher document, you might find that you occasionally need to annotate your pictures with captions. You can do so by using Publisher's Caption feature.

**LET ME TRY IT**

## Inserting a Picture Caption

You can insert a picture caption by completing the following steps:

1. Go to Publisher's Format tab.

2. Click on the picture to which you want to add a caption.

3. Click the Caption icon, located on the toolbar.

4. Select the caption that you want to add to the picture.

5. Click the default text within the caption to select it.

6. Replace the default text with your own caption.

7. Format your caption with the font, color, and style of your choosing.

You can see an example of a caption in Figure 3.8.

**Figure 3.8**   *Publisher makes it easy to add captions to pictures.*

## Changing a Caption's Color

By default, Publisher uses a background color that is based on the current theme (the default color was red in this case). You are not stuck with the default color. Before I show you how to change a caption's color, it is worth noting that a caption is really nothing more than a shape that has a text box in the middle of it. Consequentially, all the techniques I am about to show you can also be applied to shapes.

 **LET ME TRY IT**

## Changing Colors

If you refer to Figure 3.8, you will notice that our caption had some wavy lines at the top. Publisher treats each of these lines as a separate shape. As such, you will have to apply coloring to each section individually. You can change the caption's color by completing these steps:

1. Right-click on the portion of the caption that you want to modify (but not on the text box within the caption).

2. Choose the Format AutoShape command from the shortcut menu.

3. When Windows displays the Format AutoShape text box, select the Colors and Lines tab.

4. Choose the color that you want to use from the Color dropdown list, as shown in Figure 3.9.

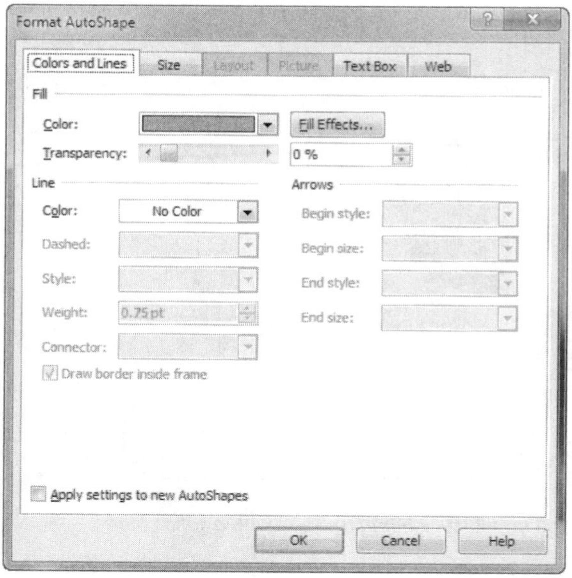

**Figure 3.9**  *You can change a caption's color.*

## Going Beyond Simple Colors

There is nothing wrong with setting a new color for a caption, but you don't have to stop there. There are numerous effects that you can apply to your caption. To get started, right-click on a section within the caption (but not on the text box within the caption), and choose the now-familiar Format AutoShape command from the shortcut menu. When you do, you will be taken to the same dialog box that I showed you a moment ago.

I have already shown you how to choose a new color, but we can do much more than that. For example, refer to Figure 3.9 and notice that the Colors and Lines tab contains a rather large section called Line. This section controls the appearance of the line that is used to separate one section of the caption from another. By default, the line is invisible, but you can make the line visible by assigning it a color. After doing so, you can also control the style and the weight of the line.

Having the ability to control the line's appearance is nice, but the reality is that this probably isn't a feature that you will use very often. You can access a more practical feature by clicking the Fill Effects button. When you do, Publisher will display the Fill Effects properties sheet shown in Figure 3.10.

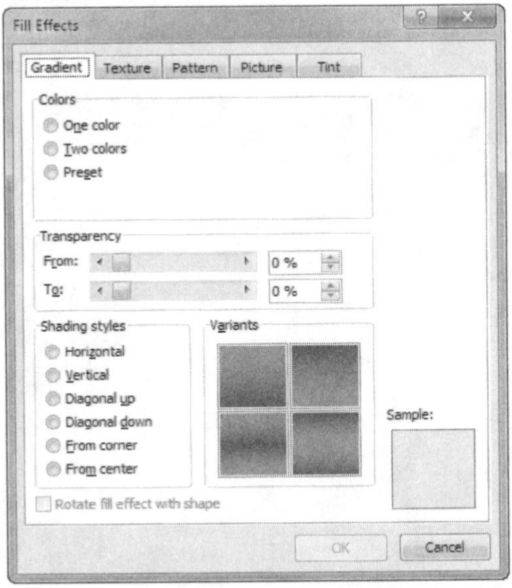

**Figure 3.10**  *You aren't stuck filling a shape with a solid color.*

# Gradients

The Gradient tab, shown in Figure 3.10, enables you to use a gradient instead of a solid color. To begin, you must tell Publisher whether you want to use a single color or two colors within the gradient. You also have the option of using a predefined gradient, but most of the predefined gradients tend to be a bit on the psychedelic side.

If you have chosen to use a single color gradient, the next step in the process is to choose the color on which you want to base the gradient. You also have the option of controlling how light or dark the gradient should be.

If you have chosen to create a two-color gradient, you will have to pick two colors instead of one. Normally, the colors that you choose should not be similar to each other. Picking colors that are too similar can cause the gradient effect to be overly subtle.

After picking your colors, you have the option of setting a range of transparency for the gradient. I tend to like to leave this option alone, but you shouldn't be afraid to experiment with it. You can achieve some rather strange results by monkeying around with the transparency.

The last step in creating your gradient is to choose the shading style that you want to use. The shading style controls the way in which the gradient is generated. Remember, a gradient is a transition from light to dark or from one color to another; therefore, a horizontal gradient might start with a light color at the top of the shape and fade into a darker color near the bottom of the shape. In contrast, a vertical gradient might place the lighter color on the left side of the screen and the darker color on the right side.

Even though you have to pick a shading style, the creation of the gradient isn't quite as rigid as the previous paragraph might lead you to believe. That's because choosing the shading style is only part of the process. If you refer to Figure 3.10, you will notice a section labeled Variants just to the right of the shading styles. This section enables you choose the specifics of how you want the gradient fill to appear with regard to the shading style that you have chosen.

One last thing that I want to mention about this tab is the Rotate Fill Effect with Shape check box that appears at the bottom of the window. Once you have selected a caption, you probably won't be rotating it very much. This isn't necessarily the case for other types of shapes, though. Sometimes you might find that after rotating a shape, the gradient no longer looks right. The Rotate Fill Effect with Shape check box enables you to preserve the effect you have created by moving the gradient along with the shape.

# The Texture Tab

The Texture tab, shown in Figure 3.11, enables you to fill a caption with a texture rather than a color. This tab is extremely simple to use. All you have to do is select the texture that you want to apply to the shape, and click OK.

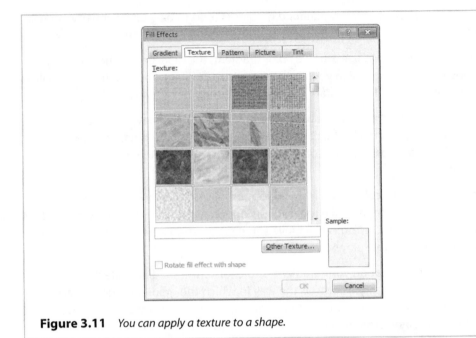

**Figure 3.11**   *You can apply a texture to a shape.*

Of course, Publisher will only show you the textures that it knows about. If you have a non-default texture that you want to use, you can click the Other Texture button and then specify the texture file you want to use.

Publisher gives you the option of rotating textures in conjunction with the movement of shapes. Doing so works in exactly the same way that it did for gradients.

## Patterns

Just as Publisher enables you to apply textures to a shape, you also have the option of filling a shape with a pattern. To do so, select the Pattern tab, shown in Figure 3.12.

As you can see in the figure, applying a pattern to a shape is a two-step process. First, you must choose the pattern that you want to apply, and then you must choose a foreground and a background color for the pattern.

## Photos

Another design element that you can include in a shape or a caption is a photograph. Filling a shape with a photo is extremely easy. As you can see in Figure 3.13, you must simply select the picture that you want to use.

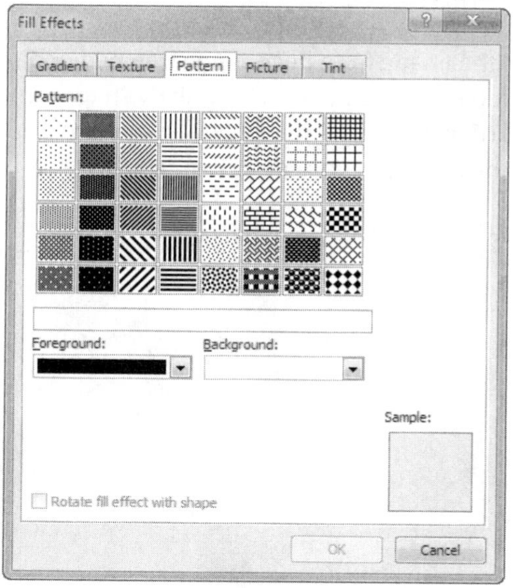

**Figure 3.12**    *You can fill a shape with a pattern.*

**Figure 3.13**    *You can fill a shape with a photo.*

The one bit of advice that I would give you regarding the use of photos within shapes is to lock the picture aspect ratio by using the check box shown in Figure 3.13. This prevents the image from becoming stretched or distorted, which can really become a problem if you have an irregularly shaped image or are trying to fill a shape that is not of uniform dimensions. When a photo is used to fill a shape, the end result looks similar to what you see in Figure 3.14.

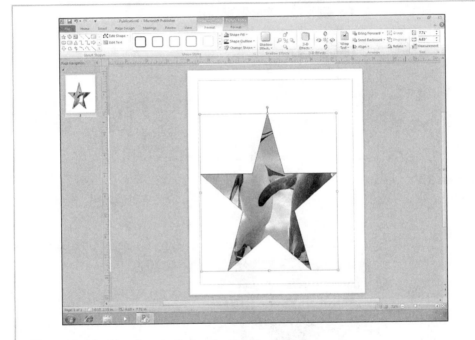

**Figure 3.14** *The photo is displayed within the shape.*

# Tint

The last option for filling a shape is to use the tint option. As you can see in Figure 3.15, tinting a shape involves picking a base color, and then deciding how dark the tint should be. The end result is similar to that of filling the shape with a solid color.

**SHOW ME** Media 3.4—Fill Effects
*Access this video file through your registered Web edition at*
**my.safaribooksonline.com/9780132182591/media.**

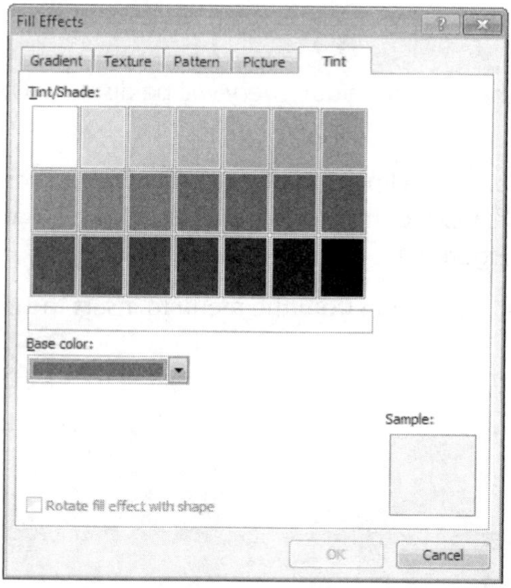

**Fill Effects**

Gradient | Texture | Pattern | Picture | Tint

Tint/Shade:

Base color:

Sample:

☐ Rotate fill effect with shape

OK | Cancel

**Figure 3.15** *Tinting is essentially the same as filling a shape with a solid color.*

# Clip Art

The process of adding clip art to a Publisher document is similar to that of adding an image, but there are a few key differences in the process. The biggest difference between adding clip art and adding a picture is that Publisher does not seem to provide you with a method for browsing all the available clip art. You need to have an idea going in of what type of clip art you want to use. You must then search for the clip art that you want to use.

 **LET ME TRY IT**

## Inserting Clip Art

The whole process of inserting clip art sounds much more difficult than it really is. To see how easy it is to work with clip art, perform these steps:

1. Go to Publisher's Insert tab.

2. Choose the Clip Art icon, located on the toolbar.

3. Enter a search term into the Search For box.

4. Click Go.

5. Any clip art that matches your query will be displayed beneath the search box.

6. Click on the piece of clip art that you want to use. When you do, a down arrow appears next to the clip art. Click this down arrow to reveal a menu, as shown in Figure 3.16.

7. Choose the Insert option from the menu to insert the clip art into your document.

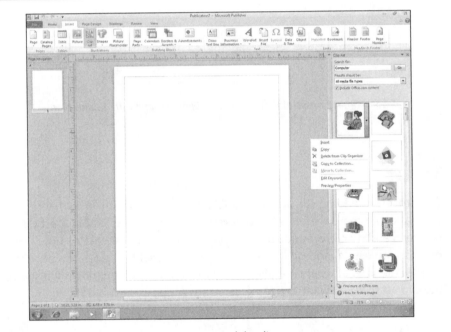

**Figure 3.16** *Click on the down arrow to reveal the clip art menu.*

## Clip Art Key Words

When you search for clip art, you are searching by entering keywords into the search engine. Although the built-in clip art is fairly well indexed, you will probably run into situations in which finding the clip that you want requires a lot of effort.

## **LET ME TRY IT**

## Reviewing Key Words

You can make it easier to find the clip in the future by revising the list of keywords that are associated with the clip art image. To do so, follow these steps:

1. Click on the image that you want to revise.

2. When the down arrow appears alongside the image, click it to reveal the clip art menu.

3. Choose the Edit Keywords option from the menu.

4. The Keywords dialog box appears and enables you to add keywords to the image.

## Copyright Issues

I need to take just a moment and discuss some of the copyright issues you will encounter while creating Publisher documents. Whenever you create a document, it is your responsibility to ensure that images used within the document do not violate someone's copyright.

You really don't have to worry about copyright issues if all you are using is clip art. Microsoft makes clip art freely available as a part of Publisher, and you are free to include it in any type of document.

Photos are another story, however. The safest way to ensure that a photograph does not violate someone's copyright is to use your own original work. For instance, the image that I used in the section on pictures was a photograph that I took on a recent trip to New York City.

Generally speaking, photographs found on the Internet are copyrighted and are usually either owned by or licensed to the owner of the website where they are displayed. There are exceptions, though. Some websites specialize in stock photography that you can use for your own purposes. A good example of such a site is Corbis (www.Corbis.com), where I have purchased several photos.

If you decide to use stock photography in a document, you must take the time to check the terms for licensing the photograph. Some of the images on Corbis and on other stock photography sites are royalty free. Other photographs are rights managed, and licensing such photographs can be tricky.

# Shapes

When you think of adding graphics to a Publisher document, you probably think of pictures or clip art. Although you can certainly add these types of graphics to a Publisher document, you can also add shapes. I talked about shapes to some degree when I covered captions. You can create other types of shapes, though.

 **LET ME TRY IT**

## Inserting a Shape

Shapes don't add a lot to a document by themselves, but they can be combined with other design elements to create some nice effects. You can add shapes to a document by completing the following steps:

1. Go to Publisher's Insert tab.

2. Choose the Shapes option from the toolbar.

3. Select the desired shape from the Shapes menu, as shown in Figure 3.17.

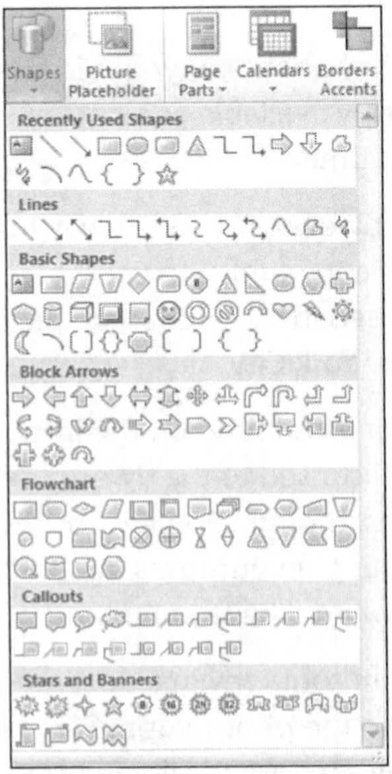

**Figure 3.17**    *The Shapes menu contains a variety of shapes to choose from.*

4. Move the cursor to the location where you want to place the lower-left corner of the shape.

5. Hold the left mouse button, and then move the cursor to the location where you want to place the upper-right corner of the shape.

6. Release the mouse button.

7. Move or resize the shape as needed by dragging the markers on the box surrounding the shape.

# Adding a 3-D Effect

As you can see, Publisher has no trouble adding a shape to the page, but in its present form, the shape is a bit lackluster. It doesn't have to stay that way, though. There are a number of things that we can do to make the shape a bit more exciting. For starters, we can make our two-dimensional shape three dimensional.

 **LET ME TRY IT**

## Creating a 3-D Shape

To convert a shape into a 3-D shape, follow these steps:

1. Click on the shape to select it.

2. Select Publisher's Format tab.

3. Click the 3-D Effects icon, found on the toolbar.

4. Choose one of the predefined 3-D shapes from the 3-D Effect menu. If you aren't sure which effect to use, you can see a preview of each effect by hovering your mouse over it. You can see a sample of a 3-D effect in Figure 3.18.

**SHOW ME**   Media 3.5—Creating 3-D Shapes
*Access this video file through your registered Web edition at*
**my.safaribooksonline.com/9780132182591/media.**

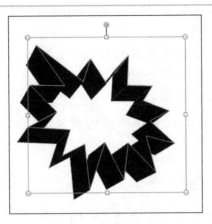

**Figure 3.18**    *This is what a shape looks like after one of the 3-D effects has been applied.*

# Coloring a Shape

Even though we have made our shape 3-D, it is still a bit boring. One way to brighten things up a bit is to add some color. There are two different techniques that I want to show you for coloring a shape.

The first technique will work for both 2-D and 3-D shapes. In the case of a 2-D shape, this technique will fill in the shape with the color that you choose. When you use this technique on a 3-D shape, the center becomes a solid color and the 3-D edges become gradients of the chosen color.

 **LET ME TRY IT**

## Adding Color to a Shape

To apply color to a shape using this method, follow these steps:

1. Click on the shape to select it.

2. Go to Publisher's Format tab.

3. Select the Shape Fill icon from the toolbar.

4. Choose the desired color from the resulting menu.

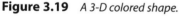

## LET ME TRY IT

## Coloring a Shape's Outer Edges

The next technique that I want to show you is applicable only to 3-D shapes. This technique colors the shape's outer edges. You can combine this technique with the one I just showed you so that you end up with a colored shape with a different colored border. To do so, follow these steps:

1. Click on the shape to select it.

2. Go to Publisher's Format tab.

3. Click the 3-D Effect icon, found on the toolbar.

4. Choose the 3-D Color option from the 3-D Effect menu, and then choose the color you want to apply to the shape. You can see the results of this technique in Figure 3.19.

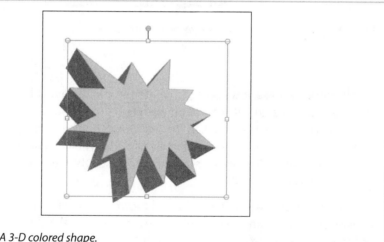

**Figure 3.19**   *A 3-D colored shape.*

# Layering

Earlier in the book, I mentioned that it is possible for visual elements to overlap each other. When done correctly, you can use this technique to produce some fairly impressive documents.

If you look at Figure 3.20, you can see that I have dummied up something like what you would see in a cheesy advertisement. This effect is the result of combining multiple layers. The bottom layer is the page's background. The middle layer is the 3-D shape that we created in the last section. The top layer is made up of word art.

**Figure 3.20** *You can add a text layer on top of a shape.*

In this particular case, it was easy to create the desired effect because the 3-D shape already existed. All I had to do was create the word art and then drag it so that it was on top of the shape. In the real world, however, things don't always go quite so smoothly. You may occasionally find that you have not created the layers in the correct order. This isn't a problem, though. Publisher enables you to arrange document layers on the fly.

Imagine, for example, that I had created the word art before I created my three-dimensional shape, and that in the process of creating the shape, the word art became covered up, as shown in Figure 3.21.

 **LET ME TRY IT**

## Pushing a Shape to the Back

In a situation like this, we would need to move the word art to the outer layer so that it is displayed on top of the shape. This actually is very easy to do. If you look at Figure 3.21, you will notice that the toolbar contains Bring Forward and Send

Backward icons. The easiest way to bring the text to the front is to push the shape to the back. To do so, follow these steps:

1. Click on the shape to select it.

2. Go to Publisher's Home tab.

3. Click the Send Backward icon found on the toolbar.

4. Choose either the Send Backward option (to move the shape back one layer) or the Send to Back option (to move the shape to the bottom layer).

**Figure 3.21**   *Layers can accidentally become covered by other layers.*

In this case, it doesn't really matter which options you choose because we have only a couple of layers. In more complex documents, though, you will most likely have to move objects one layer at a time.

## Other Objects

I want to conclude this chapter by showing you some other types of objects that you can include in your Publisher document. Generally, Publisher offers the ability to incorporate just about any design element that is supported by other Microsoft

Office applications. For example, you can import a Microsoft Word document, an Excel spreadsheet, or PowerPoint slides. These are far from being the only types of Microsoft Office objects that you can import, however.

I don't really want to get into importing Microsoft Office documents right now, because I cover the topic at length in some of the later chapters. For example, Chapter 4 deals with Microsoft Word documents (among other things). I also talk about Excel in Chapter 6, "Tables," and I even spend some time in Chapter 10, "Bulk Mail Techniques," discussing Microsoft Access.

For right now, though, I want to show you a couple of examples of other types of Microsoft Office data that you might want to include in your document.

# Drawings

If you have ever used Publisher 2007, you probably know that it includes some crude drawing tools. Microsoft seems to have removed these tools from Publisher 2010. However, that doesn't mean that Publisher no longer supports drawings.

 **LET ME TRY IT**

## Using the Paintbrush

Publisher 2010 is designed to use Paintbrush (the drawing applet that comes with Windows) as its drawing tool. If you want to doodle in Publisher, follow these steps:

1. Go to Publisher's Insert tab.
2. Click the Object icon located on the toolbar.
3. When the Insert Object dialog box appears, choose the Paintbrush Picture option, as shown in Figure 3.22.
4. Make sure the Create New option is selected, and click OK.
5. Windows will now open Paintbrush. Go ahead and create your drawing.
6. When you complete your drawing, I recommend that you save a copy of it for future reference.
7. Choose Paintbrush's Exit and Return to Document option, shown in Figure 3.23.
8. Your drawing is seamlessly imported into Publisher, as shown in Figure 3.24.

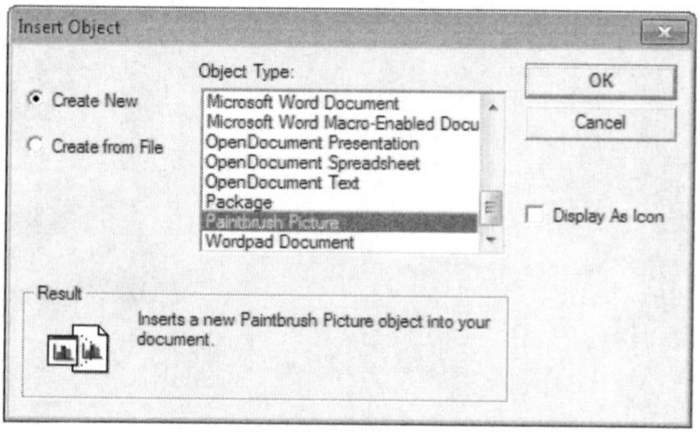

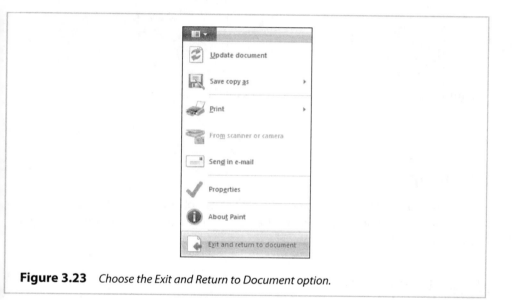

**Figure 3.22**   *Paintbrush is Publisher's new drawing tool.*

**Figure 3.23**   *Choose the Exit and Return to Document option.*

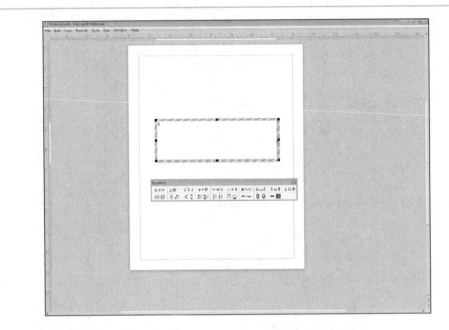

**Figure 3.24**    *Your Paintbrush drawing is imported into publisher.*

## Equations

The Equation Editor is something that a lot of people don't seem to realize exists. Because I am an engineer, I tend to use a lot of math, so I wanted to introduce you to this feature.

 **LET ME TRY IT**

## Accessing the Equation Editor

You can access the equation editor by completing these steps:

1. Go to Publisher's Insert tab.

2. Click the Object icon.

3. Choose Microsoft Equation 3.0 from the list of available objects, and click OK.

You can see what the Equation Editor looks like in Figure 3.25. At first glance, this editor probably looks a bit cryptic. However, you can use it by clicking the icon that most closely represents the symbol that you need. Doing so causes the editor to display a submenu containing individual symbols. When you select a symbol, it is displayed within the text box. Once your symbols are in place, you can begin filling in numbers and variables.

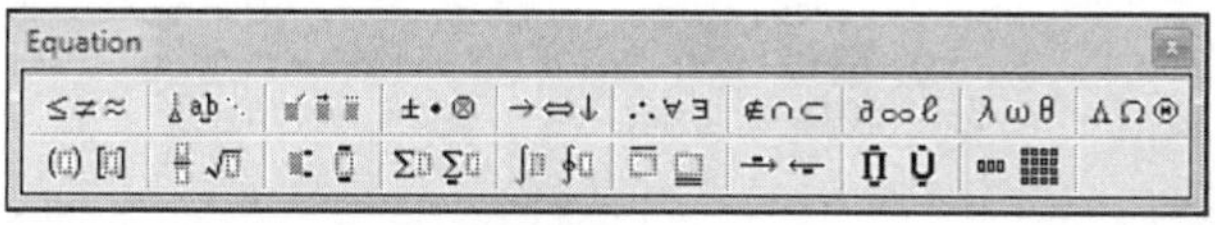

**Figure 3.25**   *The Equation Editor is one of my favorite toys.*

**TELL ME MORE**     Media 3.6—Avoiding Visual Element Overkill
*To listen to a free audio recording about avoiding visual element overkill, log on to **my.safaribooksonline.com/9780132182591/media**.*

In this chapter, you learn how to use Publisher to create postcards, calendars, and other types of documents.

4

# Designs and Layouts

In Chapter 3, I spent some time talking about templates, and I showed you how templates could be used to make a brochure. In this chapter, I continue the discussion by showing you some more creative projects that you can make by using templates. I also add a few more creative elements to your projects by talking about color schemes and word art.

## Calendars

As I explained in the previous chapter, Publisher includes predefined templates that enable you to easily produce various types of documents. One of the more useful document types that you can create is a calendar.

The easiest way to create a calendar is to open Publisher and select the Calendars option from the list of available templates. When you do, Publisher creates a document containing a blank calendar.

At this point, the first thing you must do is tell Publisher what type of calendar you want to create. Most people will probably choose to create a regular calendar, but Publisher does enable you to create academic calendars. An example of an academic calendar would be a calendar for the 2010–2011 school year.

The Other Calendars section currently contains only an option to create a calendar for Kwanzaa, but I would be surprised if Microsoft didn't eventually make additional calendars available for download.

Because regular calendars are going to be the most commonly used, watch what happens when you click the 2010 option. As you can see in Figure 4.1, Publisher gives you a choice of several different calendar formats. You can choose to create a photo calendar, a business card-sized calendar, a quarterly calendar, or any one of several other options.

When you select a calendar format, the column at the far right presents you with any available configuration options. The only option shown in Figure 4.1 is the Download button, which is used to download the template. However, some of the calendar formats enable you to alter things like fonts and color schemes.

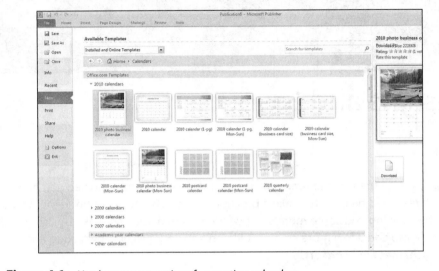

**Figure 4.1**   *You have many options for creating calendars.*

After you download the template, Publisher displays the calendar document. Each month is displayed on a separate page of the calendar, and the photographs are already included in my photo calendar. You could print out the calendar in its current form. However, the thing that sets templates apart from documents is that they are designed to be customizable.

 **LET ME TRY IT**

## Replacing a Photo

Even though I like the default pictures that Microsoft provides, two of my passions in life are travel and photography. I have been fortunate enough to have visited several dozen countries, and I have pictures from most of them, which I would like to use instead of the default pictures. There is an easy way to accomplish this. To replace a photo in the calendar, follow these steps:

1. Using the slide bar in the lower-right corner of the screen, zoom the document so that you can clearly see the photograph.

2. Click on the photograph to select it.

3. Go to Publisher's Picture Tools Format tab.

4. Click the Change Picture icon, found on the toolbar.

5. Choose the Change Picture option from the Change Picture dropdown menu.

6. When prompted, browse to the location of your replacement image.

7. Select your replacement picture, and click the Insert button.

As you can see in Figure 4.2, I have replaced the default image with a picture that I took in Portofino, Italy.

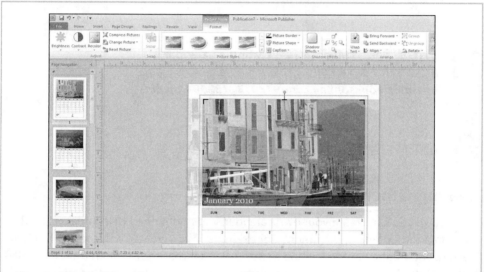

**Figure 4.2**   *Replacing an image is quick and painless.*

## Additional Customizations

In Figure 4.3, I have zoomed in on the bottom of the calendar. As you can see, Publisher provides you with text boxes that you can use to fill in the name of your business, along with some other basic information, such as your phone number and website.

Because everything that you see is based on text boxes, you have the option of adding, deleting, or modifying fields as you see fit. For example, if you were printing a personal calendar, you wouldn't need business contact information. In that case, you could just delete all the fields. You may, however, want to replace some of Microsoft's fields with a text box that you can use to describe the calendar. In this case, I might create a text box that says something like "Portofino Italy, Thanksgiving 2009."

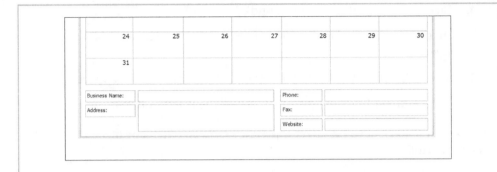

**Figure 4.3**   *You can personalize a calendar for your business.*

**SHOW ME**     Media 4.1—Creating a Calendar
*Access this video file through your registered Web edition at*
**my.safaribooksonline.com/9780132182591/media**.

**LET ME TRY IT**

# Creating Other Types of Calendars

Although you can create your own calendar, you might need to include a calendar within another type of document. For example, if you created a flyer advertising an event, you might want to include a small calendar that shows when the event takes place. Publisher makes this possible through the use of page parts, as follows:

1. Go to Publisher's Insert tab.

2. Click the Calendars icon.

3. Select the calendar component that you want to use in your document, as shown in Figure 4.4.

4. Once the calendar has been inserted into your document, adjust its size and position.

You can see an example of a flyer with an embedded calendar in Figure 4.5.

The calendar that we have just inserted into a document is really nothing more than a table. As such, you can customize this calendar using the same techniques you would use to alter the appearance of a standard table. I talk all about table formatting in Chapter 6, "Tables."

**Figure 4.4**    *Choose the type of calendar you want to insert.*

**Figure 4.5**    *A Publisher document with an embedded calendar.*

# Postcards

Postcards are another type of document that you can create using Publisher 2010. The easiest way to create a postcard is to open Publisher and select the Postcards template (see Figure 4.6).

As you can see in the figure, Publisher contains templates that you can use to create marketing postcards, as well as postcards for real estate. There are also templates for calendar postcards.

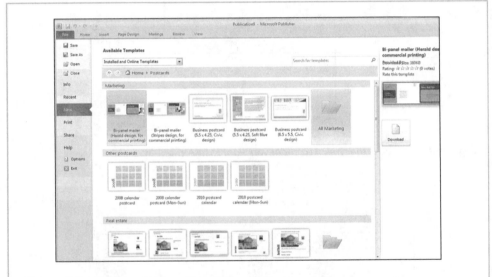

**Figure 4.6**    *Publisher 2010 enables you to create custom postcards.*

You might find that none of the templates I just mentioned will work for you. Fortunately, Publisher contains templates for 18 different sizes of blank postcards, as shown in Figure 4.7. Publisher also groups postcard templates by manufacturer as a way of helping you match your Publisher document to the paper on which you are going to print.

As was the case with calendars, you can create a postcard by selecting the template that you want to use, and then clicking the Download button (if necessary). The template is displayed as a Publisher document, as shown in Figure 4.8. You can edit any part of the postcard using exactly the same techniques that I showed you for editing a calendar.

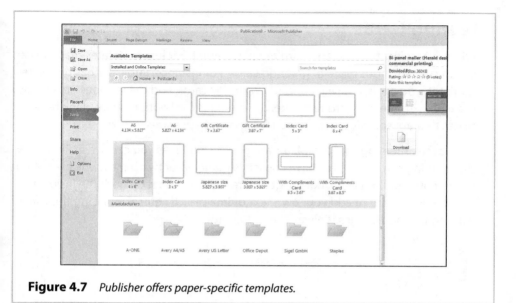

**Figure 4.7**    *Publisher offers paper-specific templates.*

**Figure 4.8**    *The postcard template is loaded as a Publisher document.*

**SHOW ME**    Media 4.2—Creating a Postcard

*Access this video file through your registered Web edition at*
***my.safaribooksonline.com/9780132182591/media.***

# Greeting Cards

When you select the Greeting Card template, Publisher lists templates that you can use to create various types of greeting cards. For instance, Publisher has templates for thank-you cards, anniversary cards, birthday cards, and the list goes on. As was the case with the postcard template, the greeting card option offers blank templates that are specifically formatted for certain paper sizes.

Most of the greeting card templates are pretty simple. As you can see in Figure 4.9, the greeting card template I have chosen is made up of two pages, which would be printed on two sides of a single page. There is ample room on both the inside and outside of the card to add your own text or images. Of course, replacing the card's existing text and images is always an option, too.

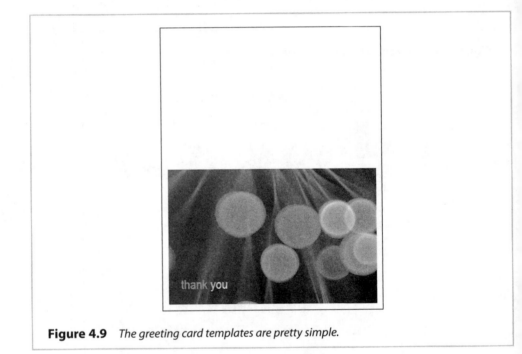

**Figure 4.9**   *The greeting card templates are pretty simple.*

# Additional Visual Elements

So far in this chapter I have shown you how to make a variety of creative projects. Sometimes, though, you can add more flair to your projects by using additional visual elements. In this section, I show you how to use things such as color schemes and word art.

# Color Schemes

When I talked about the calendar templates earlier, I mentioned that some templates contain options to modify things like fonts or business information. An element that is supported by some, but not all, templates is color schemes.

If you look at Figure 4.10, you can see that I have chosen a template that is classified as a Quick Publication. The right side of the screen displays the customizable attributes for this template, including the color scheme, font scheme, business information, and layout.

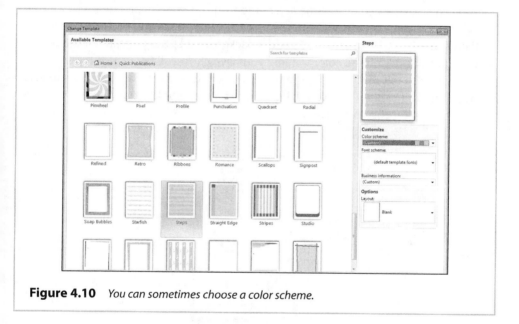

**Figure 4.10** *You can sometimes choose a color scheme.*

Keep in mind that these options are not unique to the template I have selected. I chose this particular template randomly. Many of Publisher's templates offer customizable attributes. At any rate, Publisher offers numerous color schemes from which you can pick. When you select a color scheme, the document preview above the color scheme changes to reflect the scheme you have selected. When you have made your choice, click OK and the template will be applied to your document using the color scheme and other attributes you have specified.

Even after you have chosen a color scheme, you are not committed to sticking with it. The Page Design tab, shown in Figure 4.11, displays all the available color schemes, and Publisher enables you to switch color schemes on the fly by simply clicking on a new one.

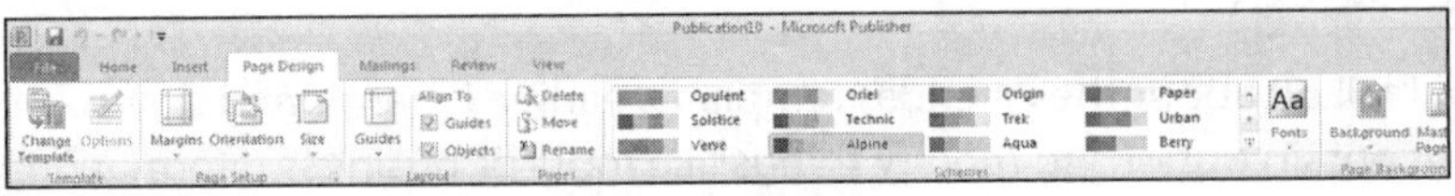

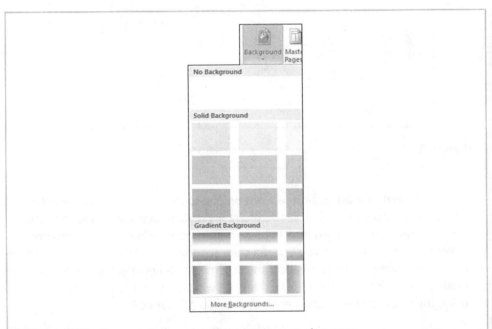

**Figure 4.11**   *You can pick a new color scheme at will.*

## Using Color Schemes in Blank Documents

You can also use a color scheme in a made-from-scratch document. If you look at Figure 4.12, for example, you can see that I have chosen a color scheme from the Page Design tab. When you go to add a background to the page, the available backgrounds match the color scheme you have chosen. Of course, it is probably really hard to tell that the colors in the screen capture match because this book is being printed in black and white, but you can always look at the Web version to get a better feel for the color scheme.

**Figure 4.12**   *You can apply a color scheme to an empty document.*

# Custom Color Schemes

You aren't just limited to using Publisher's built-in color schemes. If you have a creative side, you can define your own. If you expand the color schemes that are displayed on the Page Design tab, notice in Figure 4.13 that there is a Create New Color Scheme option at the bottom of the menu.

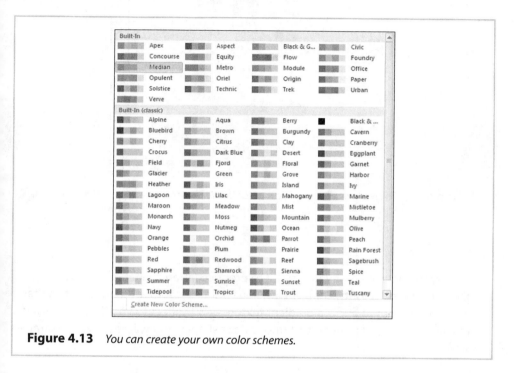

**Figure 4.13**   *You can create your own color schemes.*

The actual process of creating a color scheme is simple. As you can see in Figure 4.14, Publisher displays the colors that are currently being used and gives you a chance to replace each color with one of your own choosing. When you are done, just give the new scheme a name and click Save.

 **SHOW ME**   Media 4.3—Creating a Custom Color Scheme
*Access this video file through your registered Web edition at*
***my.safaribooksonline.com/9780132182591/media.***

Creating custom color schemes is helpful if you work for an organization that demands consistency. For example, I volunteer at charitable organizations. Their websites contain numerous documents, and all the documents use consistent formatting. Creating a custom template with a custom color scheme is an easy way of ensuring that all documents are created with a consistent look and feel.

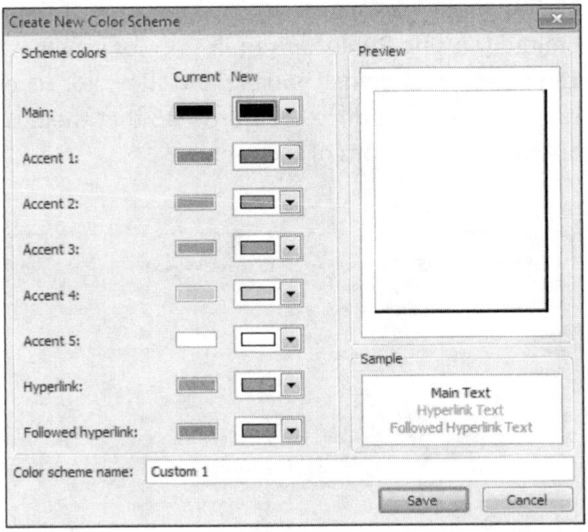

**Figure 4.14**    *To create a color scheme, replace the default colors with your own colors.*

# Word Art

Word art is a feature that you can use to produce lettering that exceeds the capabilities of standard fonts. For instance, you could use word art to form letters that appear hollow, or to apply a gradient texture or 3-D effect to your lettering. Word art can also be used to bend text into various shapes. You will see several examples of this later on.

 **LET ME TRY IT**

## Inserting Word Art

The technique that you must use to add word art to your document is similar to the techniques I have already shown you for adding things such as pictures and shapes to a document. To insert word art into a document, complete these steps:

1. Go to Publisher's Insert tab.

2. Click the Word Art icon, located on the toolbar.

3. Select the style of word art that you want to insert, as shown in Figure 4.15.

4. Enter the text that you want to transform into word art, as shown in Figure 4.16.

5.  Select the font and point size that you want to use. You can also apply the
    Bold or Italic attributes if you like.

6.  Click OK.

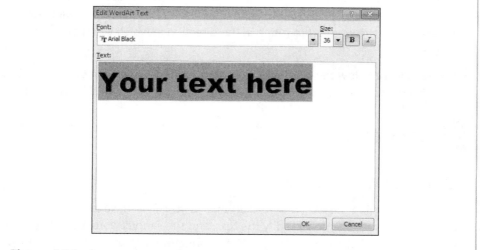

**Figure 4.15**   *Choose the word art style that you want to apply.*

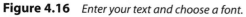

**Figure 4.16**   *Enter your text and choose a font.*

You can see a simple example of word art in Figure 4.17. The word art appears within a box, and you can use the box's now-familiar markers to stretch, move, or resize the word art box.

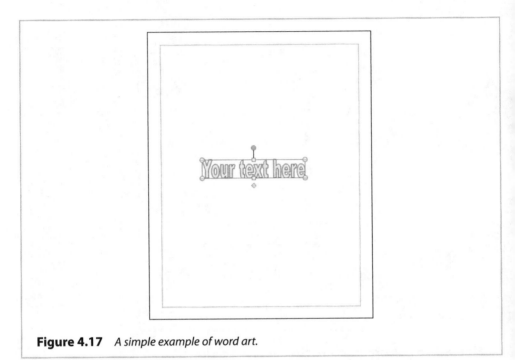

**Figure 4.17**    *A simple example of word art.*

In addition to the markers on the corners and in the middle of the word art box, there is also a green dot above the word art. Clicking this dot and moving your mouse causes the word art to rotate in the direction in which you move your mouse.

The yellow dot below the word art box is used to control the slant of the text. Dragging this dot to the left, for example, causes the text to be slanted to the right.

 **LET ME TRY IT**

## Editing the Word Art Text

If you find a typing mistake in a word art image, you don't have to re-create the image from scratch. Simply modify the text, and the various word art attributes will be applied to the corrected text. To make a correction to your word art text, follow these steps:

1.  Select the word art box.

2.  Go to the Word Art Tools Format tab.

3.  Click the Edit Text icon.

4.  Enter the corrected text, and click OK.

Keep in mind that although Publisher does a relatively good job of retaining word art attributes after text is modified, the very nature of editing text means that the size of the word art image will change. As such, you might find it necessary to resize your word art after altering the text.

**LET ME TRY IT**

## Changing Word Art Spacing

When you type regular text into the text box, the text's appearance is dictated by the font that you are using. In some ways, this is also true for word art, but you do have more control over how the text is displayed. You have the ability to change the spacing between the individual letters.

Publisher won't give you complete granular control over the text spacing, but you can set the spacing to Very Tight, Tight, Normal, Loose, or Very Loose. Letters that are spaced very tightly tend to overlap each other, whereas very loosely spaced letters tend to have big gaps between them. You can control text spacing by following these steps:

1.  Go to Publisher's WordArt Tools Format tab.

2.  Select the word art that you want to format.

3.  Click the Spacing icon, shown in Figure 4.18.

4.  Choose the spacing that you want to use.

As you create WordArt, you should always be mindful of how large the WordArt text will be when it is printed. Often images in a printed document will be smaller than they are when viewed on your monitor. Some WordArt images can be difficult to read at smaller sizes.

**Figure 4.18**    *Word art enables you to control the spacing between letters.*

**SHOW ME**    **Media 4.4—Using WordArt**
*Access this video file through your registered Web edition at*
***my.safaribooksonline.com/9780132182591/media.***

## Color Effects

Because word art is really nothing more than just a complex shape, it shouldn't come as any surprise that your options for coloring word art are practically identical to those available for coloring shapes. Because I discussed shape coloring in detail in Chapter 3, "Working with Visual Elements," I don't want to bore you by repeating myself. I do, however, want to give you a quick overview of the options that are available to you.

**LET ME TRY IT**

## Coloring Word Art

There are two primary aspects to coloring word art images. You can color the letters themselves, and you can apply a color to the outline around the letters. To change the outline color, follow these steps:

1. Select the box containing the word art.

2. Go to Publisher's WordArt Tools Format tab.

3. Click the Shape Outline icon, located on the toolbar.

4. Choose the desired outline color from the Shape Outline menu, shown in Figure 4.19.

Although the Shape Outline menu's primary purpose enables you to change the color of the outline around a word art image, there are a couple of other menu options that I want to point out. One option is the Sample Line Color option. Use this option if you want the outline color to match a color used elsewhere in the document.

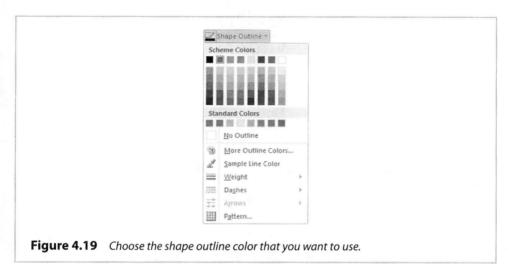

**Figure 4.19**   *Choose the shape outline color that you want to use.*

When you choose this option, the cursor changes into the shape of an eyedropper. Simply move the tip of the eyedropper over the color that you want to duplicate, and then click your mouse button.

Another option is the Weight option. The weight option enables you to control the thickness of the outline. Higher weights produce thicker lines. Similarly, the Dashes option enables you to change the outline into a dotted (or dashed) line. This usually has the effect of making the words appear fuzzy. A similar effect can be achieved by applying a pattern to the outline, but the pattern is usually visible only if you are using a high weight number and a large font size.

To apply color to the inside of the letters, you must click the Shape Fill icon, found on the WordArt Tools Format tab. As you can see in Figure 4.20, Publisher gives you the same options for coloring word art images as you have for filling in other types of shapes. You can use a solid color, a gradient color, a pattern, a texture, or even an image.

Applying an image to a block of lettering might seem like an odd concept, but you can actually create some pretty neat effects by using this technique. To show you what I mean, I have created the document shown in Figure 4.21, in which I applied a picture from a trip to Tahiti to the word Tahiti.

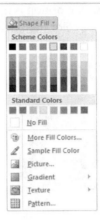

**Figure 4.20**  *Options for filling Word Art images are similar to those available for filling shapes.*

**Figure 4.21**  *You can fill a word art image with a picture.*

Incidentally, if you use this technique, you can adjust the picture's position to some degree. If you hover over a letter, the cursor changes to display four arrows. When this happens, you can hold down the mouse button and drag the picture to the desired position. Depending on the size of your lettering and the dimensions of your picture, though, you might find that you can move the picture in only one direction.

 **LET ME TRY IT**

## Creating Shadow Effects

You can add depth to your word art images by adding shadows. Publisher enables you to create anything from a subtle hint of a shadow to a large drop shadow. To create a shadow, follow these steps:

1. Select the word art to which you want to apply the shadow.

2. Go to Publisher's WordArt Tools Format tab.

3. Click the Shadow Effects icon.

4. Choose the effect that you want to apply, as shown in Figure 4.22. You can see a preview of each effect by hovering your mouse pointer over it.

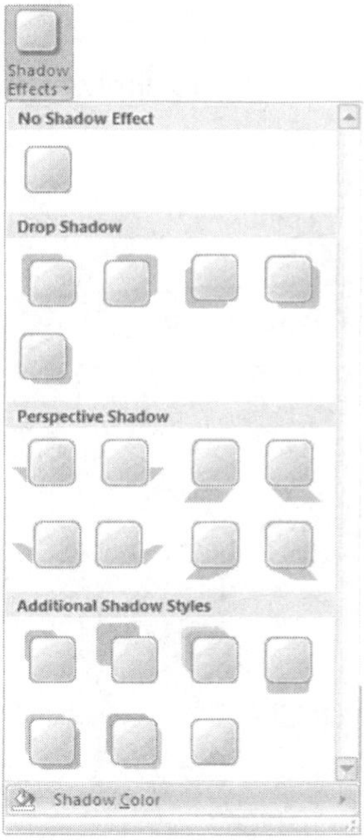

**Figure 4.22** *Choose the type of shadow that you want to use.*

It is worth noting that the Shadow Effects menu contains a Shadow Color option, which is also shown in Figure 4.22. Although you can't get quite as creative with shadow colors as you can with the color of the lettering and its outline, you do have the option of making your color of choice semi-transparent.

 **LET ME TRY IT**

# Creating 3-D Effects

I will never forget attending a Windows NT Server certification class back in the 1990s. As much great material as was presented, one of the things that I remember most was the screensavers that came with Windows. One of the screensavers allowed you to enter a word or a short phrase and then rendered your text in 3-D and made it bounce across the screen. You can use Publisher to create similar text effects. To do so, follow these steps:

1. Click on the word art image to select it.

2. Go to Publisher's WordArt Tools Format tab.

3. Click the 3-D Effect icon.

4. Choose the effect that you want to apply, as shown in Figure 4.23.

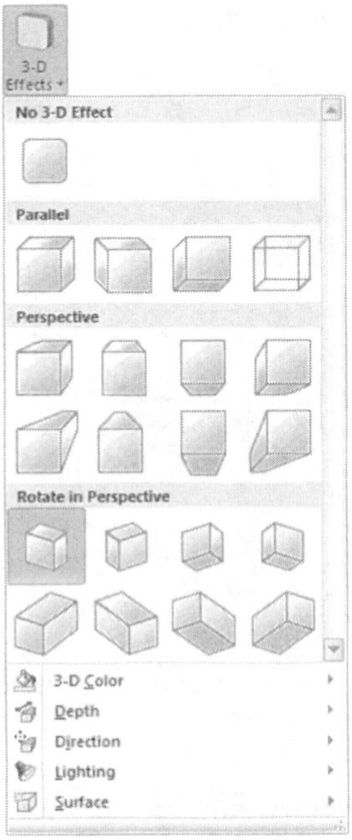

**Figure 4.23**   *You can apply 3-D Effects to word art text.*

As you can see in the figure, the options for rendering text in 3-D are identical to the options I showed you in Chapter 3 when we applied a 3-D effect to a shape. Publisher gives you total control over the depth, direction, and lighting used in rendering the 3-D text. Likewise, you can create numerous surface and coloring effects.

 **LET ME TRY IT**

## Shifting Shapes

Word art is probably best known for its ability to twist words into all kinds of wacky shapes. You already got a preview of this capability a few pages back when I showed you the screen that enables you to select the style you want to use for your word art image.

It's important to understand that selecting a word art style is only a shortcut. Any of the effects that can be chosen as a style can also be created manually. To see what I mean, perform these steps:

1. Click on your word art text to select it.

2. Go to Publisher's WordArt Tools Format tab.

3. Click the Change Shape icon, found on the toolbar.

4. Pick the shape that you want to apply to your text from the Change Shapes menu, shown in Figure 4.24. Once again, you can get a preview by hovering your mouse pointer over each shape.

As you looked at Figure 4.24, you might have noticed the yellow dots below and to the left of the word art box. As I already showed you, you can drag the dot below the image back and forth as a way of controlling the slant of the letters. The dot to the left of the image is a control for adjusting the height of the letters. Simply drag the dot up to make the letters taller, or drag it down to make the letters shorter.

## Creating Building Blocks

As you have seen, a lot of work can go into creating a shape or a word art image. If you create a shape, word art image, or even a block of text that you want to reuse in other documents, you can save those objects as building blocks.

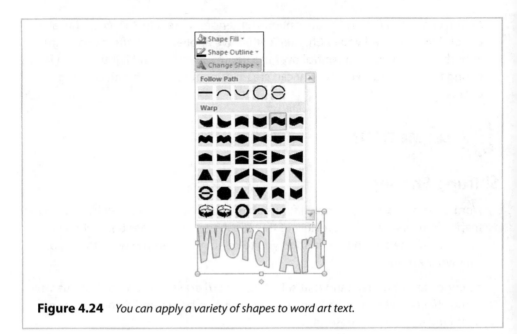

**Figure 4.24**  *You can apply a variety of shapes to word art text.*

To show you how building blocks work, I have taken one of the default shapes and applied a 3-D effect, as shown in Figure 4.25.

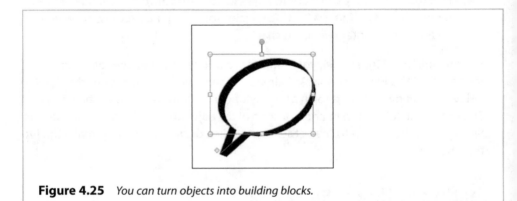

**Figure 4.25**  *You can turn objects into building blocks.*

 **LET ME TRY IT**

# Converting an Object into a Building Block

Let's pretend that we want to turn this into a building block. To do so, follow these steps:

1. Right-click on the object.

2. Select the Save as Building Block command from the shortcut menu.

3. Publisher displays the Create New Building Block dialog box, shown in Figure 4.26. Enter a title and an optional description for your building block. It is also a good idea to provide some keywords to make your building block show up in search results.

4. Select the gallery in which you want to store the building block, and click OK.

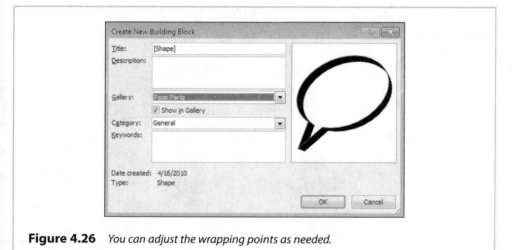

**Figure 4.26** *You can adjust the wrapping points as needed.*

You can access your newly created building block at any time by going to Publisher's Insert tab and clicking the Page Parts link. The building blocks that you create are displayed within the Pager Parts galleries, as shown in Figure 4.27.

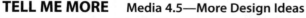 **TELL ME MORE**    Media 4.5—More Design Ideas
*To listen to a free audio recording about some additional design ideas, log on to* **my.safaribooksonline.com/9780132182591/media.**

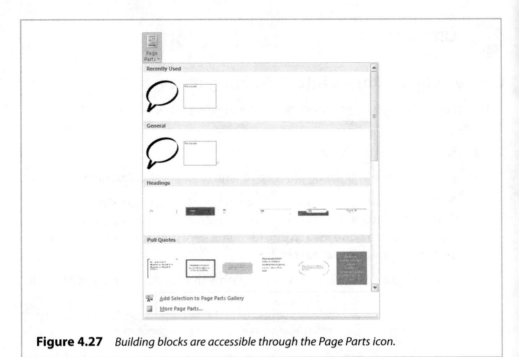

**Figure 4.27**  *Building blocks are accessible through the Page Parts icon.*

# Working with Longer Documents

The previous chapters all focused on the basics of using Publisher 2010. As you worked through those chapters, you probably noticed that we have mostly created simple, single-page documents. That doesn't mean that Publisher is only good for creating short documents, though. You can use Publisher to create some rather long documents.

You may recall that back in Chapter 1, "An Introduction to Publisher 2010," I mentioned that Microsoft Office 2010 is available as either a 32-bit or a 64-bit application. I highly recommend running the 64-bit version of Publisher if you are going to create long documents.

Last year, I wrote a book called *Brien Posey's* Guide to Practical Telecommuting (http://www.brienposey.com/Books.asp). Before the book could be published, the publisher went bankrupt. Rather than letting all my hard work go to waste, I decided to publish the book myself.

Although I had written the text and provided the publisher with all the screen captures that went along with the book, the book had not yet been laid out. My initial idea was to import my Microsoft Word document into Publisher, and use it to lay out the book. The problem was that my manuscript was too long, and Publisher ran out of memory before it could be imported.

To make a long story short, I performed the entire layout process using Microsoft Word. Word got the job done, but as you have already seen, Publisher would have been a better tool for the job had it been able to accommodate such a long document. The good news is that the 64-bit version of Publisher accommodates longer documents than the version that I was using. That's why I recommend using the 64-bit version of Publisher whenever possible.

Even if you don't plan on using Publisher to write a book, I still recommend taking the time to read this chapter. Some of the techniques that I am going to show you will save you a lot of heartache, even on shorter documents. For example, I show you how to import text from Microsoft Word what to do when your text won't fit within a text box you have created.

# Text Boxes Revisited

Because this chapter focuses on creating long documents, I am going to spend quite a bit of time talking about text boxes. You learned some methods for creating text boxes in Chapter 3, "Working with Visual Elements," and how to enter text into a text box, but now I want to come back to the topic and show you some other things that you can do with text boxes.

# Formatting

If you look at Figure 5.1, you can see that I have pasted a page of text (from my telecommuting book) into a text box. Because the text is coming from Microsoft Word, Publisher has placed a dropdown menu in the lower-right corner of the text box. This menu contains the following options:

- **Paste**—Although Publisher displays text in the text box, this is only a preview. Clicking the Paste icon makes the text permanent.

- **Keep Source Formatting**—Using this option causes the text to retain the formatting that was present in the original Microsoft Word document.

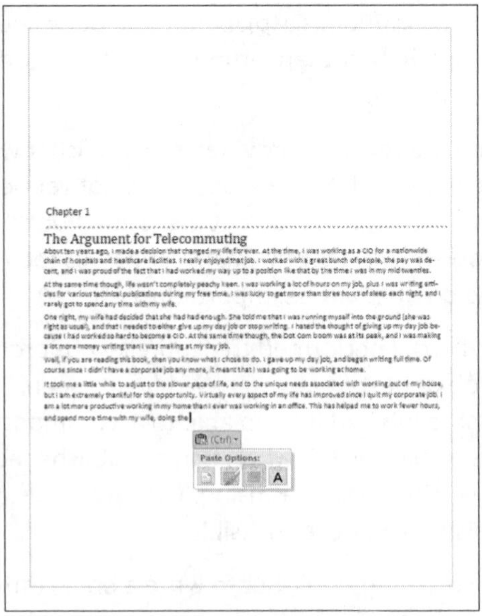

**Figure 5.1**  *You can control how the text appears once pasted.*

- **Use Destination Styles**—Using destination styles causes the text formatting to be modified to match the Publisher document's style.

- **Keep Text Only**—This option causes the text to be added to the text box using default formatting.

# Linking Text Boxes

As you look at Figure 5.1, you might notice the icon on the lower-right side of the text box. This is the overflow icon, which indicates that the text that has been pasted into the text box doesn't fit. We could fix the problem by making the text box bigger or the font smaller, but these are not always good options.

 **LET ME TRY IT**

## Connecting Text Boxes with Each Other

Another option for making text fit is to create a second text box and link it to the first. To do so, complete these steps:

1. Create a second text box.

2. Select the text box that currently contains the text.

3. Go to Publisher's Format tab.

4. Click the Create Link icon, shown on the toolbar.

5. The cursor changes to resemble a pitcher of water. Move the cursor to the new text box and click it. The text now overflows into the second text box, as shown in Figure 5.2.

By linking (sometimes called chaining) text boxes together, text flows from one text box to the other. If we were to add some text to the first text box, the overflow text would seamlessly flow to the second text box.

As a shortcut, you can click the overflow icon. When you do, the cursor changes to resemble a pitcher. Move the cursor to the area in which the overflow text should be displayed, and click the mouse button. A new text box will be created automatically.

**Figure 5.2**   *Text now overflows into the second text box.*

**SHOW ME**    Media 5.1—Linking Text Boxes
*Access this video file through your registered Web edition at*
***my.safaribooksonline.com/9780132182591/media.***

# Navigating Text Boxes

In my previous demonstration, I caused text to overflow from one text box into a secondary text box that is directly beneath it. In the real world, things are not always so well organized, though. Imagine, for instance, that you have a short newsletter divided into several columns, and that this newsletter contains three separate stories and a few clip art images. In this type of situation, there is a very good chance that at least one or two of the stories will span multiple text boxes. So how do you keep everything straight?

If you refer to Figure 5.2, notice an icon in the upper-left portion of the bottom text box. This is a link icon. If you want to find out which text box comes before this one in the chain, click the icon and you are taken to the text box that comes before it. Likewise, an arrow icon in the lower-right corner of a text box indicates that the text flows into another text box, and clicking the icon takes you to that text box.

# Layout Strategies

As handy as text box links are, you might be wondering about the recommended best practices for using them in the real world. From what I have read, it seems that everyone has their own idea of what constitutes the best practices for linked text boxes, but there doesn't seem to be much consistency.

My advice is to base your use of linked text boxes on the type of document that you are trying to create. For example, if you are creating a two-page newsletter, you probably already have a pretty good idea of what you want the newsletter to look like. In that type of situation, I think that it makes sense to lay out all the text boxes up front, before you start adding the text. You might have to make some adjustments to the text box sizes once you actually begin populating them, but you shouldn't have too much trouble sticking to your basic design idea.

On the other hand, if you are creating a longer document that will contain primarily text, but might also have some other design elements mixed in, you will probably find it easier to create text boxes as you need them, just as I did in my demonstration earlier in this chapter.

# Master Pages

As you have no doubt discovered by now, it is usually easier to compose the text for longer documents in Microsoft Word than to try to compose it in Publisher. That being the case, I want to show you how to import a Word document into Publisher. Before I do that, though, I need to teach you about master pages.

Under normal circumstances, Publisher treats each page as a blank canvas. The formatting on one page can be vastly different from the formatting used on the next. This is great if your goal is to express your creativity, but when it comes to creating longer documents, it is usually desirable to have at least some degree of consistency throughout the document. This is where master pages enter into the equation.

Master pages are designed to help reduce the amount of tedious editing work that you have to do by enabling you to apply a consistent format to each page within a document. For example, a master page might contain your corporate logo or the name of the document at the top of each page.

Besides enforcing design consistency, there is another benefit to using master pages. Publisher files can become quite large, especially when they contain many graphics. Using master pages helps limit the size of the document files because the information on the master pages exists only once within the document, rather than existing as a separate entity on each page.

**LET ME TRY IT**

## Creating a Master Page

The process for creating a master page is similar to creating any other type of document page. You have all the same visual elements and editing tools available to you. For the sake of demonstration, I am going to create a master page that has my Poker-Run-Boats.com logo in the upper-left corner. If you want to follow along and create your own master page, you can do so by completing these steps:

1.  Go to Publisher's Page Design tab.

2.  Click the Master Pages icon, found on the toolbar.

3.  Select the Edit Master Pages option from the Master Pages menu. When you do, Publisher will display a Master Pages tab, as shown in Figure 5.3, indicating that you are editing a master page.

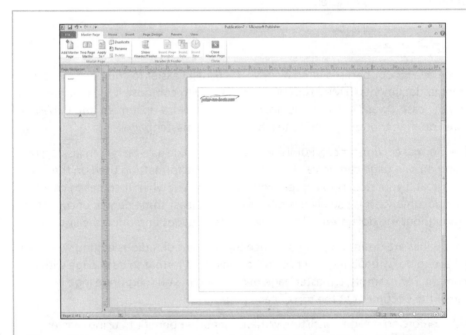

**Figure 5.3**   *Create your master page, and then click the Close Master Page icon.*

4.  Create your master page, and then click the Close Master Page icon, located on the toolbar.

**LET ME TRY IT**

# Applying Master Pages

When you close your master page, your document will look exactly like the master page that you have just created. Publisher automatically applies the master page to every page in the document. It doesn't have to be this way, though. Publisher allows you to enable and disable master pages on an as-needed basis. This is handy because you might not always want to include a master page in a document. Likewise, it is common for the first page in a document to be formatted differently from the remaining pages. As such, you might want to exempt the document's first page from master page formatting.

To control how a master page is applied to a document, follow these steps:

1.  Go to Publisher's Page Design tab.

2.  Click the Master Pages link, found on the task bar.

3.  Choose the Apply Master Page command from the Master Pages menu.

4.  Publisher should now display the Apply Master Page dialog box. If you want your master page to be used in the document, make sure it is selected, as shown in Figure 5.4; otherwise, choose the Ignore Master option from the dropdown list.

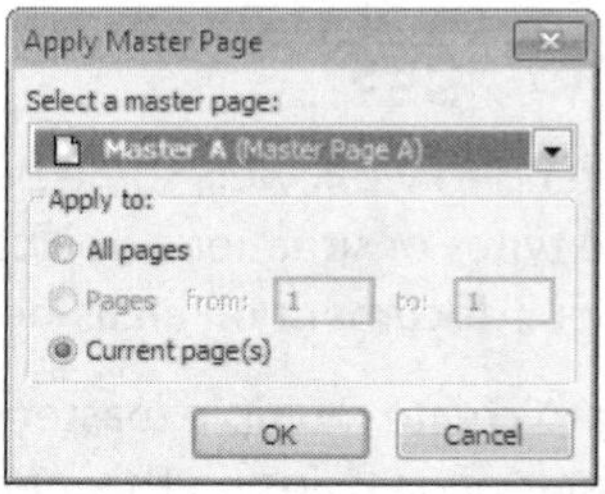

**Figure 5.4**  *The Apply Master Page dialog box allows you to enable or disable master pages.*

5.  Choose the pages to which the master page should apply. You can apply the master page to all the pages in the document, the current page only, or to a range of pages.

**SHOW ME**    Media 5.2—Creating Master Pages

*Access this video file through your registered Web edition at*
***my.safaribooksonline.com/9780132182591/media.***

**LET ME TRY IT**

# Editing Master Pages

Every once in a while, you might find that you need to update the master pages you have created. Updating master pages is done in nearly an identical manner to creating master pages. To make an update, follow these steps:

1. Go to Publisher's Page Design tab.
2. Click the Master Pages icon.
3. Verify that the correct master page is selected.
4. Choose the Edit Master Pages command from the Master Pages menu.
5. Make any necessary edits to the page.
6. Click the Close Master Page icon.

**LET ME TRY IT**

# Using Multiple Master Pages

Even though master pages tend to work well, some projects require a higher degree of flexibility. In these types of situations, you can create multiple master pages and assign them to your document on an as-needed basis.

If you find yourself needing to create multiple master pages, you will have to start out by creating a single master page by using the method I described earlier. After doing so, follow these steps:

1. Go to Publisher's Page Design tab.
2. Click the Master Pages icon.
3. Choose the Edit Master Pages option from the Master Pages menu.
4. When Publisher takes you to the Master Page tab, click the Add Master Page icon.

5.  When prompted, enter a single character to identify the page you are creating.

6.  Enter a description for the new master page, as shown in Figure 5.5.

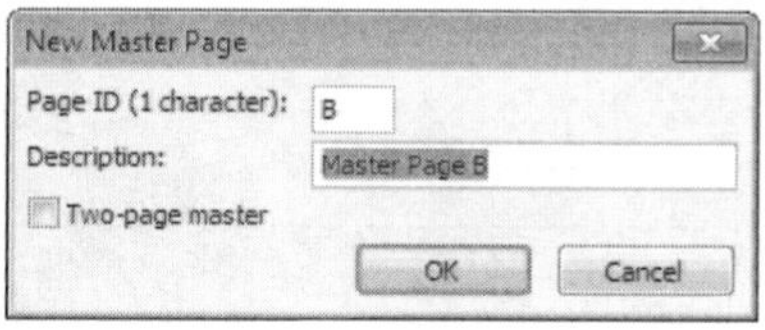

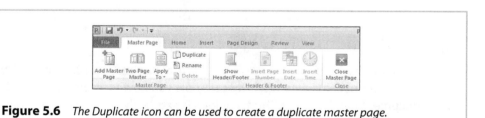

**Figure 5.5**   *You must identify the new master page that you are creating.*

7.  If the master page will be a two-page spread, select the Two-Page Master check box.

8.  Click OK.

9.  Click the Close Master Page icon.

## Additional Master Page Options

The technique I just showed you will enable you to create a blank master page. Sometimes, though, you might have put a lot of work into your previous master page, and find that the new master page needs to be a variation of the existing master page. In these types of situations, there is no need to create a new master page from scratch. As you can see in Figure 5.6, Publisher's toolbar contains an icon that you can use to duplicate an existing master page. After doing so, you can modify your new master page as your needs dictate.

**Figure 5.6**   *The Duplicate icon can be used to create a duplicate master page.*

Another handy option found on the toolbar shown in Figure 5.6 is the Two-Page Master option. Clicking this icon causes the master page to take the form of a two-page spread.

If you are planning on creating a two-page spread, I recommend that you click the Two-Page Master button before you begin designing the master page. The reason for this is that if you place design elements on a master page and then decide to create a two-page spread, Publisher will make the left page a mirror image of the right page. If you look at Figure 5.7, for example, you can see that my logo is printed backward on the left page.

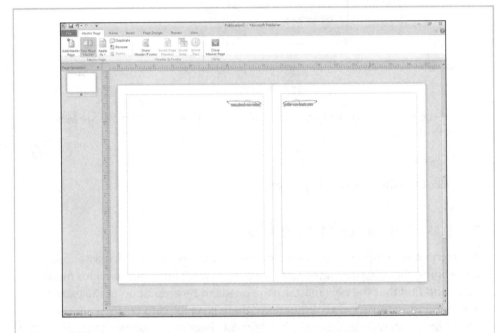

**Figure 5.7**    *You can use a two-page spread for your master pages.*

# Importing Microsoft Word Documents

Now that I have covered some of the more important points regarding using Publisher with multi-page documents, I want to show you how to import a Microsoft Word document into Publisher. This technique is extremely useful because it tends to be a lot easier to create a text document in Word than in Publisher. Therefore, you can use Word to create and proofread your document, and then lay out the document in Publisher.

## LET ME TRY IT

# Import Text from Microsoft Word

The actual process of importing a Microsoft Word document is pretty simple. To do so, follow these steps:

1. Go to Publisher's Insert tab.

2. Click the Insert File icon. When you do, Publisher automatically creates a small text box in the middle of the page and prompts you to specify the file that you want to import. You can use this same technique to import any selected text file format.

3. Select the file you are importing, and click OK. Publisher takes a moment to convert the file to its own format.

If you look at Figure 5.8, you will notice a couple of different things. First, I imported a fairly long Word document. As such, the Page Navigation section displays eleven different pages.

**Figure 5.8**   *You can import a Microsoft Word document into Publisher.*

Another thing you will notice is that because the document does not fit within the miniscule text box on the first page, Publisher automatically creates text boxes on subsequent pages and chains all the text boxes together in the appropriate order. As you can see in the figure, the text boxes on the remaining document pages each take up the entire page (but stay within the margins).

Even though Publisher has created such a small text box on the first page, we aren't stuck using the default size. If the text box is resized, the text from the next page automatically moves up to fill the void, as shown in Figure 5.9.

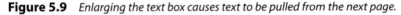

**Figure 5.9**   *Enlarging the text box causes text to be pulled from the next page.*

**SHOW ME**   **Media 5.3—Importing Word Documents**
*Access this video file through your registered Web edition at*
***my.safaribooksonline.com/9780132182591/media.***

# Adding Images to the Document

In the preceding section, I imported a chapter from a book that I wrote (but never bothered to publish) on customizing performance boats. This particular Word document contains only text, but my original intent when I wrote the book was to have lots of photos and illustrations to go along with the techniques I describe. That being the case, I want to take a look at how you would add images to a document such as the one I just imported.

If you look at Figure 5.10, you can see that I have left space within the Word docu-ment for inserting images. I could just go to the Insert tab and then use the Picture option to insert an image. The problem with doing so is that Publisher would place the image in its own box that would be layered on top of the document's text, as shown in Figure 5.11.

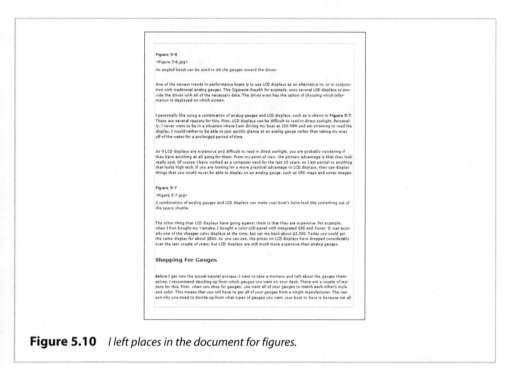

**Figure 5.10**    *I left places in the document for figures.*

So how do we deal with this dilemma? The reason why we are having the problem in the first place is because each page contains one large text box, and there is no room for an image without covering up text in the process.

One way to get around the problem is to shrink the text box to make room for the image. That is usually going to be only half of the solution, though. More often than not, you are going to end up having to place text above, below, and maybe even beside an image. You could deal with this situation by changing the image's proper-ties or adjusting the text wrapping style, or you could create multiple text boxes.

Of course, things aren't quite so simple because the text box shown in Figure 5.11 is linked to the text box on the next page. We can easily shrink the text box, add an image to the page, and create one or more new text boxes on the page, but Pub-lisher isn't going to populate those text boxes with text from the document because they are not a part of the text box chain. Because of this, we must break the text box chain, and then re-create it using the new text boxes we created.

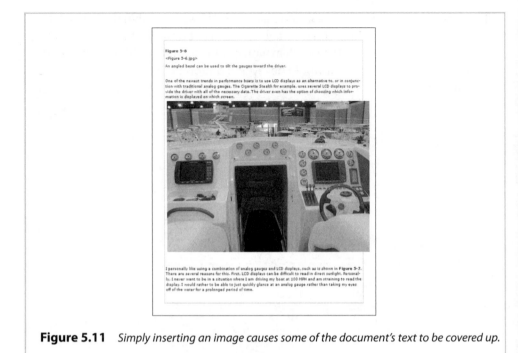

**Figure 5.11**   *Simply inserting an image causes some of the document's text to be covered up.*

If you look at Figure 5.12, you can see that I have resized a text box. I have also created a small text box at the bottom of the screen, while leaving room in the middle of the page for the image I want to insert. If you look at the page navigation section of the screen, you can see that the text continues to flow to the text box on the next page, skipping the newly created text box.

To fix this problem, it is necessary to select the text box that currently contains text. Select the Text Box Tools Tab, and then click the Break icon, located on the Format tab's toolbar. If you look at Figure 5.13, you can see that once I break the link, the text box displays the overflow icon and the document's remaining pages are now blank.

At this point, I select the text box at the top of the page and click the Create link icon. I then click the text box at the bottom of the screen. The text now flows between the two text boxes but the remaining document pages are still blank.

With the lower text box selected, I must now click the Create Link icon, and then click the text box on the next page. This causes the remaining document pages to become populated once again, as shown in Figure 5.14. Now, we can add the image to the page without covering up the text on the page, as shown in Figure 5.15.

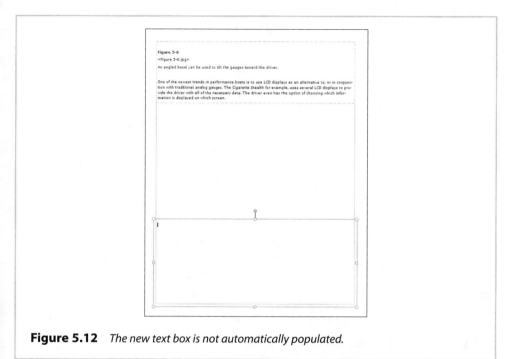

**Figure 5.12**   *The new text box is not automatically populated.*

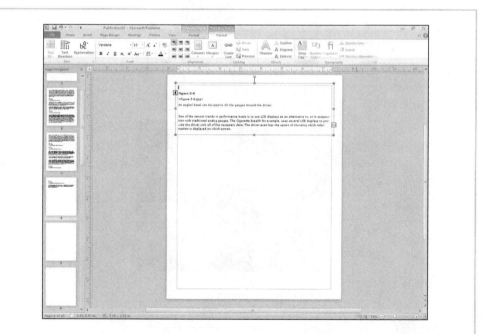

**Figure 5.13**   *Breaking a link causes the text boxes on the remaining document pages to become empty.*

**Figure 5.14** *We have restored the text on the remaining pages.*

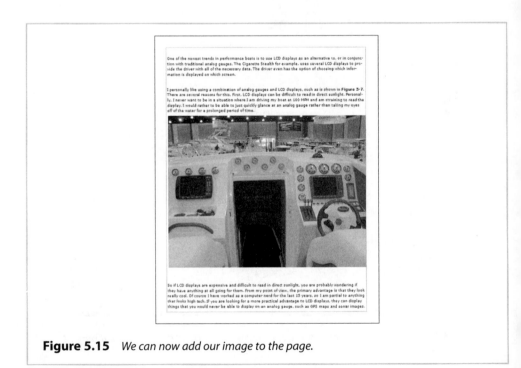

**Figure 5.15** *We can now add our image to the page.*

When you create a chain of text boxes, the text boxes retain their order regardless of where the box is located in the document. As such, it is important to arrange text boxes so that the text is displayed in the correct order.

## Word Documents with Images

In the previous section, I showed you how to add an image to an imported Microsoft Word document. As I'm sure you know, though, Microsoft Word has the ability to embed images within documents just as Publisher does. With that in mind, I wanted to show you how Publisher reacts to a Microsoft Word document that already contains images.

If you look at Figure 5.16, you can see a Publisher document that is based on a Microsoft Word document I have imported. So far, I haven't done anything to touch up the document. This is exactly how it was imported from Word.

As you can see in the figure, the document contains text, an image, and even a caption. It is important to realize, though, that Publisher has imported the document in a very unsophisticated way.

The entire page is made up of a single text box. The image is in its own box and is simply layered on top of the text box. The only reason why this approach works in this case is because the original Word document was already formatted to leave the necessary amount of space for the image. If we were to try to move this image, things would get really messy.

In this type of situation, if you want to do any editing that involves moving images around, you will most likely have to divide up the document into multiple text boxes just as we did in the previous section.

## Wrapping Text Around Images

In the previous section, I showed you how to position an image on a page full of text in a way that prevents the image from interfering with the text. In doing so, I created a couple of text boxes and left a big gap in the middle of the page so that I could insert an image. This technique works really well, and it is my preferred method for working an image into a large block of text. There are some other techniques that you can use, however.

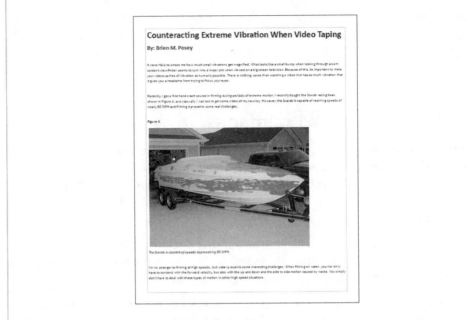

**Figure 5.16** *Some Microsoft Word documents contain images.*

One especially popular technique involves word wrapping. Word wrapping forces the words within a text box to flow around an image. To show you how word wrapping works, I am going to use the same Publisher document that I showed you in Figure 5.16.

As you can see in the figure, the image exists within its own box in the middle of a text box. There is text above and below the image. For the sake of demonstration, I am going to get rid of the captions immediately above and below the image so that the text will flow more smoothly.

When the captions are gone, I can right-click on the image and choose the Format Picture command from the shortcut menu. This causes Publisher to display the Format Picture dialog box. As you can see in Figure 5.17, the properties sheet's Layout tab contains several options for wrapping text.

As an alternative, you can double click on a picture. Doing so causes the Picture Tools, Format tab to become active. This gives you all the same options as the properties sheet, plus a few more.

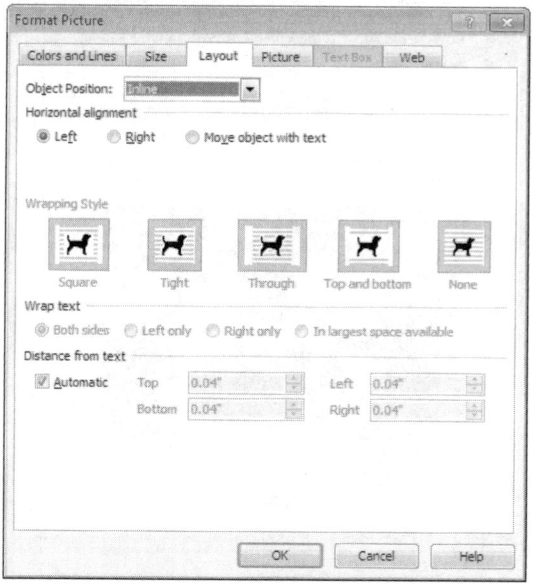

**Figure 5.17**    *The Layout tab offers several different wrapping styles.*

Right now, Publisher is configured to wrap the text on the top and bottom of the image only. However, we could format the text to form a square around the image. To do so, you must set the object position to Exact, and then set the wrapping style to Square.

Because the image was already present in the document, and a sufficient amount of blank space was provided for the image, the text isn't going to instantly wrap around the image in the way that you might expect it to. However, if I delete some of the empty space, the text begins to form a square around the image, as shown in Figure 5.18.

Granted, how I wrapped the text in the document shown previously is probably overkill. You would rarely do something quite so extreme in the real world, but I wanted to show you how the text-wrapping capabilities work.

I'm no artist, but if I were laying out this document for real, I would probably shrink the image a bit, move it to one side, and wrap text around the other side. This is actually pretty easy to pull off. If you go back and look at Figure 5.17, you will notice that Publisher gives you the option of wrapping text around both sides of the image, the left only, the right only, or placing text in the largest space available. By choosing the Right Only option and moving the picture to the left, I was able to achieve the effect shown in Figure 5.19.

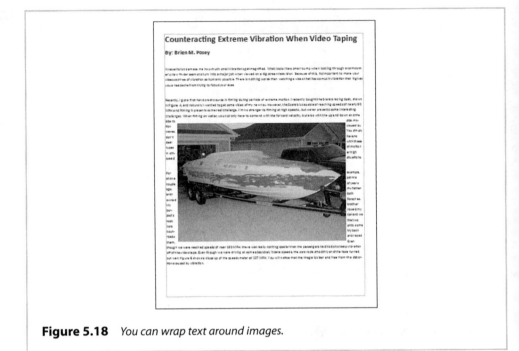

**Figure 5.18**   *You can wrap text around images.*

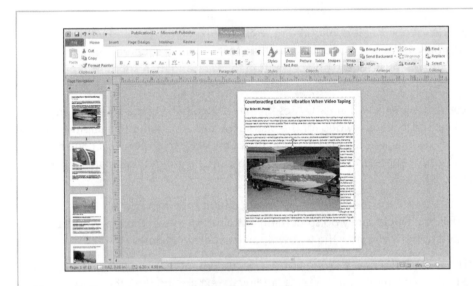

**Figure 5.19**   *You can wrap text around one side of an image.*

**SHOW ME**   Media 5.4—Text Wrapping
*Access this video file through your registered Web edition at*
***my.safaribooksonline.com/9780132182591/media.***

# Irregularly Shaped Images

Back in Figure 5.17, you saw that Publisher gives you several different wrapping styles to choose from. I have already shown you how the Square and the Top and Bottom styles work, but I haven't mentioned the Tight and the Through styles yet. Both of these styles work best with irregularly shaped images.

## Tight Wrapping

To show you how Tight wrapping works, I have created a text box and then filled it with a block of text. Next, I added a shape to the middle of the page. Upon doing so, my text wraps itself around the shape, as shown in Figure 5.20.

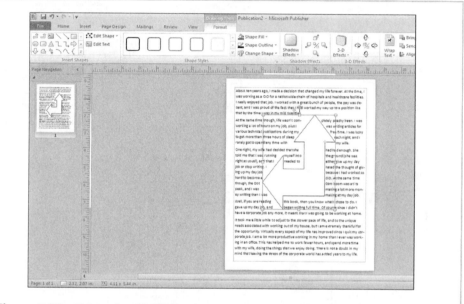

**Figure 5.20**    *This is what it looks like if you overlay a text box on a shape.*

Now I am going to right-click on the shape and choose the Format AutoShape option from the shortcut menu. This brings up a properties sheet that is similar to the one used for formatting pictures. When I select the Layout tab, the wrapping style is set to Through, as shown in Figure 5.21. In other words, the Through option lets the text run through the box around the image (or shape in this case), whereas when we used the Square wrapping style, the text stopped at the square around the object. It might have been a little bit difficult to tell that this is what was going on because I was using a square image. However, you can see an example of the Square wrapping style in Figure 5.22.

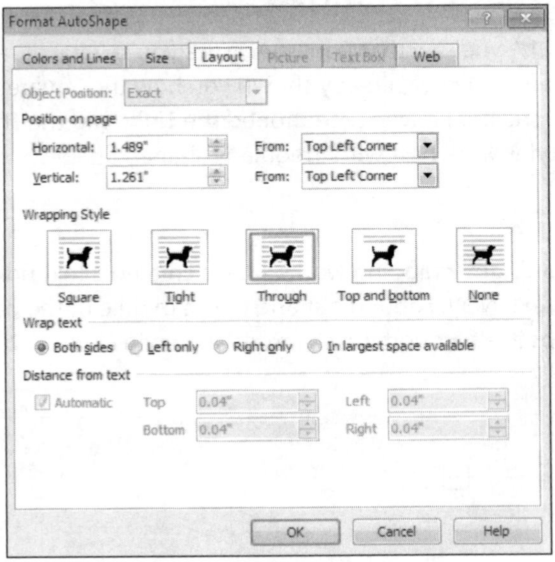

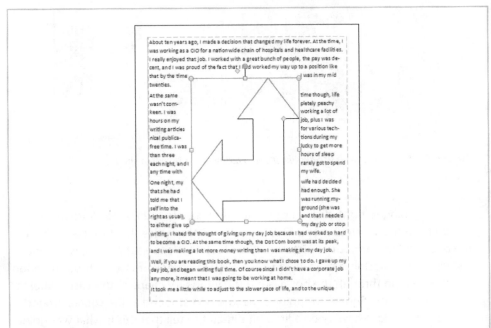

**Figure 5.21**   *The Through style lets text run through the image.*

**Figure 5.22**   *The same document with the Square wrapping style applied.*

# Adjusting the Wrapping

When we apply the Through wrapping style, Publisher seems to do a pretty good job of wrapping text around the image. This might not always be the case, though, especially for nonstock images or word art. There is a way to tell Publisher how the text should be wrapped, however.

If you look at Figure 5.23, you can see that I have wrapped some text around a word art image. After doing so, I right-clicked on the word art. Notice that when I do, a series of icons appears. The Text Wrapping icon contains an option for editing wrapping points.

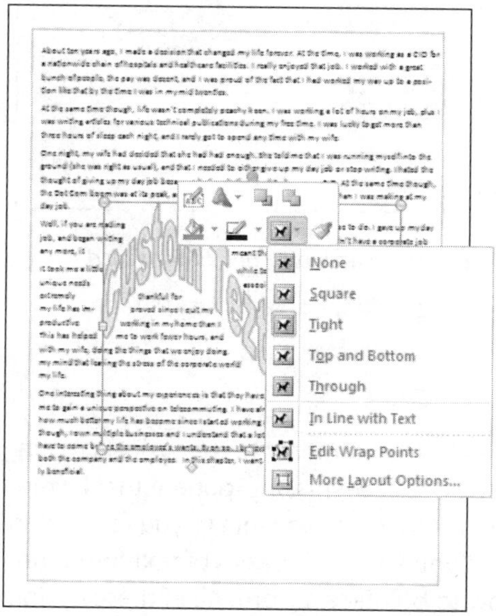

**Figure 5.23**　*Wrapping points give you granular control over text wrapping.*

When I choose this option, a series of wrap points surround the word art. If you look at the bottom toward the left side of the word art, you will see that I have pulled one of these wrap points away from the word art. This has the effect of moving the text farther away, as shown in Figure 5.24.

In the top-right portion of the figure, there is an area above the word art in which the text is loosely wrapped, and there are no wrapping points that can be adjusted. You can easily create your own wrapping points, however. Simply click on the dotted line and drag it into the position where you want the new wrapping point to appear.

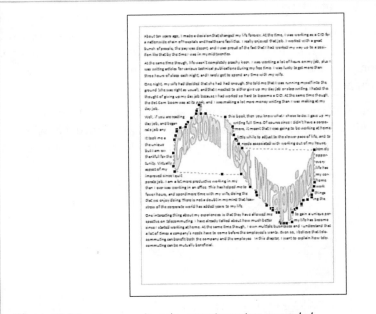

**Figure 5.24**   *You can adjust the wrapping points as needed.*

## Formatting Text Boxes

I have dedicated this chapter primarily to the task of creating long, mostly text-based documents. As such, it seems appropriate that I wrap things up by showing you some of the options that are available to you for formatting text boxes. In this section, I assume that you know the basics of text formatting, such as how to change a font or how to boldface a word. All of these options can be found on the Text Box Tools, Format ribbon.

## Text Fitting

Earlier in this chapter I showed you how to chain text boxes together as a way of dealing with overflow text. Sometimes, though, creating additional text boxes might not be an option because the design constrains mandate that the text has to fit on one page. When this happens, you can use text fitting.

I have a block of text that simply doesn't all fit in the text box. The Text Box Tools Format tab contains an icon named Text Fit, shown in Figure 5.25. If you click this icon, you are presented with several options for making the text fit in the box. Most of the time, the best option is going to be to use the Best Fit option, which shrinks the text to make it fit in the box. Another option is to grow the text box to accommodate the text.

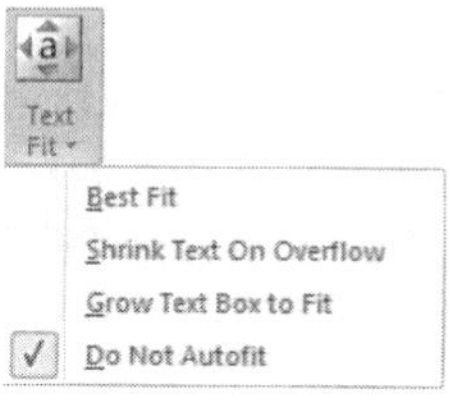

**Figure 5.25**  *Text fitting can help you accommodate overflow text.*

# Text Direction

Occasionally, you might need to display text sideways on a page. To do so, all you have to do is select the text box, and then click the Text Direction icon, as shown in Figure 5.26. When you do, the text changes directions.

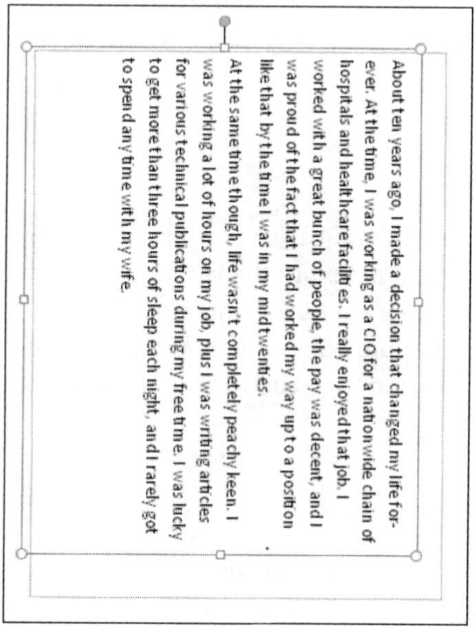

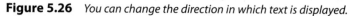

**Figure 5.26**  *You can change the direction in which text is displayed.*

# Hyphenation

One way to cram a lot of text into a small text box is to use hyphenation. Hyphenation enables you to make better use of space by splitting words that otherwise wouldn't fit at the end of a line of text. Of course, hyphenation is completely inappropriate for certain types of documents, so Publisher allows you to enable or disable hyphenation.

When you click the Hyphenation icon, Publisher displays the dialog box shown in Figure 5.27. As you can see in the figure, you can enable or disable automatic hyphenation by selecting or deselecting a check box. You also can control how far the page's hyphenation zone extends.

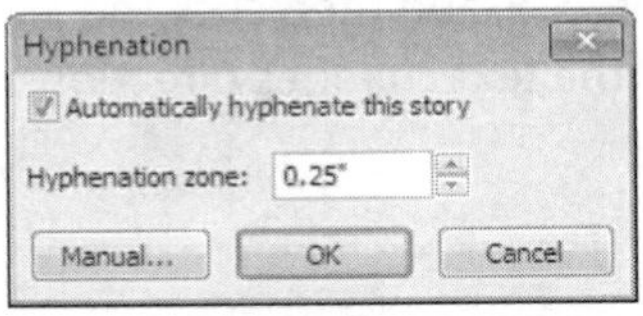

**Figure 5.27**   *Hyphenation can help you save space in a text box.*

# Alignment

If you have used Microsoft Word very much, you probably are familiar with the icons that enable you to align text to the left, right, or center. Publisher also offers a text alignment tool, but there are a few more options. If you look at Figure 5.27, you can see that Publisher provides nine different toolbar icons for aligning text. You can select a text box and then click one of these icons to get the look that you want.

# Columns

You can sometimes achieve some nice visual appearances by splitting blocks of text into multiple columns. Publisher makes it extremely easy to use columns. All you have to do is select your text box, and then click the Columns icon and choose the number of columns that you want to create. You can see an example of a two-column text box in Figure 5.28.

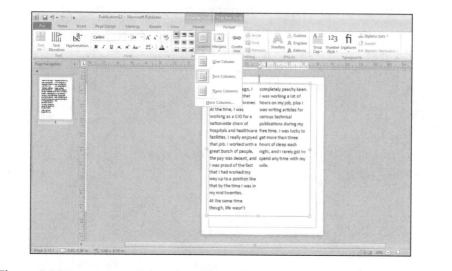

**Figure 5.28**   *You can display text as multiple columns.*

## Word Art Lite

If you really want to get fancy with your text, you pretty much have to use word art. However, you have some options for changing the way in which basic text is displayed, beyond just changing fonts, point sizes, and colors. The Effects section of the toolbar enables you to apply a shadow, outline, engrave, or emboss effect to your text with the click of a mouse. You can see what each of these effects looks like in Figure 5.29.

## Drop Cap

The last time I was in Dublin, Ireland, I took time out to see the Book of Kells, an ancient illuminated manuscript that is on display at Trinity College. It was common for illuminated manuscripts to be written in a way that caused the first character of a paragraph to be displayed as big and fancy, while the remaining characters appeared normally.

You can achieve this same effect in Publisher by using the Drop Cap feature. All you have to do is select your text box, click the Drop Cap icon, and then pick the effect that you want. You can see an example of the effect that the Drop Cap feature produces in Figure 5.30.

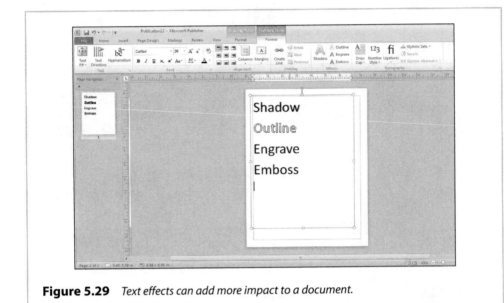

**Figure 5.29**   *Text effects can add more impact to a document.*

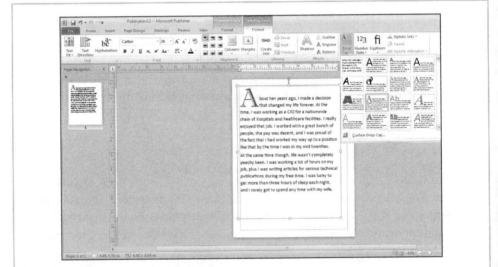

**Figure 5.30**   *The Drop Cap feature causes the first character to appear larger than the other characters.*

# Number Styles

The Number Style option provides you with several different options for controlling how numbers are displayed within the document. Although Publisher provides five different options, as shown in Figure 5.31, there is very little difference in the appearance that the styles produce. The document shown in the figure actually uses all five different styles, but you would be hard pressed to tell the difference between most of them.

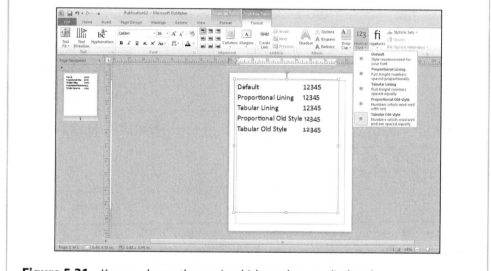

**Figure 5.31** *You can change the way in which numbers are displayed.*

 **TELL ME MORE**   Media 5.5—Keeping Large Documents Reasonable

*To listen to a free audio recording about keeping large documents reasonable, log on to **my.safaribooksonline.com/9780132182591/media.***

In this chapter, you learn techniques for creating
and formatting tables within your document.

6

# Tables

If you read Chapter 4, "Designs and Layouts," recall that I mentioned that calendars
were actually nothing more than tables to which some nice visual effects had been
applied. Making calendars isn't the only thing you can do with tables, though.
Tables can also be used as a means for importing data from an Excel spreadsheet.
In this chapter, I show you everything you need to know about working with tables
in Publisher 2010.

## What Are Tables?

In case you aren't familiar with tables, they are simply a grid that you can use to
display data. Tables are made up of individual cells (rectangles) that are arranged
into rows and columns. You can see an example of a table in Figure 6.1.

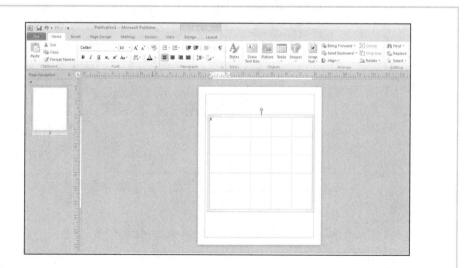

**Figure 6.1**  *An example of a table.*

It is worth noting that even though a table looks a lot like a spreadsheet, it is not a spreadsheet. So what's the difference between a table and a spreadsheet? Well, one of the most important differences is that tables do not support the use of formulas. Another difference is that spreadsheets number each cell, whereas table cells are not numbered.

# Creating Tables

Creating tables in Publisher couldn't be any easier. The process is similar to what was used in previous versions of Publisher and in other Microsoft Office applications.

 **LET ME TRY IT**

## Create a Table

To create a table, follow these steps:

1. Go to Publisher's Home tab.

2. Click the Table icon (the Table icon located on the Insert tab can also be used).

3. Use your mouse to select the number of rows and columns you want to include in the table, as shown in Figure 6.2.

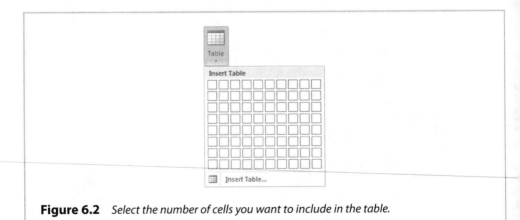

**Figure 6.2**   *Select the number of cells you want to include in the table.*

# Formatting Tables

As you can see, Microsoft makes it really simple to create a table. As you have prob-ably already figured out, though, we aren't stopping there. There are several differ-ent things that we can do to change the table's appearance. Some of these tech-niques are identical to things you have already learned in previous chapters. For example, fill effects work similarly for tables as they do for shapes. Other cosmetic effects, such as border art, are unique to tables.

# Resizing a Table

At its simplest, resizing a table works the same way as resizing a shape or resizing a text box. All you have to do is select the table that you want to resize, grab the table's edges, and drag them to the desired location. Likewise, you can click on the lines that make up a cell and drag them to increase or decrease the cell's size.

I generally recommend making your table the desired size before you begin popu-lating the table's cells. I say this because when you resize a table, the text within the table's cells does not automatically increase in size along with the table. It is up to you to manually increase the font size. It is possible, however, to select multiple cells and then increase the font size for the selected cells simultaneously.

 **LET ME TRY IT**

## Resize a Table

As I hinted earlier, although you can grab a table's edges with the mouse and then drag the edges so that the table grows to the desired size, this isn't the only way to resize a table. You can achieve a higher degree of control over how large the table becomes. To do so, follow these steps:

1.  Right click on the table.
2.  Choose the Format Table command from the shortcut menu.
3.  When the Format Table properties sheet appears, select the Size tab.
4.  Set the new table size, and click OK.

If you look at the Size tab, shown in Figure 6.3, you can see that you can change a table's size by entering the desired height and width. These values are entered in inches and can include several decimal positions.

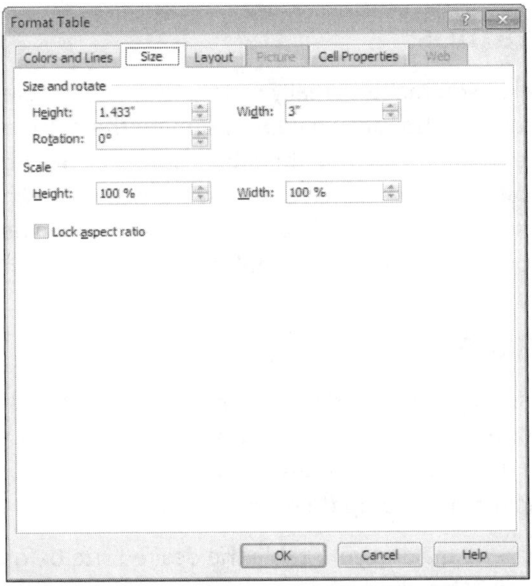

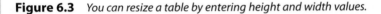

**Figure 6.3**  *You can resize a table by entering height and width values.*

In a lot of my examples, I tend to accomplish the task at hand by right-clicking an object and then choosing a command from a resulting shortcut menu. It is worth mentioning however, that right-clicking is rarely the only way to accomplish a task in Publisher. One of Publisher 2010's new features is the ribbon, and nearly everything that I talk about can be done by clicking an icon on the ribbon. The only reason my examples often use right-click instead of the ribbon is because I normally write about server products, which don't have a ribbon, and I have gotten in the habit of using the right mouse button.

You might have also noticed in the figure that you can resize a table by scaling it. Rather than entering height and width dimensions, you can simply scale the height and width based on a percentage of the table's current size. For example, if you wanted to make the table 50% larger, you could set the height and width to 150%.

Sometimes scaling a table can cause the table to become stretched. You can use the Lock Aspect Ratio check box to prevent the table from changing shapes as you change its size.

**SHOW ME**    Media 6.1—Creating a Table
*Access this video file through your registered Web edition at*
**my.safaribooksonline.com/9780132182591/media.**

# Fill Effects

Fill effects work in exactly the same way for tables that they do for shapes or word art. If you want to change a table's background, select the Format Table properties sheet's Color and Lines tab, and click the Fill Effects button. Doing so displays the Fill Effects properties sheet, which gives you the options for filling the table's background with a solid color, a gradient, a texture, a picture, or a pattern.

# Borders

The Colors and Lines tab, which is shown in Figure 6.4, isn't only used for controlling the table's background through the use of fill effects. This tab is also used to control the table's borders.

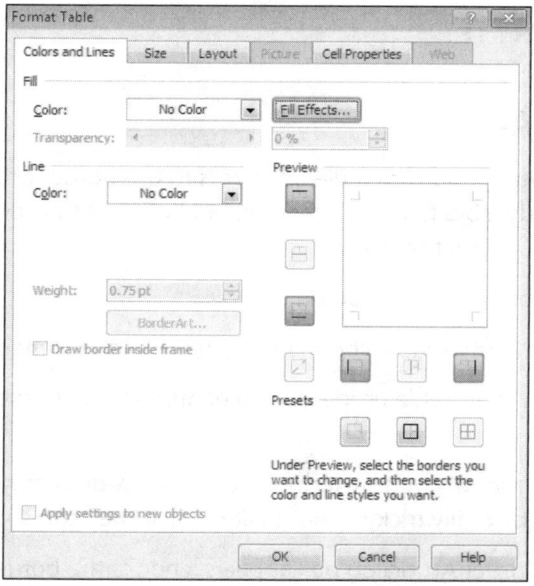

**Figure 6.4**    *The Color and Lines tab can be used to control the table borders.*

Formatting a table's borders can actually be a little bit tricky. I have found border formatting to be one of Publisher's least-intuitive functions.

Although border formatting is a table-level function, the formatting actually is applied to individual cells. With that in mind, the first step in the process is to select the cells for which the border changes should apply. After doing so, right-click on the area that you have selected, and then choose the Format Table command from the shortcut menu. When the Format Table properties sheet appears, select the Colors and Lines tab, shown in Figure 6.4.

As you look at the figure, you will notice a preview area surrounded by a series of smaller squares. These smaller squares act as toggle buttons. Each button represents a portion of the border for the selected cells. You can click a button to enable that portion of the border, and then click the button again to disable it. As you pick border elements, the preview area will remain mostly blank.

Once you have selected the portions of the border that you want to customize, pick a line color and line weight. This causes the preview area to show you what your cells will look like. When you are happy with the preview, click OK and your changes will be applied to the table.

 **LET ME TRY IT**

## Using Border Art

Another thing you can do with table borders is to use border art. I have to confess that I'm not exactly a big fan of this feature, but I wanted to show you how it works. To use border art, follow these steps:

1. Right-click on your table's border.

2. Choose the Format Table command from the shortcut menu.

3. When the Format Table properties sheet appears, go to the Colors and Lines tab.

4. Click the Border Art button. If the Border Art button is grayed out, start over. It can be really tricky to right-click in just the right spot.

5. When the Border Art dialog box appears, choose the border you want to use, as shown in Figure 6.5.

6. Click OK twice, and then the selected border will be applied to your table, as shown in Figure 6.6.

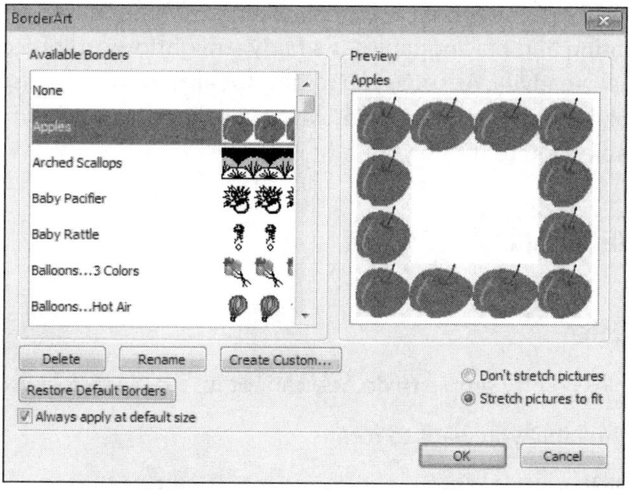

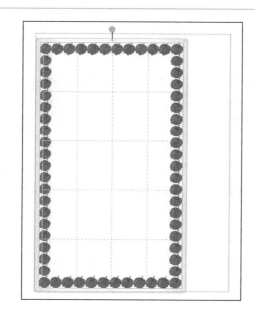

**Figure 6.5**    *Select the border you want to use.*

**Figure 6.6**    *The border art you have chosen is applied to the table.*

# Table Rotation

Although creating and placing tables is a fairly straightforward process, Publisher is all about visual creativity. As such, you might not always want to display tables in the traditional manner. For those times when you want to be a bit more creative, Publisher enables you to rotate your tables.

 **LET ME TRY IT**

## Rotate a Table

Rotating a table is pretty simple to do. You can rotate a table by following these steps:

1. Select the table you want to rotate.

2. Right-click on the table, and choose the Format table command from the shortcut menu.

3. When Publisher displays the Format Table properties sheet, select the Size tab.

4. Enter your desired angle of rotation into the Rotation field, as shown in Figure 6.7.

5. Click OK to rotate the table.

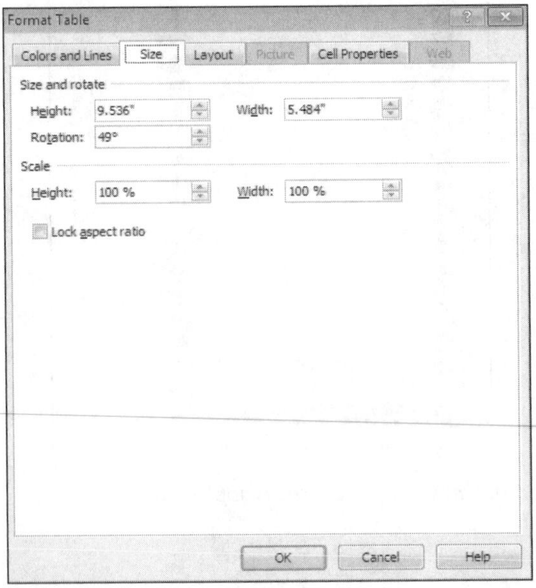

**Figure 6.7**  *Enter your desired angle of rotation.*

As an alternative, you can drag the rotation handle in the direction that you want to rotate the shape. Using the dialog box however, is a better option for those requiring precision control.

You can see an example of what a table looks like after being rotated in Figure 6.8. In this figure, I have left the border art in place to make the table easier to see.

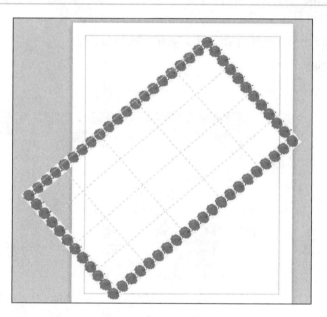

**Figure 6.8**    *This is what a table looks like after being rotated.*

## Text Wrapping

I spent quite a bit of time talking about text wrapping in Chapter 5, "Working with Longer Documents," so I don't want to repeat everything that I have already talked about. I do, however, want to at least mention that you can wrap text around a table. The method for doing so is nearly identical to what you have already learned.

**LET ME TRY IT**

## Wrapping Text Around a Table

To enable text wrapping for a table, complete these steps:

1.  Right-click on the table, and choose the Format Table command from the shortcut menu.

2.  When the Format Table properties sheet appears, select the Layout tab, as shown in Figure 6.9.

3.  Choose the wrapping style that you want to apply.

4.  Click OK.

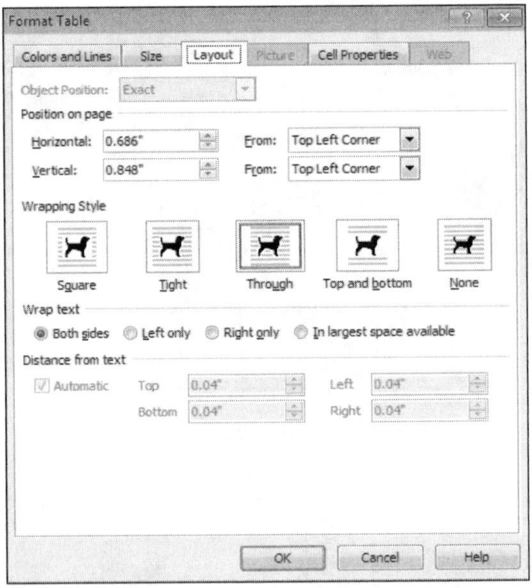

**Figure 6.9** *Choose the wrapping style that you want to apply to the table.*

## Cell Alignments and Margins

As I'm sure you know, a table's purpose is to display rows or columns of information in an organized manner. Without the proper cell formatting, though, the table can take on a messy (dare I say, illegible) appearance.

Thankfully, Publisher is configured by default to keep this from happening. Publisher automatically sets a 0.4 inch margin at the top, bottom, left, and right of each cell. That way, the text that is displayed in one cell doesn't bump right up against the text in the next cell. These margins go a long way toward making table data legible.

 **LET ME TRY IT**

## Adjusting Table Margins

In most cases, you probably won't have to adjust table margins, but you can should the need arise. To do so, follow these steps:

1. Right-click on the table.

2. Choose the Format Table command from the shortcut menu.

3. When the Format Table properties sheet appears, select the Cell Properties tab.

4. Enter the new margin sizes into the Left, Right, Top, and Bottom fields.

5. Click OK.

## Text Rotation

Although the Cell Properties tab, shown in Figure 6.10, is designed primarily for changing cell margins, there are a couple of other handy things you can use it for. One thing is to rotate text within the table, but without rotating the table itself. To rotate the text within the table, just select the Rotate Text Within AutoShape by 90° check box.

## Text Vertical Alignment

The other thing you can use the Cell Properties tab for is to adjust the vertical alignment of the text within a cell. By default, table data is aligned along the top of the cell (minus the area reserved for the cell's margins). You can, however, align the table data to the middle or to the bottom of the cell.

Changing a cell's vertical alignment isn't going to make much difference if you are using small cells or if the cells are completely filled with text. The effect becomes much more noticeable with large or sparsely populated cells. You can see an example of the effect of changing a cell's vertical alignment in Figure 6.11.

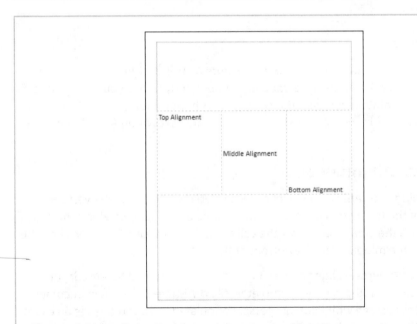

**Figure 6.10**   *You can rotate the text by 90 degrees.*

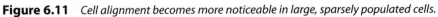

**Figure 6.11**   *Cell alignment becomes more noticeable in large, sparsely populated cells.*

# Table Design

So far, I have shown you how to adjust a number of different table formatting options through the Format Table properties sheet. However, most of the options I have shown you are also accessible through the toolbar. When you select a table, Publisher displays a tab called Table Tools. This tab is subdivided into a Design and a Layout tab. Most of the functions I have discussed so far are accessible through the Design tab.

## Table Formats

One thing you can do through the Design tab that I haven't talked about yet is to change the table's format. A table's format is essentially just a stylized layout that controls the table's colors and controls which rows and columns are used as table headers. The Design tab displays a few available table formats by default, but clicking the down arrow next to the Table Formats section causes many more choices to be displayed, as shown in Figure 6.12. In the figure, I have applied one of the formats to a table so you can see what the result looks like.

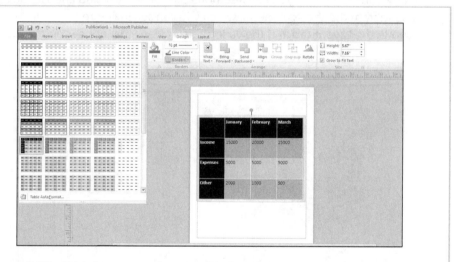

**Figure 6.12**   *Table formats can change a table's appearance.*

# Table Layout

The Table Tools tab's Table Layout subtab contains a number of options for controlling the table's appearance and functionality. I have already shown you how to perform many of the Layout tab's functions through the Table Properties sheet, but there are a few functions that are not available on the Properties sheet, including such things as inserting and deleting rows and columns.

# Inserting Rows and Columns

I have found that when I work with tables, inserting rows or columns is one of the tasks that I seem to perform the most often. Even the best-planned tables just seem to evolve as I begin working with them. Thankfully, Publisher makes it simple to insert a row or a column.

Regardless of whether you are going to be inserting a row or a column, the first step is to click on the cell that is going to act as your starting point. Next, decide where the new row or column is going to be located relative to the cell that you have selected. For example, if you are going to be inserting a row, the new row will be placed either just above or just below the cell you have selected. Likewise, a new column would be inserted either to the left or to the right of the selected cell.

After you have selected the cell that will act as your starting point, simply click one of the Insert icons (Insert Above, Insert Below, Insert Left, Insert Right) found on the toolbar. As an alternative, you can also right-click on the cell and choose the Insert command from the shortcut menu, which you can see in Figure 6.13. This figure also shows the Layout tab and the various Insert icons that appear on the toolbar.

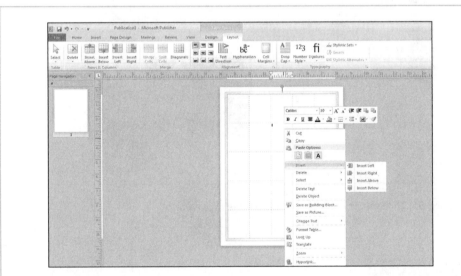

**Figure 6.13**   *Right-click on a cell and choose the Insert command from the shortcut menu.*

# Deleting Rows and Columns

The process of deleting a row or column works similarly to that of inserting a row or column. To perform a deletion, click on a cell that will act as your starting point. Next, click the Delete icon, found on the toolbar. As you can see in Figure 6.14, the Delete menu gives you the choice of deleting the currently selected row or column. There is also an option to delete the entire table, so be sure to exercise caution when using the Delete option. If you accidentally delete something you shouldn't have, remember that Publisher has an Undo function.

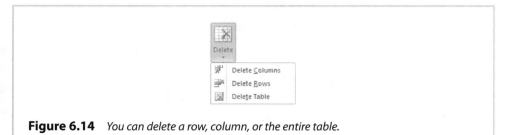

**Figure 6.14** *You can delete a row, column, or the entire table.*

The delete functions are also available by right-clicking on a cell and choosing the Delete command from the Start menu. Doing so causes Publisher to display a submenu with options for deleting the currently selected row or column, or the entire table.

# Diagonals

If you have worked with tables in any other Microsoft Office product that has been released in the past 10 years or so, I probably haven't shown you anything you didn't know. Something that you might never have run into before, however, is the Diagonals option, which enables you to split a cell diagonally.

To use the Diagonals function, all you have to do is select the cell you want to split, and then click the Diagonals icon. When you do, Publisher asks you if you want to divide up or divide down. You can see what these options look like, along with a couple of examples of cells that I have split diagonally in Figure 6.15.

# Merging and Splitting Cells

When you create a table, it is common to find that you need to combine some cells into one big cell. Likewise, you might need to split a cell into a bunch of smaller cells. Both of these tasks are very easy to accomplish through Publisher.

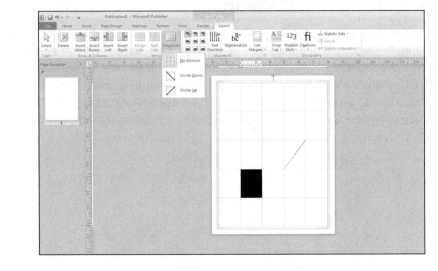

**Figure 6.15**  *Publisher enables you to split cells diagonally.*

You can merge cells by selecting the cells you want to merge and then clicking the Merge Cells icon. Figure 6.16 shows an example of cells that have been merged to create one large cell.

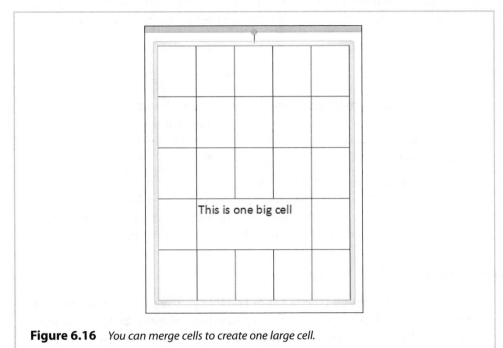

This is one big cell

**Figure 6.16**  *You can merge cells to create one large cell.*

Just as you can merge cells, you can also split a cell into many smaller cells. To split a cell, select the cell you want to split and click the Split Cells icon. You can only split cells that have been previously merged. Splitting the cells returns them to their original layout.

**SHOW ME**    Media 6.2—Formatting Tables and Cells
*Access this video file through your registered Web edition at*
***my.safaribooksonline.com/9780132182591/media.***

# Importing Excel Spreadsheets

So far, I have shown you how to work with tables in Publisher 2010. As I have explained, though, tables have a lot of limitations compared to a full-blown Excel spreadsheet. Should the need ever arise, however, you can insert an Excel spreadsheet into a Publisher document. In this section, I show you how.

**LET ME TRY IT**

## Creating a Blank Spreadsheet

I want to start out by showing you how to insert an empty Excel spreadsheet into your Publisher document. To do so, follow these steps:

1. Go to Publisher's Insert tab.

2. Click the Object icon, located on the toolbar.

3. Choose the Microsoft Excel Worksheet option from the list of available objects, as shown in Figure 6.17.

4. Click OK.

You can see what the recently inserted Excel Worksheet looks like in Figure 6.18. There are a couple of different things you should pay attention to in the figure. First, the spreadsheet exists within a box, which means you can resize and position it using exactly the same techniques you would use for repositioning or resizing any other type of object.

More importantly, though, take a look at what has happened to the menus and the toolbar. We have inserted a true Excel worksheet. As such, any time the worksheet is selected, Publisher essentially becomes Excel. All the menus and the toolbars that are displayed while the spreadsheet is selected belong to Excel. You can go back to the normal Publisher menus and toolbars by clicking outside the spreadsheet.

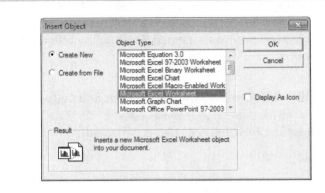

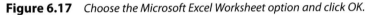

**Figure 6.17**   *Choose the Microsoft Excel Worksheet option and click OK.*

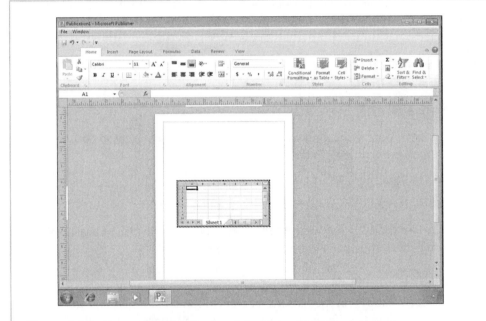

**Figure 6.18**   *You can insert an Excel worksheet into a Publisher document.*

## Importing a Spreadsheet

Although you can add a blank Excel spreadsheet to a Publisher document, it is usually going to be more useful to import a spreadsheet that has some data in it. To
show you how the import process works, I am going to import a spreadsheet that
was related to a recent failed expedition to Antarctica. My Antarctic expedition was

the very definition of irony because my trip to the coldest place on the face of the earth was canceled due to a freak blizzard in Atlanta, Georgia, of all places. Supposedly it was the first time that Atlanta had seen snow in 16 years.

 **LET ME TRY IT**

# Inserting a Spreadsheet into a Publisher Document

At any rate, you can insert an existing spreadsheet into a Publisher document by following these steps:

1. Go to Publisher's Insert tab.

2. Click the Object icon, located on the toolbar.

3. Choose the Microsoft Excel Worksheet option from the list of objects.

4. Choose the Create From File option.

5. Click OK.

6. Click the Browse button.

7. Choose the spreadsheet that you want to import, and click Open.

8. Click OK.

Often, you might find that even very small spreadsheets, such as the one shown in Figure 6.19, exceed the size of the Publisher document. In these cases, it will be necessary to resize the spreadsheet or adjust the page orientation to make the spreadsheet fit properly.

As you look at Figure 6.19, you might notice that most of the spreadsheet's space is being consumed by unused rows and columns. You can delete unwanted rows or columns by double-clicking them and using the Delete command.

If all your data is located in contiguous cells, you can open Excel and select the cells that you want to copy into your Publisher document. After doing so, press Ctrl+C to copy the cells to the clipboard. Next, switch over to Publisher and press Ctrl+Z to copy the selected cells into the Publisher document, as shown in Figure 6.20.

If your spreadsheet doesn't use formulas, you might consider pasting its contents into a table. Publisher gives you a higher degree of control over a table's appearance than it does over the appearance of a spreadsheet.

If you decide to use a table, there is one major drawback of which you need to be aware. If you try to copy and paste an entire spreadsheet into a table, you must have the same number or rows and columns in your table as the spreadsheet that you are importing.

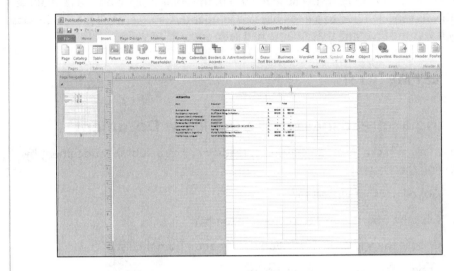

**Figure 6.19**   *Spreadsheets don't always fit properly when imported.*

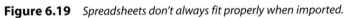
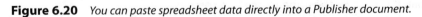

**Figure 6.20**   *You can paste spreadsheet data directly into a Publisher document.*

Publisher limits you to using a maximum of 128 rows and 128 columns in a table.

**SHOW ME** Media 6.3—Importing Spreadsheets

*Access this video file through your registered Web edition at*
*my.safaribooksonline.com/9780132182591/media.*

## Link Options

Although you can import a spreadsheet into a Publisher document using the method I have shown you, Publisher gives you a couple of other options as well. If you look at Figure 6.21, for example, you will notice a Link check box. Selecting this check box causes Publisher to display a picture of the spreadsheet rather than actually importing the spreadsheet in its native form. However, the Publisher document remains linked to the spreadsheet, so any changes you make to the spreadsheet are also reflected in the picture of the spreadsheet.

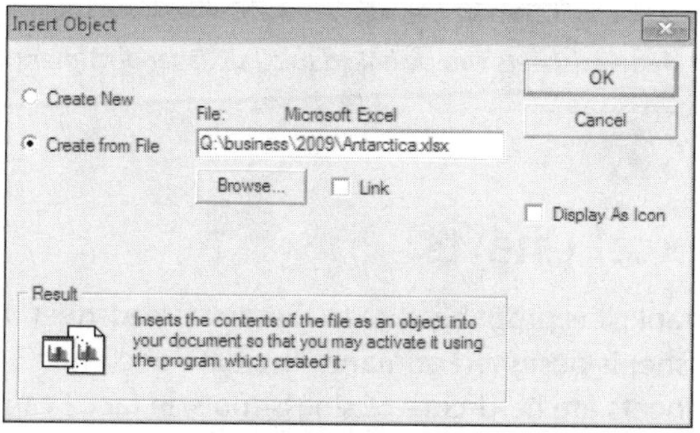

**Figure 6.21** *The spreadsheet can be linked to a Publisher document.*

## Display Spreadsheet as Icon

Another option that you might have noticed in Figure 6.21 is the Display as Icon check box. Selecting this check box causes an Excel icon to be placed into the Publisher document instead of having the document display the spreadsheet's contents. You would normally use this option only if you were using Publisher to create web content. I talk all about using Publisher as a website creation tool in Chapter 9, "Publishing Online." In the meantime, you can see an example of a spreadsheet that is linked as an icon in Figure 6.22.

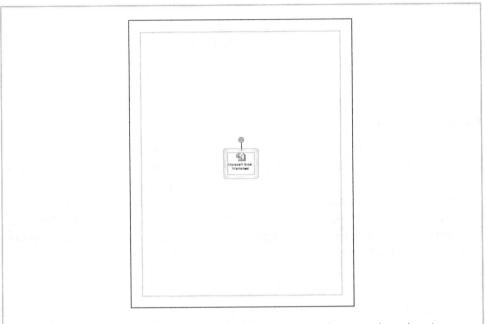

**Figure 6.22**   *Excel spreadsheets can be linked to a Publisher document through an icon.*

# Importing Excel Charts

To be perfectly frank, it is probably rare to import spreadsheet data into a Publisher document. Publisher is designed primarily to create documents with visual appeal, whereas spreadsheets are hard-core business tools. In fact, I can recall only one situation in which real-world circumstances required me to display raw spreadsheet data within a Publisher document. That isn't to say that I never use Excel and Publisher together, however. Excel can create some rather nice-looking charts, and Publisher offers the perfect medium for displaying them.

## LET ME TRY IT

# Creating a Chart Within Publisher

As with a spreadsheet, you have a choice of either importing an existing chart or creating a new chart directly through Publisher. I start out by showing you how to use Publisher to create a chart, and then I show you how to import an Excel chart. With that said, you can create a chart by completing these steps:

1. Go to Publisher's Insert tab.

2. Click the Object icon, located on the toolbar.

3. Choose the Microsoft Excel Chart option from the list of available object types.

4. Click OK.

Upon completing these steps, Publisher creates a new chart, as shown in Figure 6.23. As you look at the figure, you might wonder what data the chart is reflecting. If you look just beneath the chart, you will notice two tabs, one labeled Chart1 and the other labeled Sheet1. The Chart1 tab contains the actual chart, whereas the Sheet1 tab contains the spreadsheet that was used to create the chart.

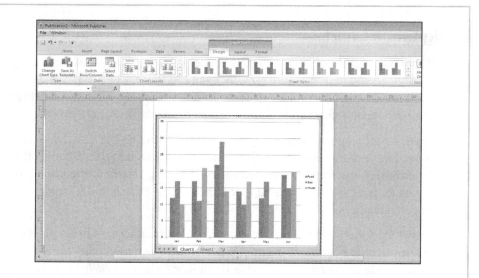

**Figure 6.23**    *You can create a brand-new chart directly through Publisher.*

As you can see in Figure 6.24, the Sheet1 tab contains a generic spreadsheet, which exists only as a way of helping you get started with creating your chart. Microsoft fully expects you to change all the column headings and replace the data with your own.

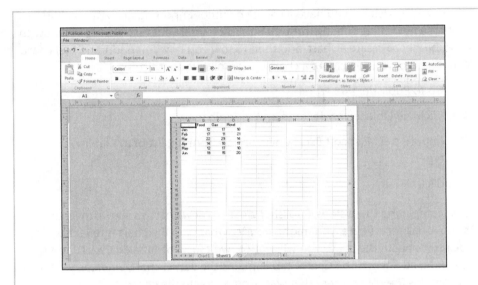

**Figure 6.24**   *Charts are linked to a generic spreadsheet.*

# Designing a Chart

Publisher provides a nearly unlimited set of options for customizing the chart you are creating. If you look at Figure 6.25, for example, you can see that the Design subtab beneath the Chart Tools tab contains options for changing the chart type and selecting a new chart style, and an option to change the chart layout.

In addition to the options that are geared toward changing the chart's appearance, there are two very useful icons on the Design toolbar. One of these icons is the Switch Row/Column icon. Sometimes you may find that the chart function plots your data incorrectly. When this happens, clicking the Switch Row/Column icon often corrects the problem.

The other icon you need to know about is the Select Data icon. Clicking this icon brings up a dialog box that enables you to choose which rows and columns you want to include in the chart. You will find this icon to be especially important after you alter the spreadsheet to include your own data, because your data will rarely use the same number of rows and columns as the generic spreadsheet that Microsoft provides.

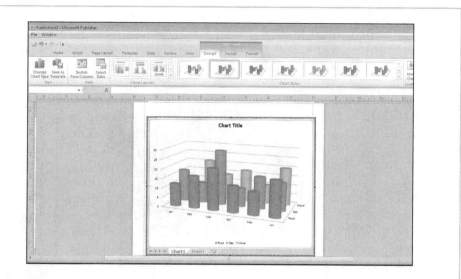

**Figure 6.25**   *The Design toolbar contains a variety of options for changing the chart's appearance.*

## Changing the Way a Chart Is Displayed

The Chart Tools tab's Layout subtab is almost as important as the Design tab. This tab enables you to control things such as the chart's title and how the chart's legend and axis are displayed. You can also do really cool things, such as changing the chart's 3-D view or filling the chart's backdrop with a picture. The options found on the Layout tab are pretty self-explanatory, but I have used the tab to customize the chart shown in Figure 6.26, just so you can see what is possible.

Although not required, it is helpful to have some experience with creating charts in Excel.

In this figure, I used the default spreadsheet data but selected a different chart type. I replaced the chart wall with a picture that I took in St. John last month, and I replaced the chart floor with a solid color.

.
.

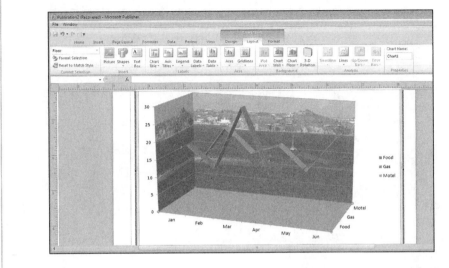

**Figure 6.26**  *The Layout tab enables you to customize a chart.*

## Controlling Text Within a Chart

The Format tab isn't quite as important as the Design and Layout tabs. It is primarily used to control the style of text used within the chart. As you can see in Figure 6.27, this tab enables you to select shape styles or word art styles. You can also use this tab to format things such as the chart's legend and axes.

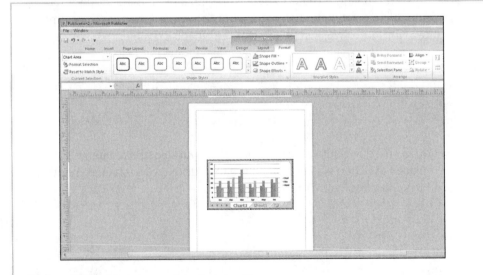

**Figure 6.27**  *The Format tab is of minimal importance.*

**SHOW ME**    Media 6.4—Creating a Chart
*Access this video file through your registered Web edition at*
*my.safaribooksonline.com/9780132182591/media.*

# Importing an Existing Chart

Various methods can be used to import an existing chart into Publisher. I have
found that the easiest method is also the least sophisticated. All you have to do is
open Excel and select the chart that you want to import. Excel enables you to
select either the chart itself, the legend, or the chart and the legend together, so
make sure you select the portion that you need. After doing so, press Ctrl+C to
copy the chart to the clipboard. Then, switch over to Publisher and press Ctrl+V to
paste the chart into your Publisher document. As you can see in Figure 6.28, the
chart is imported seamlessly.

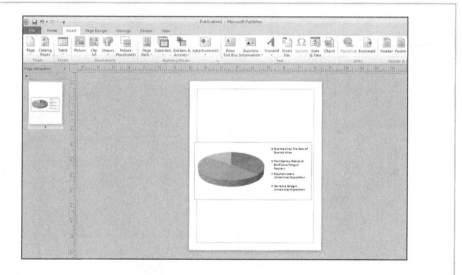

**Figure 6.28**    *Excel charts can be pasted into Publisher documents.*

**TELL ME MORE**    Media 6.5—The Practicality of Using Spreadsheet
**Data in Publisher**
*To listen to a free audio recording about how realistic it is to include*
*spreadsheet data in a Publisher document, log on to*
*my.safaribooksonline.com/9780132182591/media.*

In this chapter, you learn techniques for properly finalizing your publication.

7

# Finalizing Your Publisher Document

It's already time for me to begin talking about techniques for finalizing Publisher documents. Sure, there are a few chapters left after this one, but those chapters deal with printing, web publishing, and mass distribution of Publisher documents. Because each of those chapters deals with completed documents, I wanted to take this opportunity to show you how to finalize your document.

## A Visual Inspection

By far the most important thing you can do to prepare your document for completion is to give it a thorough visual inspection. First and foremost, this means proofing and reproofing the document's text.

Generally, I tend to think that proofreading Publisher documents is even more important than proofing Microsoft Word documents. Don't get me wrong...it is always important to proofread your work. It's just that Microsoft Word documents can become so long that some grammatical mistakes are bound to go unnoticed. I have found that grammatical mistakes are more likely to cause problems in Publisher documents because of the way Publisher tends to be used.

To give you an idea of what I'm talking about, there is a charitable organization for which I do a lot of volunteer work. One of the projects I helped out with was a brochure that helps explain the organization services. I wrote about half the text and helped lay out the document in Publisher. Because I take pride in my work, I proofread the text several times. Even so, some of the organization's other members found some minor grammatical faux pas the first time they read it. Even as I corrected the grammatical mistakes that were pointed out to me, I began finding a few other minor things that needed to be corrected.

So is my grammar really that terrible? Well, maybe. That isn't really the point, though. My point is that even something as short as a brochure requires multiple editing passes before the grammar is perfect. Always remember that in short documents, your readers are likely to pick up on mistakes you have overlooked. This is a problem because creating documents that are full of grammatical errors has a direct impact on your credibility.

When I was creating the brochure I just described, I visited the websites for several similar organizations. I wasn't out to plagiarize anyone's work, but I was looking for a bit of inspiration. What I found was eye-opening. Some of the websites I visited were very well done and contained highly polished text. Other sites took on the amateurish feel of a fly-by-night organization simply because the website's text was so poorly edited. I'm not talking about a small, mom-and-pop outfit either. I don't want to name names, but these are charities you are likely to have heard of.

# Proofreading Techniques

Because proofreading is essential to the success of a Publisher document, I think it makes a lot of sense to spend a moment talking about some best practices for proofreading.

## You've Got to Have Friends

Proofread your document to the best of your abilities, and then ask a friend to review it. A second set of eyes can work wonders. When I have asked friends to review something I have written, I am often amazed at the things they pick up on that I have missed.

## Dictation Software

When I proofread my own work, one of the problems I have the hardest time spotting are missing words. Sometimes when I'm writing a document, I will stop mid-sentence to think about what I want to say next. Once in a while, this ends up causing me to leave out a word or two in the middle of a sentence. When I go back and reread my work, I sometimes skim right over the missing words.

A technique that I have found for combating this problem is to use Dragon Naturally Speaking to help with my proofreading. If you're not familiar with Dragon Naturally Speaking, it is an application that enables you to dictate your work rather than type it. In fact, everything I have written in this chapter so far has been dictated.

The reason why I recommend using dictation software for proofing is because Dragging Naturally Speaking has a built-in text-to-speech engine that is capable of reading your work back to you. That way, you can hear your work as it was written, rather than reading your work as your brain interprets it.

## Go Back to Elementary School

When I first started writing professionally, the company I was working for assigned me a mentor whose job it was to critique my writing and help me improve it. After reading my first few submissions, my mentor gave me an elementary school grammar book and told me to read it.

I have to admit that at first, I was really put off. However, my mentor explained to me that the single biggest thing that any of us can do to improve our grammar is to focus on the basics. Using an elementary school textbook helped me learn the basics quickly. It only took me about half an hour to read the book, and yet I can honestly say that I learned a lot. My grammar still wasn't perfect, but thanks to this simple technique, my grammar is much better than it used to be.

## Adjusting Document Spacing

Although spelling and grammatical problems are the single most important issue to address in Publisher documents (at least in my opinion), document spacing comes in a close second. Sometimes, you have trouble fitting everything onto the document page.

Depending on how severe your spacing problems end up being, there might not always be a solution for cramming everything onto a single page while still keeping the page legible. There are, however, some techniques you can use to address minor document-spacing issues.

## Use a Compact Font

One of the most effective techniques for reducing the amount of space that a block of text or a headline consumes is to use a compact font. In most cases, I would recommend that you never use more than three different fonts on a page. Using an excessive number of fonts has a tendency to make a document page seem cluttered and messy. Having said that, though, there is a time and a place for everything. If switching to a compact font helps you overcome otherwise insurmountable space issues, that is what you should do.

To give you an idea of what a difference a compact font can make, I have created the screen capture shown in Figure 7.1. The document shown in the figure contains two lines of text. The first line of text uses a font named Bodini MT, and the second line uses a variation of the Bodini MT font called Bodini MT Condensed. Both lines of text were created using the same font size, and yet you can see that the condensed font takes up a lot less space.

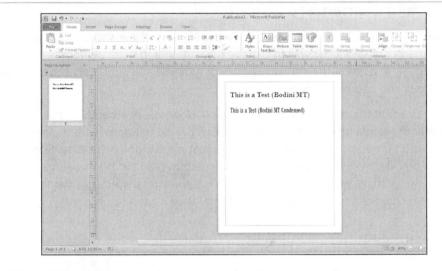

**Figure 7.1**  *Using compact fonts can save a lot of space.*

The nice thing about the condensed font is that it is a direct variation of the font that I used in the first line. As such, the two fonts are similar to each other. This means that if you have to use a condensed font, you can do so without completely sacrificing the overall feel of the font that you had originally chosen (assuming that you own a condensed version of the font you originally used).

## Text Boxes

In Chapter 5, "Working with Longer Documents," I showed you how you could use techniques such as hyphenation and word wrapping to help large amounts of text fit into a small text box. Sometimes, these techniques alone might not be enough. There are a few other things you can do, though.

When you have too much text for the amount of space you have to work with, the most obvious solution to the problem might seem to be to reduce the size of the font. In some cases, this may be a viable option. Reducing the font size isn't always a good idea, however.

There comes a point at which a font simply becomes too small to read. You could also consider a font to be too small if it looks ridiculous within the context of the document. In other words, if your document contains a large headline and a huge picture but uses little bitty text, the document probably is going to look pretty silly (unless, of course, you are using the small print to append a legal disclaimer to the document). In those types of situations, it is probably better to shrink some of the other design elements so that you don't have to use a font size that feels out of balance with the rest of the document.

The design aesthetics aren't the only problem with shrinking a document's font. If the text whose font you are shrinking exists within a single text box, and you can shrink the font without making it too small, decreasing the font size probably won't be a problem. The same cannot always be said for situations in which multiple text boxes are chained together. That's because the changes that you make in one text box altered the contents of other text boxes. Believe me when I say that refitting the contents of all those text boxes after a font change can truly be a frustrating experience.

The approach you will have to take to making text fit within a text box varies depending upon how much space you need to reclaim. If the text you are trying to fit only slightly exceeds the allotted space, you might consider editing the text. You might find that by rewording a sentence or two, you can make the text fit. Another idea is to use the built-in thesaurus to replace some of the longer words with shorter words that have the same meaning.

In Publisher you can adjust the font sizes in 0.1 point increments. Sometimes such a slight adjustment to a font size may be all that you have to do to make the text fit.

## Overlapping Frames

In Chapter 3, "Working with Visual Elements," I showed you how you can use word wrapping to wrap text around an image or a shape. Although word wrapping is an effective technique, it doesn't always produce a result that is consistent with the look and feel you are trying to achieve for the document. It is possible, however, to get some of the same space benefits by using a similar technique, but without actually having to resort to using word wrapping.

To see what I am talking about, take a look at Figure 7.2. In this figure, I have created a document containing a text box and a clip art image. As it stands, there is no shortage of space in the document (although I did intentionally overflow the text box). I left the document uncluttered so that I could more easily demonstrate the technique I want to show you.

As you look at the figure, you can't see the outline for the text box, but you can pretty much tell where it is because of the way the text flows. You also can see the box that surrounds the clip art image. If you look at the lower-left corner of the clip art image, you will notice that there is some wasted space. The box extends far beyond the boundary of the image. If necessary, we can make our text box overlap the unused portion of the clip art box. That way, the text box can become a little bit bigger without us having to shrink our clip art image.

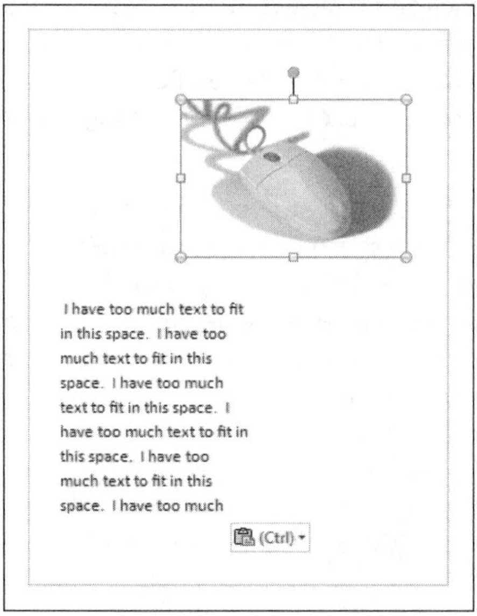

**Figure 7.2**   *Sometimes the boxes used for design elements contain wasted space.*

If you decide to use this technique, you will have to remember what you have learned about layering. You will need to use the Bring Forward icon (shown in Figure 7.2) to make sure the text box is layered on top of the clip art box. Figure 7.3 shows what this technique might look like when implemented.

In the figure, the text box actually overlaps the clip art box. Because this overlapping was done in a responsible manner, the final document looks nice, and you would never know that some of the design elements overlap with each other.

# Coming Up Short

So far, I have spent most of the chapter talking about how to make various types of design elements fit on the page when they are too large. Sometimes, however, you may find that you have the opposite problem. Just as an overcrowded page can be a problem, a page that is too empty can also cause problems.

You can see an example of such a document in Figure 7.4. As you can see in the figure, this document contains a heading, a small block of text, and an image. Even though I am using three different design elements, the document looks funny because the design elements appear to be scattered across a vast area of empty white space.

**Figure 7.3**   *You can save space by overlapping the unused portions of design elements.*

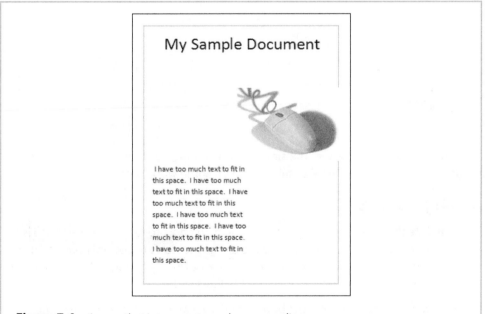

**Figure 7.4**   *A page that is too empty can be unappealing.*

Assuming that the document doesn't need any additional visual elements, you might wonder what you can do to fill in the remaining space, aside from increasing the size of the fonts and the clip art image.

# Subheads

One especially effective technique is to add a subhead to the document, which goes directly beneath the document heading. The subheading's font size isn't quite as large as the font used for the main heading, but it is larger than the body text font, and that helps take up space. You can see an example of a subhead in Figure 7.5.

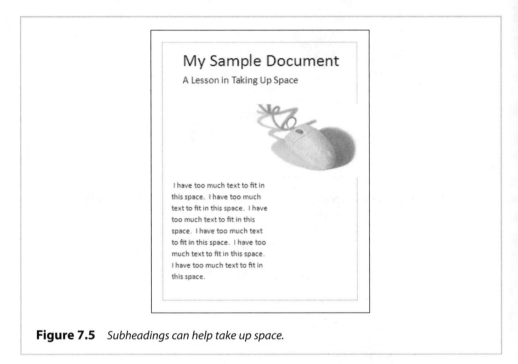

**Figure 7.5**   *Subheadings can help take up space.*

As you can see in the figure, the simple act of adding a subhead is already helping the document look better. We still need to do some work, though.

# Adding Borders

Another technique you can sometimes use in an effort to take up some space is to add a border around the images you are using. You don't necessarily have to use border art, however. You can create a very nice border by telling Publisher to color the line around the image and increase the line's thickness.

I don't really think that adding a border works very well for this particular document. One of the few appealing things about the document is that the image I am using has the same background color as the rest of the page, giving it a very clean look. Borders tend to work best around square or rectangular images. A perfect example of a situation in which using a border might be helpful would be framing an Excel chart.

## Relocating Design Elements

Another technique you can use to make a sparsely populated document page more appealing is to rearrange some of the design elements. I will be the first to admit that I am not an artist, and I have absolutely no formal training in laying out documents. Having said that, I have always found that sparsely populated documents seem to take on a nicer appearance if most of the empty whitespace appears at the outer edges of the document rather than in the middle.

To show you what I mean, check out Figure 7.6. The document shown in this screen capture still has all the same design elements as the previous figure. I haven't resized anything; all I have done is move some things around.

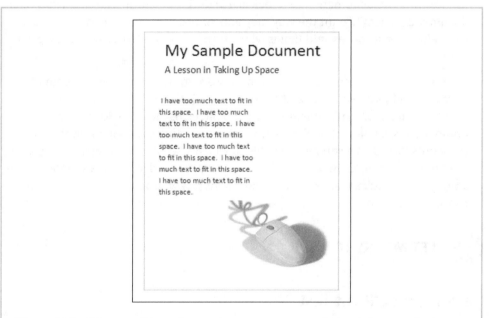

**Figure 7.6**    *When possible, push excessive empty space to a document's outer edges.*

As you can see, I have moved the text box to the upper-left portion of the document, just below the subhead. I did this because the natural tendency is for people to read a document beginning in the upper-left corner. Because the text box was moved to the upper-left corner, I balanced the document by moving my image to the lower-right corner. I also avoided moving the image too far away from the text box in an effort to prevent too much empty whitespace in the middle of the document.

**SHOW ME** Media 7.1—Adjusting Design Elements
*Access this video file through your registered Web edition at*
***my.safaribooksonline.com/9780132182591/media***.

# Test Printing the Document

After you have finished proofreading your document, I recommend printing it. I realize that your intent may be to have the document printed professionally. I talk about both professional and in-house printing at length in the next chapter. For right now, though, I suggest printing the document yourself so that you can get a feel for what the document might look like in its finished form. Although Publisher documents generally print the way they appear onscreen, printing does occasionally yield some surprises, and that is why it is so important to perform a test print right now.

Of course, in some cases, test printing may prove to be impossible. For example, I have a good friend who is an architect in New Orleans. He routinely has to print architectural documents on extremely large paper. Because he does not own a printer that is capable of working with such large paper sizes, all his print jobs have to be outsourced. In a situation like this, in which special paper is being used, a test print may prove to be impossible. Assuming you are working with a standard page size, though, a quick test print right now might save you some money and some heartache later on.

**LET ME TRY IT**

## Performing a Print Test

As I said earlier, I discuss printing at length in the next chapter. If you want to perform a quick and dirty print test, however, you can do so by completing these steps:

1. Go to Publisher's File tab.

2. Click the Print option, shown in Figure 7.7.

3. Verify that the correct printer is selected.

4. Click the Print button.

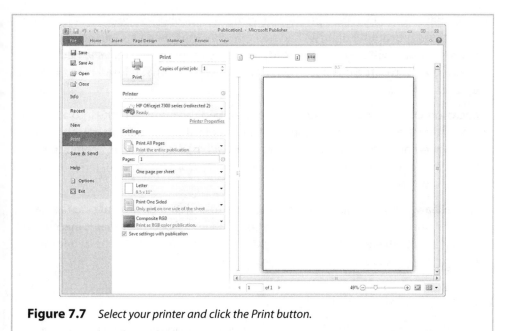

**Figure 7.7** *Select your printer and click the Print button.*

# Document Metadata

A lot of people incorrectly assume that Publisher documents are made up solely of things like text boxes, images, shapes, and word art. Although these types of design elements are the most visible part of a Publisher document, there are other parts to the document that are not generally seen.

These often-unseen document attributes are called metadata. Metadata (which is sometimes referred to as "metadata tags" or just "tags") can include many different things. For example, a document's metadata might contain the name of the author, a copyright notice, or even a set of search keywords.

Taking the time to find out what is embedded in a document's metadata can potentially save you from an embarrassing situation. I will never forget how I learned this lesson for myself.

Several years ago, my wife and I lost someone who was very close to us. After the funeral, my wife found a poem on the Internet that she thought might bring comfort to some of our friends. Because the poem's author was listed as unknown, my wife pasted the poem into a Microsoft Word document and emailed it to a couple of friends.

Later that afternoon, I got a phone call from a friend who was amazed at my ability to write such beautiful poetry. I had no idea what my friend was talking about, because I don't write poetry—ever. My friend explained to me that she had received a Microsoft Word document from my wife, and that it listed me as the document's author!

Microsoft Office documents automatically embed the author's name into any documents that are created. The author's name is set to the name of the person who was logged on to the computer. Because my wife had borrowed my computer when she sent the poem to our friends, Microsoft Word listed my name as the document's author.

The takeaway is that unless you take the time to review a document's metadata, you may inadvertently include information with your document that is inaccurate, or that is potentially sensitive. You might want to remove your personal information from the metadata.

# Working with Metadata

Metadata is not a bad thing. In most situations, the opposite is actually true. Metadata can help search engines to locate a document. This is especially true if the document is to be stored in a SharePoint document library.

The trick to working with metadata isn't to completely scrub all metadata from the document. Instead, you should focus on deciding what metadata is appropriate for use in the document given its intended purpose.

## Save As

Publisher doesn't expose all the available metadata in one place. Some metadata is manually entered when a Publisher document is saved for the first time. To show you what I mean, take a look at the Save As dialog box, shown in Figure 7.8. If you look just beneath the Save As Type dropdown list, you can see that the Authors field has automatically been set to Administrator. This is because I am currently logged in to the computer as Administrator. If you need to enter a different name or add the name of an additional author, you can do so by clicking the author's name and entering the correction into the resulting text box.

As you look at the figure, also notice a section called Tags that appears directly across from the Authors section. If you click the Add a Tag link, you are given the opportunity to add keywords to the document.

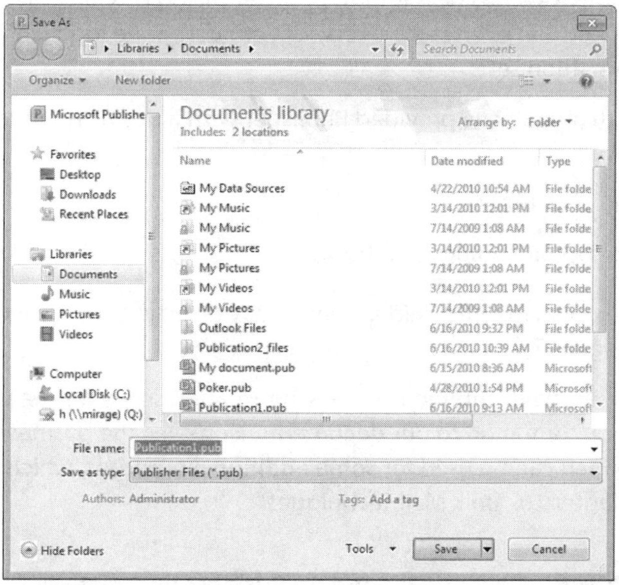

Figure 7.8   *Some metadata is automatically created when a document is saved.*

**SHOW ME**   Media 7.2—Adding Metadata
*Access this video file through your registered Web edition at*
***my.safaribooksonline.com/9780132182591/media.***

**LET ME TRY IT**

# Creating Business Information

In addition to the metadata that is created when a document is saved, metadata
related to your organization can also be stored within Publisher. To do so, complete
the following steps:

1. Go to Publisher's File tab.

2. Choose the Info option.

3. Click the Edit Business Information button.

When the Create New Business Information Set dialog box appears, populate the various fields. You can even store a copy of your corporate logo within your business information set:

1. Ensure that you have provided Publisher with a business information set name.

2. Click the Save button.

3. Click the Update Publication button.

When you are done, the Info field automatically displays your business information, as shown in Figure 7.9.

For right now, we have entered business information solely for the purpose of adding owner information to our documents. However, the business information we have provided can be used for some additional purposes, which I will be showing you in Chapter 10, "Bulk Mail Techniques."

**SHOW ME**     Media 7.3—Adding Business Information
*Access this video file through your registered Web edition at*
***my.safaribooksonline.com/9780132182591/media***.

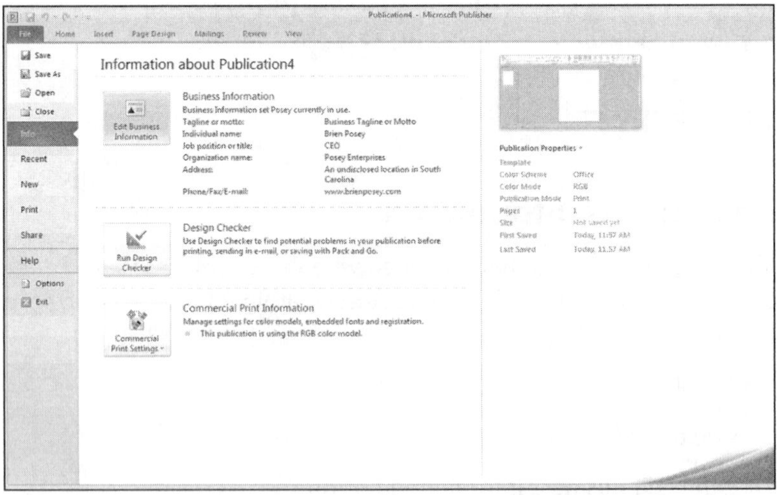

**Figure 7.9** *You can store business information directly within Publisher.*

# The Design Checker

One of the most important steps in finalizing your Publisher documents is to run the Design Checker, which is a tool is built in to Publisher. Its purpose is to check Publisher documents for issues that could pose problems later on.

 **LET ME TRY IT**

## Accessing the Design Checker

You can access the Design Checker by following these steps:

1. Go to Publisher's File tab.

2. Click the Info option.

3. Click the Run Design Checker button, which you can see in Figure 7.9.

As you can see in Figure 7.10, there are four different types of checks you can run against a document. By default, Publisher runs a general design check, which looks for any type of problem that might prevent the document from being displayed or printed correctly. Additionally, you can run a commercial printing check (which I discuss in the next chapter), a website check (which I cover in Chapter 9, "Publishing Online"), or an email check (see Chapter 10). For right now, though, I want to give you an overview of what the Design Checker is and how it works.

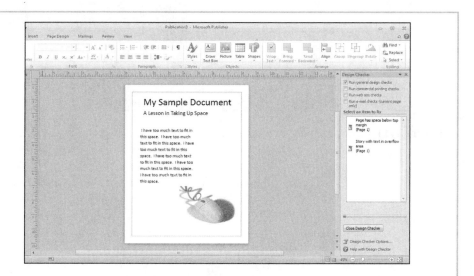

**Figure 7.10**  *You can run four different types of design checks.*

As you can see in the figure, Publisher has detected two different issues with my sample document. The errors that the Design Checker detects are not always catastrophic; in many cases, they are nit-picky things. A perfect example of this is the first error message, which tells me that there is space below the top margin.

I am starting the document a bit low on the page. In this case, it isn't a big deal—after all, I used this document earlier when I was trying to show you how to take up space in a sparsely populated document. What if the reverse were true, though? If you were having a hard time fitting everything onto the page, knowing that you were starting below the page margin might be very helpful.

For the sake of demonstration, let's pretend that this error is something we want to correct. Let's also pretend that we don't know what the error message means. By clicking on the error, Publisher displays all the individual display elements that make up the document, as shown in Figure 7.11. You can finally see how the text box and the image overlap, as I talked about earlier.

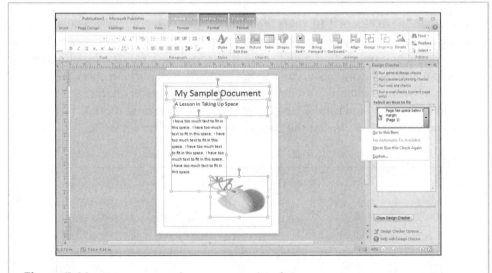

**Figure 7.11**    *Using compact fonts can save a lot of space.*

More importantly, this figure displays a dropdown menu that appears when you click on an individual design error. This menu provides you with four choices, as follows:

- **Go To This Item**—This option takes you directly to the object within the document that is causing the problem.

- **Fix**—The Automatic Fix option corrects the error automatically. However, as you can see in the figure, automatic fixes are not always available.

- **Never Run This Check Again**—In this case, I placed my header below the margin intentionally. Because this isn't really an error, I could get rid of the error message by choosing the Never Run This Check Again option.

- **Explain**—Clicking the Explain option opens Internet Explorer, which takes you to a web page explaining the error. At the time this book was written, Microsoft had yet to publish any of the explanatory text, but it should be available soon.

I wanted to conclude this section by showing you how the Design Checker could provide helpful advice. You might have noticed in Figure 7.10 that the second error that was reported indicated that there was a story with text in the overflow area. As you may recall, I talked about overflow text in Chapter 5, but if you look at the figure, there is no obvious text overflow problem.

The error exists because when I created the document, I inserted several blank spaces after the document's title specifically for the purpose of causing the text to overflow the text box. Now that you know that little tidbit of information, watch what happens when I choose the Go To This Item option from the error's dropdown list.

If you look at Figure 7.12, you can see that Publisher has automatically selected the text box in which the problem exists. You can also see that the text box is displaying the overflow icon, which indicates that some of the text is not being displayed because it exceeds the text box's capacity.

I also want to point out that you can't always depend on the option to automatically fix a design error. Not only is the Fix option not always available, but sometimes it backfires. After all, Publisher has no idea what your intentions are; it only knows the easiest way to correct what it sees as a problem. In this case, for example, automatically fixing the problem causes the text box to become linked to another text box on an empty page, as shown in Figure 7.13.

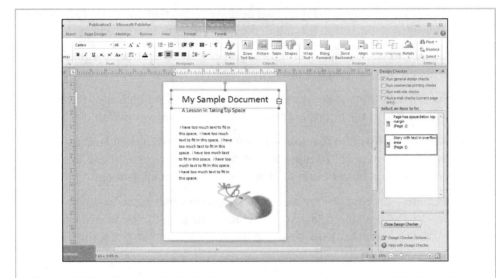

**Figure 7.12**   *Choosing the Go To This Item option selects the object in which the problem exists.*

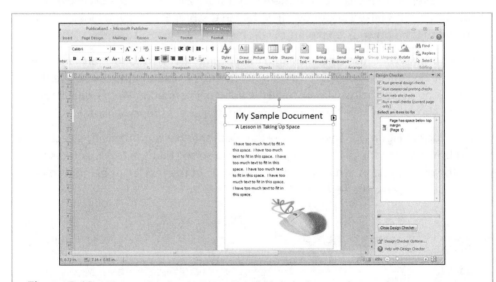

**Figure 7.13**   *The text box has been inadvertently linked to another text box on an empty page.*

**SHOW ME** Media 7.4—Design Checking
*Access this video file through your registered Web edition at*
***my.safaribooksonline.com/9780132182591/media**.*

# Creating PDF and XPS Files

Although the purpose of this chapter has been to help you prepare your document for printing, not every Publisher document gets printed. Sometimes you might only want to export the finished document to a PDF or an XPS file. If you aren't familiar with XPS files, they are similar to PDF files but are a Microsoft standard.

## LET ME TRY IT

## Exporting a Document as a PDF or XPS File

Exporting a document as a PDF or an XPS file is simple. To create a PDF file, follow these steps:

1. Go to Publisher's File menu.

2. Click the Save As option.

3. Choose the PDF option (or the XPS Document option) from the Save As Type dropdown list.

4. Click the Options button.

5. Choose the desired options from the Publish Options dialog box, shown in Figure 7.14. These options affect the size and quality of the document that you are creating. I discuss these options in more detail in the next chapter.

6. Click OK.

7. Enter a path and filename for the document that you are creating.

8. Click the Save button.

**TELL ME MORE** Media 7.5—Final Thoughts on the Design Checker
*To listen to a free audio recording about the design checker, log on to*
***my.safaribooksonline.com/9780132182591/media**.*

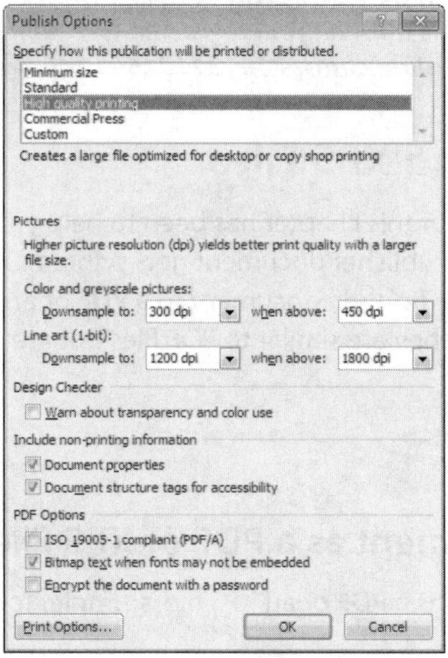

**Figure 7.14**    *The options that you choose affect the size and quality of the output file.*

Although desktop printing is a simple process, Publisher documents often are printed profession-ally. This chapter provides you with a background in commercial printing.

8

# Printing Your Documents

It might seem a bit odd for me to include an entire chapter on printing. After all, printing is a common function in all the Microsoft Office products and can be accomplished in a matter of a few mouse clicks.

Publisher documents are unique in that they are often sent to professional print shops. You never hear of anyone paying a premium price to have an Excel spread-sheet or a PowerPoint slide deck professionally printed, and yet this is the norm for Publisher documents.

Because professional printing can be expensive, I want to dedicate this chapter to teaching you about having your documents professionally printed. I also discuss in-house printing in a greater degree of detail than I did in the last chapter.

## Design Checking Your Document

In Chapter 7, "Finalizing Your Publisher Document," I showed you how to use the Design Checker to spot potential problems with your document. As I previously mentioned, the Design Checker includes a function that is specifically designed to look for printing issues.

 **LET ME TRY IT**

## Checking for Print Issues

To check for printing issues, complete these steps:

1. Go to Publisher's File tab.

2. Click the Run Design Checker button.

3. Select the Run Commercial Printing Checks check box, as shown in Fig-ure 8.1.

4. Correct any issues that are detected, and then click the Close Design Checker button.

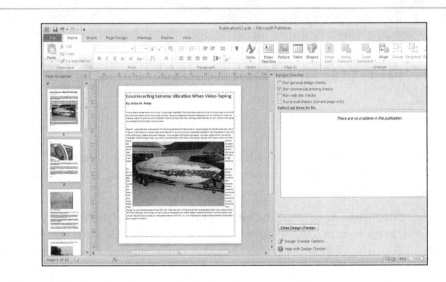

**Figure 8.1**   *You should run the Design Checker prior to printing a document.*

## Printing Documents Yourself

In many cases, you will likely end up printing Publisher documents to your own printer. Even if you are planning on having your document professionally printed, I still recommend printing your own copy if possible, just so you can get a feel for how the finished document will look. I have run into a couple of situations in which the printed document didn't look like what Publisher showed onscreen. Printing the document myself allowed me to spot the problem and correct it before sending the document to the printers.

I want to take a few moments and talk about how to print Publisher documents on your printer. Later, I turn my attention to professional printing.

## Basic Printing

At its simplest, printing a document involves going to Publisher's File tab, and then selecting the Print option. From there, you can click the Print button, shown in Figure 8.2.

Your Publisher document will automatically default to another printer. As you can see in the figure, though, there are quite a few different options you can set. Most of these options are pretty self-explanatory, but I will go through them anyway.

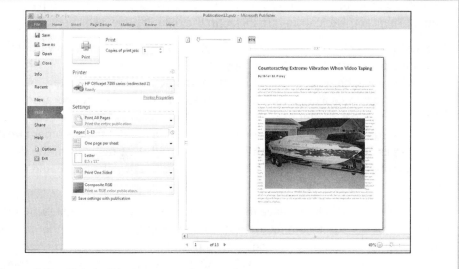

**Figure 8.2** *Click the Print button to print your document.*

## Page Range

If you look at the Settings section in Figure 8.2, the first option you see enables you to select which pages will be printed. By default, Publisher is configured to print the entire document. However, you can enter a custom page range. If you click the down arrow on the Print All Pages button, Publisher even provides you with some built-in options that enable you to do things such as printing only select pages or printing only the current page.

## Page Layout

If you look beneath the page range in Figure 8.2, you will see a button labeled One Page Per Sheet. This means that Publisher will print the document using only one side of each sheet of paper, and each document page will be treated as one printed page. There are, however, a number of other options you can use. For instance, if you wanted the page to print like a greeting card, you could click on the One Page Per Sheet button and select one of the Booklet options. As you select various page layouts, the document preview changes to reflect how the document will be printed.

## Paper Size

The third option in the Settings section enables you to choose the type of paper on which the document will be printed. Publisher automatically sets the paper size to match the template that you used when your document was created. For example,

I created my document using the template for an 8.5 x 11-inch page in letter orientation. That template choice is reflected in the default paper selection.

Earlier I said that if you are going to have your document commercially printed, you should start out by printing a copy yourself "if possible." The reason why I said that is because the page size is tied to the template, and not all printers are equipped to handle all page sizes. In this case, everything meshes because my default printer has no trouble printing 8.5 x 11 documents. Had I used an A3 template, though, my printer would not have been able to print the document unless I changed paper sizes. Changing the page size would allow me to print the document locally, but my printout would not be representative of what I could expect from a commercial printer.

Incidentally, not all printers have the same capabilities. If your default printer is unable to print your document in the desired way, but you have another printer that is capable of printing your document in the way you intended, you can change your printer selection by clicking on the listing for the printer and then choosing a different printer.

## Duplex Printing

The second-to-last option in the Settings section is the duplex printing option. By default, Publisher performs single-sided printing. If your printer supports duplex printing, though, you can click the Print One-Sided button and choose to print on both sides of the page.

## Color Model

The last option in the Settings section enables you to choose the color model that will be used when you print your document. Publisher will only display color models that are compatible with your printer. In this case, for example, the only available color models are Composite RGB and Composite Grayscale. In other words, these options enable you to print the document either in color or in black and white. I talk a lot more about color models later in this chapter.

# Professional Printing

Now that I have talked about how you can print your own Publisher document and about some of the printing options that are available to you, I want to turn my attention to commercial printing. As I do, I will be talking about all the things that you need to do in preparation for having your document printed. I start out by discussing some questions that you need to ask the print shop.

Because Windows makes it so easy to print just about any type of document to your printer, it might seem strange that professional printing can be so tricky. As such, I wanted to provide this section for the benefit of those who have never had to deal with a commercial printing service before.

# What Will the Job Cost?

Fifteen years ago, I needed to get some invitations printed for my wedding. I had a friend who had a friend who owned a printing company, so that seemed like the way to go.

One afternoon, my friend came over with samples of various wedding invitations that his buddy could print. My wife and I spent a couple of hours looking over the various styles of invitations, and finally decided on something that we liked. We told my friend of our decision, and he contacted the print shop for us.

I think that my exact words when my friend called me to confirm the order were "HOW MUCH?!!!!!"

I learned an important lesson that day. Commercial printing can be expensive, and using things like color, embossing, and special paper can dramatically increase the costs.

OK, so it isn't every day that you need to have wedding invitations printed. More than 15 years later, my wife and I are still married, and I am happy to say that I haven't had to print any more wedding invitations. At the same time, though, the same types of factors that drove up the cost of my wedding invitations can also impact other types of print jobs. Any time you use color or special paper, you can expect the printing costs to increase.

Because printing costs can be significant, it is important to know upfront how much a print job is going to cost you. That way, if the costs are too high, you can make adjustments to your job before it is printed.

Today, most printing companies will allow you to submit print jobs over the Internet. Every printing company does things differently, but most of the ones I have used recently have their websites set up so that you can select the desired printing options as you submit your document. These sites will typically calculate printing costs on the fly. If the cost is too high, you can choose different printing options until you get the price to fit within your budget.

For print jobs that are more specialized (or for companies that do not allow you to submit jobs online), it is important to talk with someone at the print shop in person. Be sure to bring along a copy of your document, and be prepared to talk about your plans for it. The person you talk to should be able to give you advice on how to get the desired results without exceeding your printing budget.

# How Long Will It Take?

It kind of goes without saying that when you submit a document for printing, you need to know how long the printing process is going to take. Almost every project has a deadline, and you need to make sure you aren't going to miss your deadline because of a slow printing company.

# How Long Will It Take to Correct Printing Mistakes?

This is an important question that a lot of people forget to ask. Although I have never personally had a printing company make a major mistake on one of my print jobs, I used to live next door to a woman who seemed to be jinxed when it came to printing. Consequently, she learned early on the importance of asking printing companies how long it would take to fix their mistakes in the event that something should go wrong.

# Is There Anything That You Won't Print?

This probably seems like a strange question to ask, but it is extremely important. I have encountered several different situations in which a commercial printing company refused to print my document based on content. Don't get the wrong idea—I wasn't trying to print anything obscene. It's just that each printing company has its own policies regarding what they will and will not print.

One example of such a situation was a flyer that I tried to print a few years ago. The problem was that the flyer contained a photograph. Although I had taken the photograph myself, the publisher refused to print the flyer because I had no way of proving that I owned the copyright for the photo.

In another situation, I tried to print a vinyl graphic for one of my boats. The graphic depicted a 1940s-style pin-up model. Although the model was fully clothed and was not depicted in an obscene manner, the print shop refused to print it. When I asked why, I was told that the woman who owned the print shop was a hard-core feminist and considered the image to be degrading to women.

One last situation that I want to tell you about involved a friend who had recently finished writing a fictional novel. The publisher to which my friend wanted to submit the novel required a hard copy. As such, my friend tried to have the novel printed. Much to his (and my) surprise, the printing company he tried to use actually scanned the document for content prior to printing it. They ultimately refused to print the novel because it contained a few swear words.

None of the situations I just described were catastrophic. In each case, it was easy to find someone else to do the print job. However, had I been on a tight deadline and the printer rejected the print job, it might have posed a problem. I therefore believe that it is prudent to ask about content restrictions ahead of time.

## In What Format Should Materials Be Submitted?

You can't just burn your Microsoft Publisher document onto a DVD and expect a print company to print it. Some printing companies might very well accept Publisher documents on DVD, but many do not. Remember that Publisher is only one of countless applications that are capable of creating printed documents. A print shop can't realistically support every application in existence. They must pick and choose which applications they will support. Some print shops will gladly accept Publisher documents. Others might accept Publisher documents, but may only support documents created with older versions of Publisher.

> If you find that a printing company accepts only documents created with an older version of Publisher, you can use the Save As option to save the document in an older format. Keep in mind, however, that doing so can have unexpected side effects. Always back up your document before saving it in a different format.

Because a print shop can't support every imaginable file type, most will accept documents in a standardized format. For example, if the printing company that you are using does not accept Publisher documents, they might tell you to use Publisher to convert your document to a PDF file or to a Postscript file.

Keep in mind that although it is important to inquire as to the document formats that a print shop accepts, it is equally important to find out what mediums the shop will accept for document delivery. For example, the last time I had to have something printed, I had planned on putting my document onto a DVD or a flash drive and giving it to the print shop. However, after a phone call to the print shop, I learned that the company only accepted documents that were uploaded through their website. When I asked why this was the only acceptable delivery method, the shop's owner explained to me that he didn't want any of his systems to become infected with viruses, so he chose not to accept removable media or email as a document delivery method.

## Color Models

Today, almost every low-cost, consumer-grade printer supports color printing, so it probably seems a bit odd to talk about the challenges of color printing. In some instances, color printing really isn't any big deal. For example, if you want to print a couple of party invitations, you can just use the print option and print those invitations to your printer.

In this type of situation, your printer isn't going to give you professional-quality results, but the quality of the hard copy that your printer produces will almost certainly be good enough for your purposes. If you hold up the printout to the computer monitor, though, you will see that the colors on the page do not exactly match the colors on the screen.

Computer monitors are notorious for displaying colors incorrectly. Most monitors will display colors accurately enough to allow you to get a feel for what a project will look like when printed, but neither the image on the monitor nor the image on the printed page will exactly reflect what the document will look like when it is professionally printed.

Because there is so much inconsistency in the way colors are reproduced, there are several different ways you can define colors to help ensure a more consistent experience.

Printing colors accurately is difficult if the colors are not being displayed accurately on your monitor. I recommend using one of the many free utilities available on the Internet to calibrate your monitor.

# Grayscale

I hesitate to even refer to grayscale as a color model, because the very word "grayscale" means black and white. Even so, grayscale (which Publisher refers to as Single Color) is one of the available choices, so I wanted to at least mention it.

# RGB

One of the oldest color models is RGB. The RGB color model produces colors by combining the colors red, green, and blue in various ways. This color model was adapted from the way in which CRT televisions work. The screen on a CRT television is made up of thousands of red, green, and blue phosphors. A cathode ray gun is aimed at specific phosphors in rapid succession. When the cathode rays strike the phosphors, it causes them to illuminate. By lighting up the correct combination of red, green, and blue phosphors, the television is able to provide the illusion of displaying other colors.

# HSL

The HSL color model defines colors by their hue, saturation, and luminance. A color's hue is essentially its position within the color spectrum (the rainbow). The color's saturation is a measure of how vivid the color is. Colors become more saturated (they become more vivid) as white is mixed with the color. A color's luminance is based on the color's brightness. Luminance is different from saturation in that while saturation is based on the amount of white that is mixed with the color, luminance is based on the amount of black that is mixed with the color. In other words, if you want to decrease a color's luminance (make it darker), you add more black to the color.

# CMYK

The CMYK model is similar to RGB, except it uses four colors instead of three. While RGB is made up of red, green, and blue, CMYK is made up of cyan, magenta, yellow, and black.

A variation of the CMYK color model is CMYKOG, which uses six colors of ink instead of four. Like CMYK, CMYKOG still uses cyan, magenta, yellow, and black, but it also uses orange and green. These two additional colors help compensate for the CMYK model's difficulty in printing faint color tints.

Before digital printing started becoming so popular, CMYK printing (also known as process printing) was the primary standard used in commercial color printing.

# PANTONE

The PANTONE Matching System (also known as PMS) was created for use in situations in which precise color reproduction is essential. All the color reproduction models that I have described so far rely on color mixing. PANTONE is different, though.

The best way that I can think of to describe the PANTONE Matching System is to compare it to a paint store. Most paint stores offer swatches of color that you can take home to see how they look in your house. Once you decide on a color, you can go back to the paint store and order it. Now here comes the really important part. When you place the order, you order the paint color by name. In other words, you tell the clerk at the paint store that you want a gallon of harvest green, not that you want paint that is 20% red, 42% green, and 38% blue.

The PANTONE Matching System works in exactly the same way. PANTONE colors are not defined as combinations of other colors. Instead, each individual PANTONE color is numbered. This number allows the print shop to know exactly what color you are intending to use.

## Choosing a Color Model

So which color model should you use? Well, it really depends on how you plan on printing your document. If you are going to be printing the document yourself on a regular printer, you will get the best results by using the RGB color model, which is Publisher's default setting. If you are going have your document professionally printed, though, you should use either CMYK or PANTONE. It is a good idea to speak to someone at the print shop ahead of time and find out what their preferred color model is.

## Offset Printing

Before I show you how to choose a color model, I need to introduce you to the concept of offset printing. Offset printing (also called offset lithography) isn't a color model, but rather a process that many commercial printers use for high-volume printing.

The process is based on the use of plates. The page that is to be printed is transferred to an aluminum plate. The polymer-based image is then etched in a way that divides it into what is known as hydraulic regions. A hydraulic region is an area on the plate that can be flooded with water. When ink is applied to the plate, it only sticks to the areas in which no water is present. The ink is then transferred from the plate to either a roller or to a rubber blanket (think of it like a rubber stamp) and then to the paper.

Although this process was originally developed for monochromatic prints, it can also be used for color printing. Color printing requires a separate plate to be created for each color that is to be used. The colors themselves are known as spot colors.

Color offset printing is often based on the CMYK color model. In doing so, cyan, magenta, black, and yellow are each treated as spot colors. Some printing houses use two additional spot colors, which usually are orange and green but can be anything.

**LET ME TRY IT**

# Choosing a Color Model

Publisher makes it easy to choose a color model. To do so, follow these steps:

1. Go to Publisher's File tab.

2. Click the Commercial Print Settings icon.

3. Select the Choose Color Model option from the Commercial Print Settings menu, as shown in Figure 8.3.

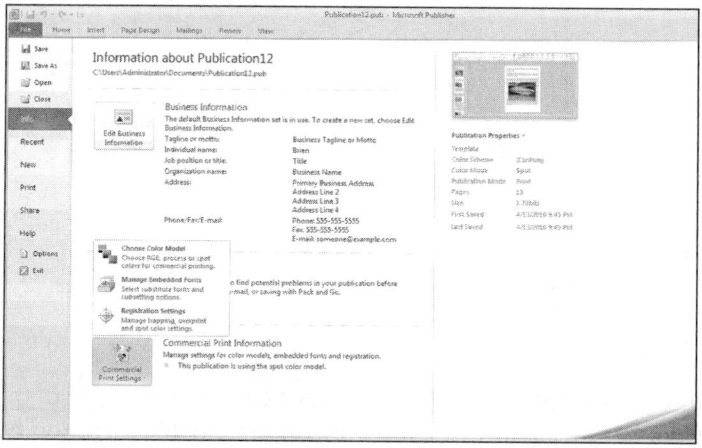

**Figure 8.3**   *Choose the Color Model option.*

4. Choose your preferred color model from the Color Model dialog box, shown in Figure 8.4.

5. Click OK.

**SHOW ME**   Media 8.1—Choosing a Color Model
*Access this video file through your registered Web edition at*
**my.safaribooksonline.com/9780132182591/media**.

Most of the books I have written have been printed in black and white. A while back, I wrote a book that was to be printed in color. I created screen captures in .TIF format. Later, the publisher asked me to convert all the images from RGB to the CMYK color model. I remember being really surprised at how different some of the colors appeared after the conversion. My point is that if possible, it is a good idea to select your color model before you start creating a Publisher document. That way, you won't have to worry about your document's appearance changing if you end up selecting a nondefault color model later.

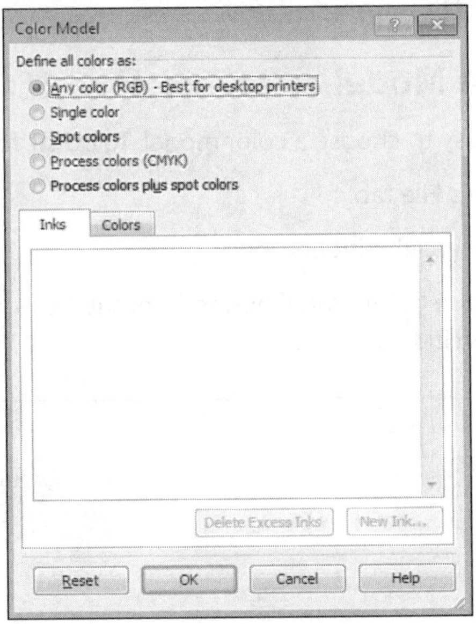

**Figure 8.4**   *You can select a color model from the Color Model dialog box.*

# Spot Colors

When I showed you the options for selecting a color model, some of the choices probably looked familiar to you. For instance, the Color Model dialog box, shown in Figure 8.4, clearly displays choices for RGB and CMYK. It's also pretty easy to figure out that the Single Color option is used for monochrome printing. However, some of the color modeling options that I have talked about, such as HSL and PANTONE, are nowhere to be found.

If you think back to the section on offset printing, you will recall that offset printing involves the use of spot colors. Sometimes these spot colors and CMYK are one and the same, but they don't have to be.

If you look at Figure 8.4, notice that the menu option for CMYK is listed as Process Colors (CMYK). The next menu option is Process Colors Plus Spot Colors. This is the option you would use if you were going to use a six-color variation of CMYK, such as CMYKOG. Similarly, there is also a Spot Colors option, which enables you to explicitly define the inks that you want to use.

To see how ink selection works, watch what happens when you choose the Process Colors Plus Spot Colors option. As you can see in Figure 8.5, when you select this option, the Inks tab displays the four inks used in process color (CMYK).

Because we have chosen to use process colors plus spot colors, we have the option of defining additional inks by clicking the New Ink button. Doing so causes Publisher to display the New Ink dialog box, shown in Figure 8.6.

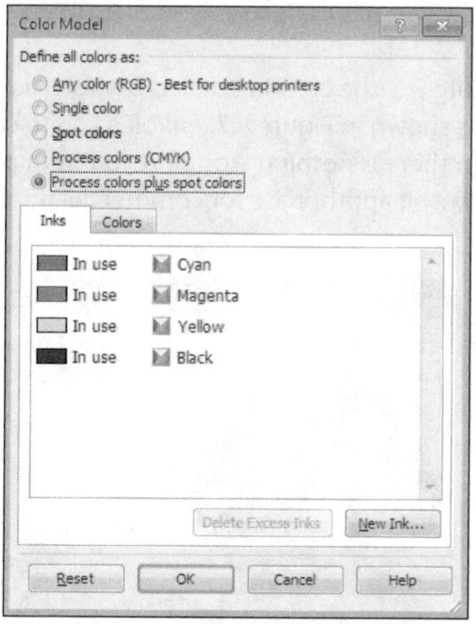

**Figure 8.5**    *Publisher displays the inks used in CMYK printing.*

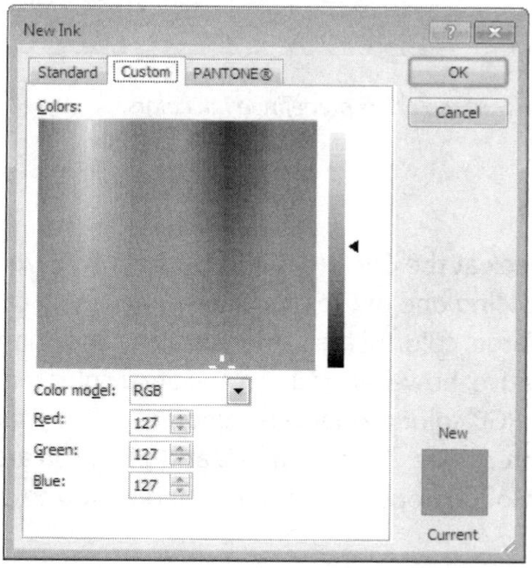

**Figure 8.6**    *The New Ink dialog box enables you to choose the ink color you want to use.*

**SHOW ME**    Media 8.2—Using Spot Color
*Access this video file through your registered Web edition at*
*my.safaribooksonline.com/9780132182591/media.*

## The Standard Tab

As you can see in Figure 8.6, the New Ink dialog box is divided into three tabs. The Standard tab, which is shown in Figure 8.7, enables you to choose from 128 predefined colors. Although there is nothing stopping you from picking a standard ink color, doing so usually isn't appropriate for commercial printing.

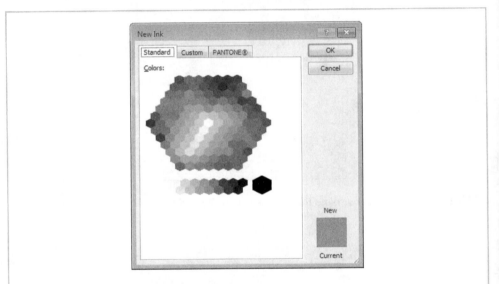

**Figure 8.7**    *The Standard tab offers predefined ink colors.*

## The Custom Tab

You already got a peek at the Custom tab in Figure 8.6. As you saw, this tab does not limit you to choosing one of the predefined inks—you can define your own. The tab contains a large, colorful area, and you can click on the color that you want to use. As an alternative, however, you can specify a color manually. In the earlier screen capture, the RGB color model was selected, and the tab provided fields where you could enter values for red, green, and blue. You aren't stuck using RGB, though. The Color Model dropdown list also enables you to use the HSL or CMYK color models.

## The PANTONE Tab

The PANTONE tab, shown in Figure 8.8, enables you to choose a PANTONE-defined ink color. PANTONE arguably provides the most accurate color reproduction.

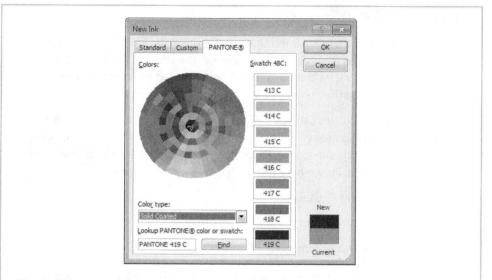

**Figure 8.8**   *The PANTONE tab enables you to choose a PANTONE-defined ink.*

## What a Printing Company Expects

Just as you expect the print shop to complete your print job on time and on budget, the staff at the print shop will also have certain expectations of you. Every printing company does things a little bit differently, but generally speaking, there are four main expectations you will be required to meet:

- You must provide the print shop with a document that is in a supported format. The file you provide must be free from viruses.

- You must adhere to the print shop's guidelines for getting the document to them. Don't expect to be able to just walk in the door and hand them a DVD (although some print shops do allow this).

- The document must be ready for printing. Don't expect the print shop to catch grammatical mistakes in your document or correct other types of content issues. The print shop's job is to print the document. That's it.

- The print shop will expect you to provide them with everything they need to be able to print your job. In some cases, this may mean providing the print shop with a copy of the fonts and the images that you use in your document.

# Packaging Your Print Job

In the previous section, I explained that some print shops might require you to provide them with all the fonts and images used in the document you are trying to print. Of course, this raises the question of how you can provide the printing company with everything they need.

Believe it or not, Publisher can actually help you with the document assembly process. Although it is always important to follow the printing company's guidelines, Publisher includes an option for bundling together everything that a print shop is likely to need. To see how this works, follow these steps:

1. Go to Publisher's File tab.

2. Click the Save and Send option.

3. Click the Save for a Commercial Printer link.

At this point, Publisher gives you a few options. As you can see in Figure 8.9, the Commercial Press option enables you to prepare the document for printing. This option often produces very large files, but it also provides the best possible quality.

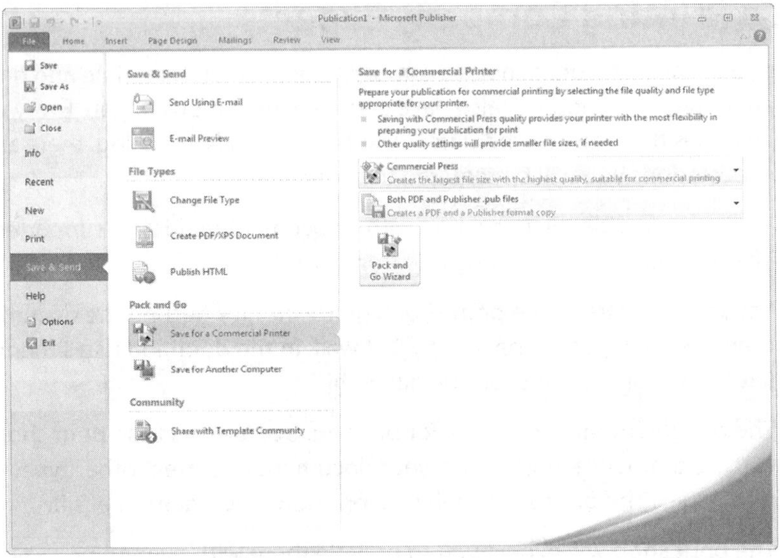

**Figure 8.9**    *Publisher provides several commercial printing options.*

If you click the Commercial Press button, you are provided with several additional options that provide a tradeoff between the document's file size and its quality. For example, the High Quality Printing option produces a large file (but not as large as the Commercial Printing option), and the document's quality is optimized for desktop or commercial printing. In contrast, the Minimum Size option creates the smallest possible file size, but the resulting quality is only suitable for draft printing. There is also a Custom option you can use to manually strike a balance between quality and file size.

The next option you see enables you to control the contents of the package that you are creating. By default, Publisher includes both a PDF file and a Publisher file (a .PUB file) in the package, but you have the option of only including one file type or the other.

**LET ME TRY IT**

## Using the Pack and Go Wizard

After you have made your selections, the final step in the packaging process is to run the Pack and Go Wizard. This wizard actually walks you through the packaging process. To run the wizard, complete these steps:

1. Click the Pack and Go Wizard button.

2. When prompted, either insert a blank DVD into the specified drive or provide Publisher with an alternative path it can use to save your packaged document.

3. Click Next.

4. The wizard copies all the necessary components into the location you have specified. When the process completes, you should see a dialog box similar to the one shown in Figure 8.10, telling you that the publication was successfully packaged.

5. Verify that the Print a Composite Proof check box is selected, and click OK.

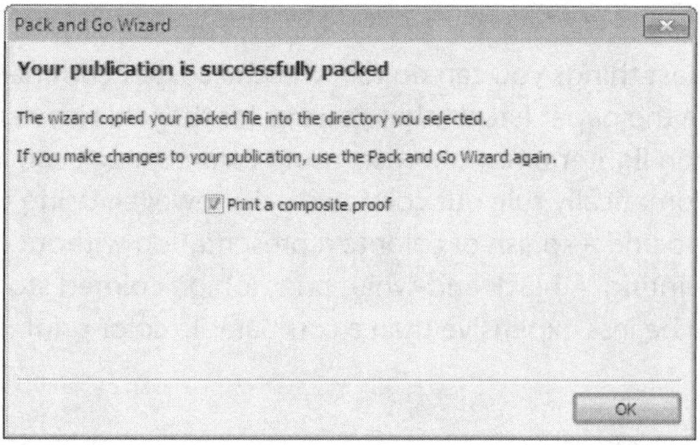

**Figure 8.10**  *You should receive confirmation that the publication was successfully packaged.*

**SHOW ME**    Media 8.3—Using the Pack and Go Wizard
*Access this video file through your registered Web edition at*
*my.safaribooksonline.com/9780132182591/media.*

In case you are wondering, the packaged publication is nothing more than a ZIP file. At a minimum, it contains your Publisher document in .PUB format, a PDF version of your document, and an XML file. The ZIP file may contain additional elements depending on the nature of the document. Normally, your fonts will be embedded into the document.

## The Importance of a Proof

When you click OK, Publisher prints a copy of your document to your default printer. It is important that you take the time to thoroughly review this proof, because it provides the best possible representation of what you can expect to get back from the print shop based on the packaged publication's contents.

When you turn your package over to the print shop, you are not completely at their mercy, though. Most print shops will provide you with a proof for large, costly, or complex print jobs (although you might have to ask for the proof). This proof will show you exactly what the finished document will look like when printed. Your review of the proof is your last chance to find and correct any issues with the document before it is printed.

# How to Save on Printing Costs

As you know, the costs of commercial printing can be astronomical. As such, I thought that I would wrap up this chapter by showing you some ways that you can reduce the cost of commercial printing.

## Stock

One of the biggest things you can do to lower the cost of commercial printing is to carefully choose the paper (stock) that you use for the job. Heavier papers cost more money than lighter ones. Likewise, using colored stock can increase printing costs. Don't automatically rule out colored stock, however. Using colored stock can be a great way to add a splash of color to a presentation without incurring the costs of color printing. A black-and-white print job on colored stock is almost always going to be less expensive than a comparable color print job on white stock.

# File Preparation

A few years ago, I contacted a print shop about having some business cards made. Even though I had created the document in Publisher and had everything the print shop needed, they tried to hit me with a hefty surcharge for setting up my file in their system. If a print shop tries to pull a stunt like this, it is usually time to go somewhere else.

# Quantity

Generally, the price that you pay per printed page decreases as the size of the print job increases. That being the case, it can be a good idea to group your orders whenever possible.

For example, I once worked for an organization that was constantly printing marketing brochures. Although the organization burned through countless brochures, they ordered only 100 brochures at a time. The organization almost certainly could have saved money in the long run if they had ordered several thousand brochures at a time rather than placing numerous small orders. Of course, this approach to saving money works only if the document's content is unlikely to change anytime soon, and if you can realistically expect to use all the documents you have printed.

# Ink Colors

Try to stick to using CMYK whenever possible. Any time you ask the printer to add nonstandard spot colors to your document, the price goes up considerably. If you absolutely must add special spot colors to a document, consider printing more copies than you think you will need. Remember that your document requires the printing company to use a special printer configuration, and every time you come back and ask for additional copies, the printer must be reconfigured. The print house will almost certainly bill you for the reconfiguration.

# Deadlines

Some print shops charge the same amount of money regardless of when a print job is needed, but many charge extra for expedited jobs. Try to avoid printing at the last minute.

# Use the Correct Printing Device

Finally, one way to really save some money is to become familiar with the equipment that your print shop of choice operates, and what types of jobs each piece of equipment is best suited for. This enables you to make sure your Publisher documents are formatted for the best possible printer for the job.

To give you a better idea of what I mean, imagine that you wanted to print 500 single-color business cards. You probably wouldn't want to do a job like that on a high-volume offset printer. Remember that offset printers require metal plates to be made for the print job, and this increases costs. On the other hand, if you had to print 50,000 copies of an advertisement, an offset printer might be the best choice because it is specifically designed for high-volume jobs.

**TELL ME MORE**     Media 8.4—Considerations for Commercial Printing

*To listen to a free audio recording about commercial printing, log on to*
***my.safaribooksonline.com/9780132182591/media****.*

# Publishing Online

Back in the mid 1990s, I started a mail order business. Although my business model revolved primarily around catalog sales, I knew that the Internet was going to be the next big thing, and I wanted to create an online store. The problem was that I didn't know anything about web programming (never mind the fact that online stores weren't yet possible).

Because I didn't really know anything about web development, I talked to a long-time friend who knew something about programming on the Web (today he owns a web development company). My friend told me that if I didn't want to take the time to learn a programming language, I could create web pages by creating Microsoft Word documents and saving them in HTML format.

My friend was correct, but I ended up selling the business before my website was complete. What is interesting, though, is that this technique for building a website could still be used today. Most, if not all, of the Microsoft Office 2010 products have the capability to convert documents into web pages, and Publisher is no exception.

Before I jump right in and show you how to create web content using Publisher, I need to point out that Microsoft Publisher is not a web development tool. Yes, you can use Publisher to create web pages, but this capability is not one of Publisher's primary features. As such, Publisher is very limited in its web development capabilities.

Although Publisher can be used to create a website, it is not exactly the best development tool available. If you decide to create a website using Publisher, you will have to use Publisher to make any future edits or updates to the site; otherwise, you might find yourself having to re-create the site from scratch. Likewise, it is also worth noting that if you delete the .PUB file, you won't be able to use Publisher to edit the site.

If you need to create a website that is more elaborate than what Publisher is capable of creating, I recommend using Microsoft Office SharePoint Designer. Of course, SharePoint Designer is a consumer-grade web development product. If you need professional-grade development capabilities, you will be better off using Microsoft Visual Studio. I have created many websites over the years, and Visual Studio is my development tool of choice.

# Creating a Website

There are two different ways in which you can create a website in Publisher. The first method involves creating a Publisher document using exactly the same methods I have been showing you throughout this book. After doing so, you can save the document as a web page.

The other option involves using a predefined template to create a website. If you are interested in creating more than just a single web page, using a template is far easier than using Publisher to develop the entire site manually.

I start out by showing you how to convert a document into a web page. Afterward, I show you how to use a template to build a more full-featured website. Finally, I conclude the chapter by showing you how you can use the Design Checker to make sure your newly created website is ready to be published.

Sites created with Publisher might work correctly only with Internet Explorer because they rely on Microsoft's VML markup language.

 **LET ME TRY IT**

## Creating a Simple Web Page

Publisher makes it really simple to turn a document into a web page. To show you how this process works, I have created the sample document shown in Figure 9.1. As you can see in the figure, this document contains an image and a text box. The document shown in the figure is a standard Microsoft Publisher document.

You can convert a document into a web page by following these steps:

1. Go to Publisher's File tab.

2. Choose the Share option from the File menu.

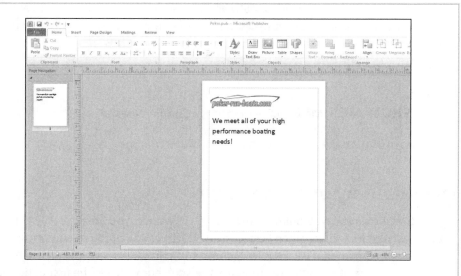

**Figure 9.1**  *You can start off with a normal Publisher document.*

3.  Click the Publish HTML button, shown in Figure 9.2.

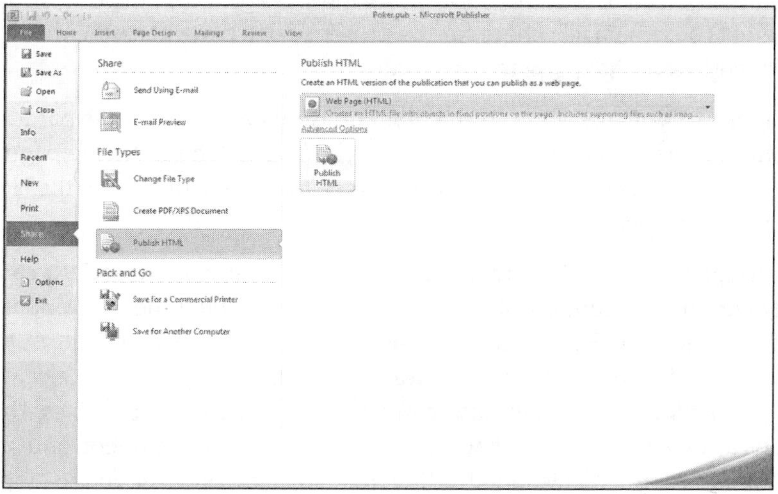

**Figure 9.2**  *Use the Share option to publish your document in HTML format.*

4.  Verify that the Web Page (HTML) option is selected within the Publish HTML section.

5.  Click the Publish HTML button.

6. When prompted, provide a path and filename for the web page you are creating. The path will normally be a folder on your local hard drive or on a network drive.

7. Click the Save button.

 **SHOW ME**     **Media 9.1—Creating a Simple Website**
*Access this video file through your registered Web edition at*
***my.safaribooksonline.com/9780132182591/media***.

# The Anatomy of a Web Page

Now that we have saved our document as an HTML file, you are probably curious to see what it looks like. When I created an HTML version of the document shown in Figure 9.1, I named it INDEX.HTM. I chose this particular name because when you create a website, it is traditional to name the site's home page (the first page that visitors see when they visit the site) Index.

The home page's name is actually more important than you might think. When someone enters a website's address into their browser, they do not usually enter the name of the page they want to view. That being the case, the server that is hosting the website has to have a way of knowing which web page to display. Most web servers automatically check for the presence of a page named either Index or Default, and serve that page to site visitors.

If you look at Figure 9.3, you can see that Publisher has created a file named Index.htm, which contains HTML code that can be used to render the page within a web browser. You can see what some of this HTML code looks like in the Notepad window that is open in the figure.

Even though the HTML file I created contains a huge amount of code, it cannot render my Publisher document all by itself. Recall that my Publisher document contained an image. The HTML language can be used to display an image, but you must provide the image file that you want to display. In Figure 9.3, notice that the folder containing my HTML file also contains a folder named index_files. This folder contains a copy of the image that is used in my Publisher document, and an Extensible Markup Language file (an XML file) that helps the browser understand what to do with the various elements. You can see the folder's contents in Figure 9.4.

Although the folder containing the support files for the web page is named Index_Files, it won't always use this name. Each HTML file you create will have its own separate folder containing its support files. The folder's name directly reflects the HTML file's name. For example, if I created an HTML file named SALES.HTML, Publisher would automatically create a support files directory named SALES_FILES.

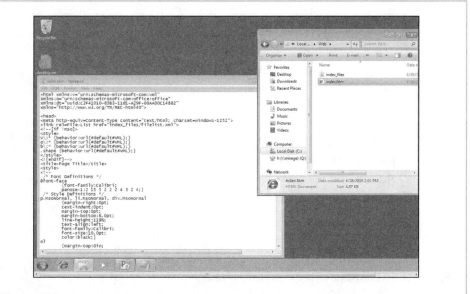

**Figure 9.3**    *The HTML file can render the Publisher document in a web browser.*

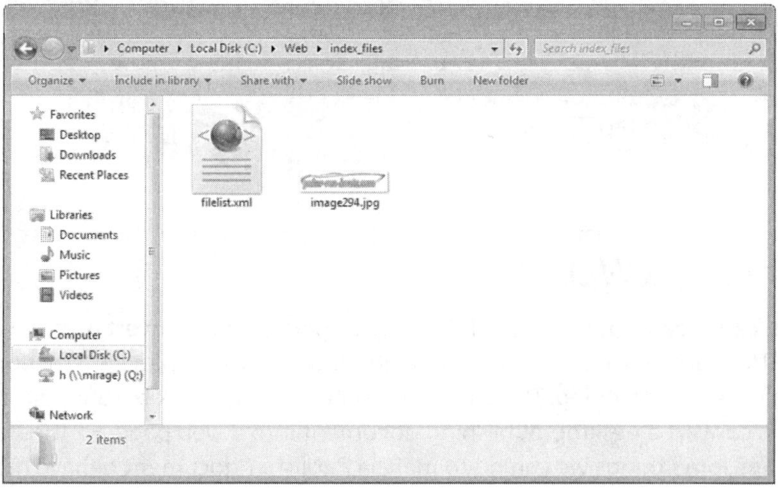

**Figure 9.4**    *Support files are placed into a separate folder.*

With that said, you are probably curious as to just how good of a job Publisher does of converting a document into an HTML file. You can preview an HTML file in your web browser by double-clicking on the file. If you look at Figure 9.5, you can see that the web page I have created looks nearly identical to my original Publisher document.

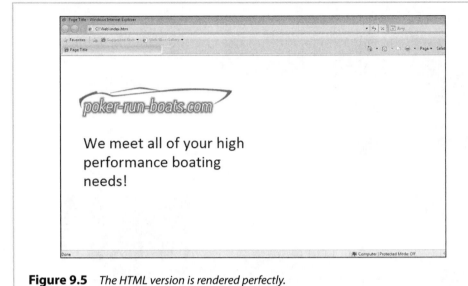

**Figure 9.5** *The HTML version is rendered perfectly.*

When you publish an HTML page, Publisher gives you the option of creating a single file rather than creating an HTML file and a separate folder containing support files. When you use this option, Publisher creates an MHT file (also known as an MHTML file), which is basically an HTML file with the support files embedded. I recommend that you avoid using this technique because not all browsers support MHTML files.

## Enhancing a Web Page

As you can see in Figure 9.5, Publisher does a good job of converting a document into HTML format. Even so, you have to admit that my web page is a bit boring—it doesn't even do anything. This shouldn't come as a big shock because all I have done is convert a desktop publishing document into a web page. Fortunately, there are some things we can do to make a Publisher document behave more like a web page.

 **LET ME TRY IT**

## Adding Alternative Text

If you are planning on creating a web page from a Publisher document, one of the first things I would recommend doing is to add alternative text to each of the document's images. In the early days of the Web, not all web browsers could display images. Alternative text was used to provide a description of the image to users with text-based browsers.

Today, nobody uses text-based browsers anymore, but alternative text is still important. The alternative text is displayed within the browser window when you hover over an image. More importantly, though, search engines use alternative text to enhance the way in which websites are indexed.

To add alternative text to a Publisher document, follow these steps:

1. Right-click on the image for which you want to provide alternative text.

2. Choose the Format Picture command from the shortcut menu.

3. When the Format Picture properties sheet appears, go to the Web tab.

4. Enter the alternative text for the image into the place provided, as shown in Figure 9.6.

**Figure 9.6**   *Use the Web tab to enter alternative text for the image.*

5. Click OK.

6. Repeat the process for any remaining images within the document.

**LET ME TRY IT**

# Creating Hyperlinks

Almost every web page contains links that take you to another page or to another site. These links are known as *hyperlinks*. You can include hyperlinks in your Publisher documents. The method for creating a hyperlink varies slightly depending on whether you are attaching the link to text or to an image.

To hyperlink a word or phrase, follow these steps:

1. Select the word or phrase that you want to hyperlink.

2. Go to Publisher's Insert tab.

3. Click the Hyperlink icon.

4. When the Insert Hyperlink dialog box opens, enter the URL you want to use within the hyperlink, as shown in Figure 9.7.

5. Click OK to create the hyperlink.

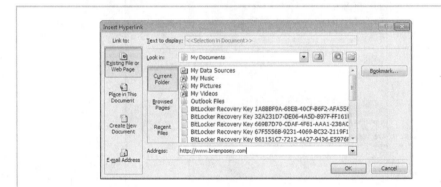

**Figure 9.7**    *Enter the desired URL into the Insert Hyperlink dialog box.*

The technique for hyperlinking an image is almost identical to what I have just shown you, but with one minor difference. Rather than selecting a word or phrase, you select an image.

# More Hyperlinking Techniques

In the previous section, I showed you how to create a basic hyperlink. In doing so, I assumed that the selected text or image was being linked to an existing web page. You do have some other options, however. For instance, you can actually create a new web page as you create the hyperlink for it.

**LET ME TRY IT**

# Creating a New Page

So far, I have shown you how to link a design element to a web page. However, you don't have to link to an existing page. You can create a new page and a link to it, all at the same time.

Imagine, for example, that I wanted to link the logo in my sample document to a Contact Us page. Rather than creating the page manually and then going back to my original page to create the hyperlink, I could create the new page and the hyperlink in a single action. To do so, perform these steps:

1.  Click on the design element that you want to hyperlink.

2.  Go to Publisher's Insert tab and click the Hyperlink icon.

3.  When the Insert Hyperlink dialog box appears, click the Create New Document icon.

4.  Enter the name and path for the new document into the space provided, as shown in Figure 9.8.

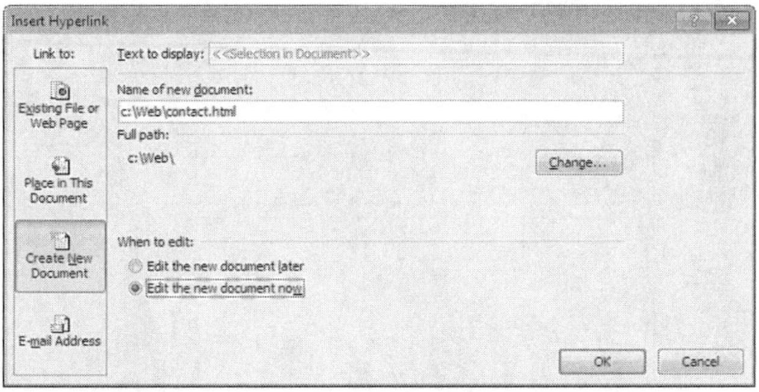

**Figure 9.8**    *Enter the name and a path for the new document.*

5.  Choose whether you want to edit the new document now or later.

6.  Click OK.

When you click OK, the hyperlink is created and a new document is also created. This document is displayed within a separate instance of Publisher.

 **LET ME TRY IT**

## Creating Email Links

Although hyperlinks are most commonly used as a way of connecting web pages, hyperlinks can also be used as a way of linking an email address to a web page. When a visitor to the website clicks on an email address link, Windows opens their mail client (such as Outlook) and begins composing a new message to the specified address. You can create an email link by completing these steps:

1. Select the design element to which you want to bind the hyperlink.

2. Go to Publisher's Insert tab, and click the Hyperlink icon.

3. When the Insert Hyperlink dialog box appears, click the E-Mail Address button.

4. Enter the email address that you want to bind to the hyperlink, as shown in Figure 9.9.

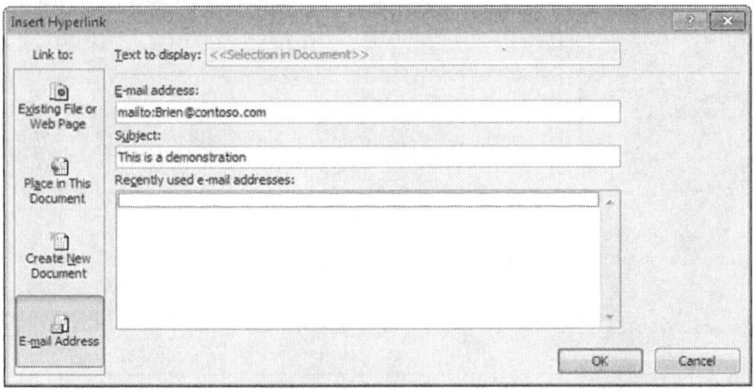

**Figure 9.9**    *Enter the email address that you want to bind to the hyperlink.*

5. You have the option of pre-populating the Subject line if you want.

6. Click OK to create the hyperlink.

Figure 9.10 shows the hyperlink within the web page, as well as the new message window that Outlook displays when I click on the hyperlink.

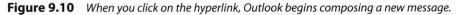

**Figure 9.10**   *When you click on the hyperlink, Outlook begins composing a new message.*

# Bookmarks

So far, we have been inserting hyperlinks into short, demonstration documents. As you have already seen, though, not all Publisher documents are short.

When you create a long Publisher document, you can use bookmarks as a way of making it easy to instantly go to a specific location within the document. Once you have created one or more bookmarks, you can create hyperlinks to them.

 **LET ME TRY IT**

## Creating a Bookmark

To create a bookmark, perform these steps:

1. Go to the exact location within the document that you want to bookmark. Be sure to click on that location.

2. Go to Publisher's Insert tab, and click the Bookmark icon.

3. When the Bookmark dialog box appears, enter a name for the bookmark that you are creating, as shown in Figure 9.11.

4. Click the Add button.

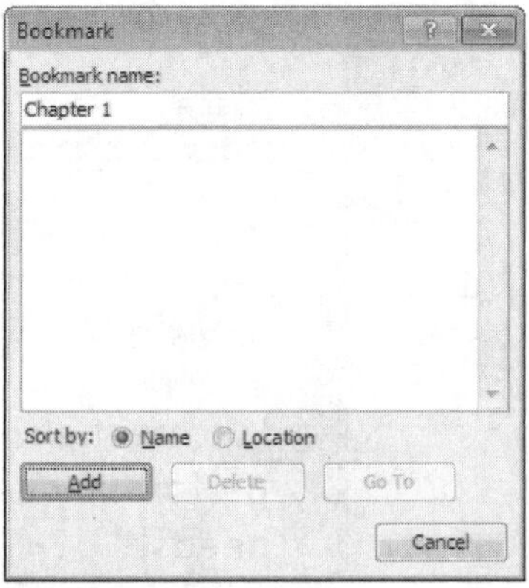

**Figure 9.11** *Enter a name for the bookmark that you are creating, and click the Add button.*

 **LET ME TRY IT**

## Hyperlinking a Bookmark

Now that we have created a bookmark, we can hyperlink to it from anywhere in our document. For example, you might create an interactive table of contents in which clicking on an entry takes you to a specific bookmark within the document. To hyperlink to a bookmark, follow these steps:

1. Click on the location within your document where you want to create the hyperlink.

2. Go to Publisher's Insert tab, and click the Hyperlink icon.

3. When the Insert Hyperlink dialog box appears, click the Place in This Document button.

4. Select the bookmark that you want to link to, as shown in Figure 9.12.

5. Click OK.

**SHOW ME**    **Media 9.2—Adding Elements to a Web Page**
*Access this video file through your registered Web edition at*
***my.safaribooksonline.com/9780132182591/media**.*

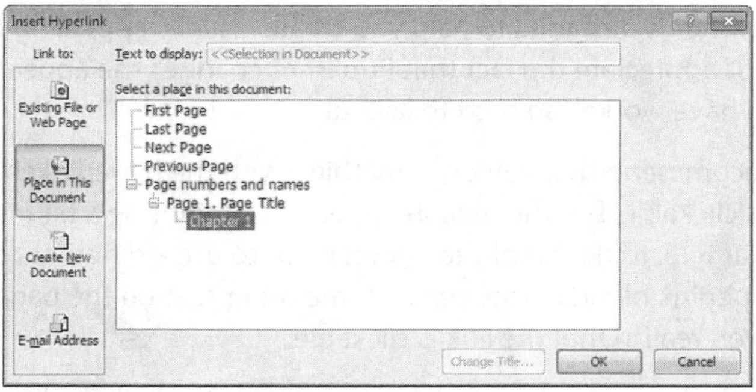

**Figure 9.12**   *Select the bookmark that you want to link to.*

## Editing Hyperlinks

After creating a new hyperlink, you may sometimes find that it isn't exactly what you had in mind. Fortunately, Publisher makes it easy to modify or even delete a hyperlink. All you have to do is right-click on the hyperlink and choose either the Edit Hyperlink or Remove Hyperlink option from the resulting shortcut menu.

If you choose the Edit Hyperlink option, Publisher takes you to the Insert Hyperlink dialog box that you used when you originally created the hyperlink. From there, you can make any desired changes to the link.

## Changing a Hyperlink's Appearance

When you hyperlink text, Publisher changes the text color to blue and underlines it, as shown in Figure 9.13. This is Publisher's way of letting you know that the text is clickable (that it has been hyperlinked).

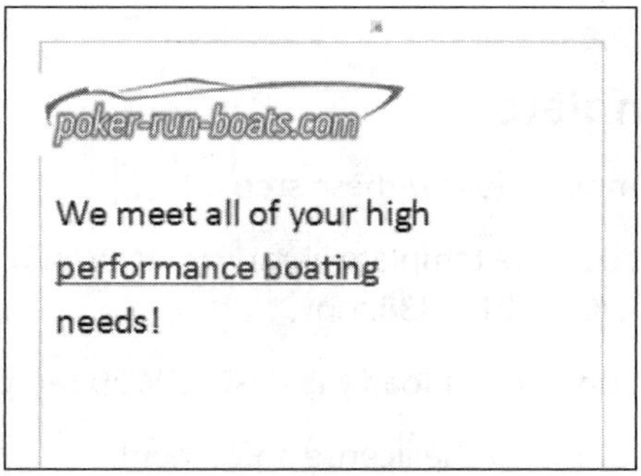

**Figure 9.13**   *Hyperlinked text is underlined and colored blue.*

In some cases, the appearance of hyperlinked text might not be an issue. However, because Publisher is designed to help you create visually appealing documents, you might not appreciate the fact that Publisher changes the appearance of the text that you have worked so hard to lay out.

I generally recommend that you do something with the hyperlinked text to indicate that it is clickable, but the default appearance might be a bit much. You might prefer, for example, to get rid of the underline or to use a different color. Just don't make the hyperlink blend in too well with the other text on the page, or others might not even realize that the link is clickable.

Publisher makes it easy to change the appearance of hyperlinked text. All you have to do is select the text, and then go to Publisher's Home tab. From there, you can remove the underline, change the text color, change the font, or make any other desired changes. Publisher enables you to modify the appearance of hyperlinked text in exactly the same way that you change the appearance of any other text.

# Using a Web Template

Up to this point, I have shown you some techniques for converting a website into a web page. If you use the option to create new pages as you generate hyperlinks, you can even create a multipage website. As I said in the beginning, however, Publisher isn't a full-blown web development tool. That being the case, you will likely find it to be impractical to create sites containing more than just a few pages by using Publisher.

If you do have to create a multipage website by using Publisher, there is an easier method than what I have shown you so far. Publisher 2010 offers a built-in template that is specifically designed for creating websites. In this section, I show you how to use the template.

 **LET ME TRY IT**

## Opening the Template

To access the web template, follow these steps:

1. Go to Microsoft's online template library at http://office.microsoft.com/en-us/templates/CT010104338.aspx.

2. Choose the option to download the desired Web template.

3. When prompted, accept the license agreement.

4. The new template will be downloaded and opened in Publisher.

# Working with the Template

As you can see in Figure 9.14, Microsoft has done most of the work for you. This template contains a Publisher document that is specifically designed to be exported as a multipage website.

As you can see in Figure 9.14, the template makes it relatively easy to create a website. All you have to do is replace the text and images used in the template with your own text and images. As you refine your website, you can also add or remove visual elements as you deem necessary.

Having said that, I have to say that I think Microsoft really dropped the ball when it created this template. I say this because the template does not make use of master pages. This means that if you want to change a visual element, you will have to manually change it on every page that uses the object. For instance, I tried changing the color of the menu bar, but Publisher only made the modification to the document's first page.

**Figure 9.14**  *This is what the website template looks like.*

# Previewing Your Website

Before I get too far into the subject of modifying the template website, I want to take a moment and show you how you can preview the template site within a web browser. That way, you can get a better feel for how the site will look and feel once you convert it to a web page.

You might have noticed in Figure 9.14 that when I opened the template website, Publisher added a Web tab to the menu bar. If you want to preview your website, simply go to the Web tab and click the Web Page Preview button. When you do, Publisher displays the template web page within a browser, as shown in Figure 9.15.

**SHOW ME**    Media 9.3—Creating a Full-Blown Website
*Access this video file through your registered Web edition at*
**my.safaribooksonline.com/9780132182591/media**.

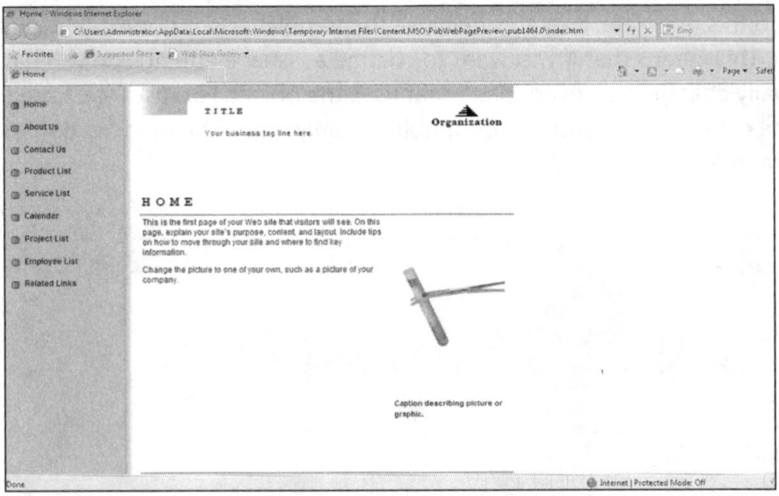

**Figure 9.15**    *You can preview a web page within a browser by clicking the Web Page Preview button.*

## The Web Tab

Now that I have shown you how to preview the template website, I want to turn my attention to the Web tab that I mentioned in the previous section. This tab, which you can see in Figure 9.16, is available only when you open a web document. The tab doesn't contain a lot of options, but the options that do exist are really handy.

## Hot Spot

Because you are already familiar with the Web Page Preview option and the Hyperlink option, I want to start out by talking about the Hot Spot icon, which provides you with another way of creating a hyperlink.

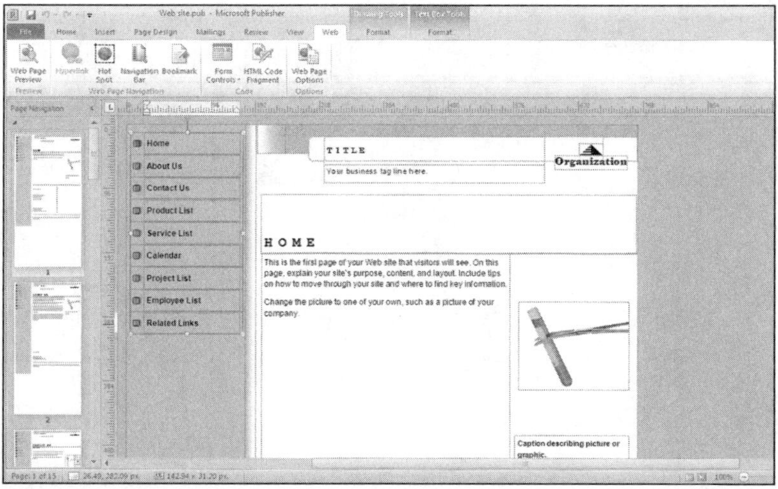

**Figure 9.16**  *The Web tab offers options designed to help you turn a Publisher document into a website.*

When I talked about hyperlinks earlier, I showed you how to hyperlink a word, phrase, or image. Publisher doesn't limit you to creating only these types of hyperlinks, however—you can create hot spot hyperlinks instead.

To create a hot spot hyperlink, simply click the Hot Spot icon, and then use the cursor to draw a rectangle around the area that you want to hyperlink. When you do, Publisher displays the Insert Hyperlink dialog box, which you can use to link the hot spot to a page, bookmark, or email address in exactly the same way I showed you earlier.

## Navigation Bar

When I showed you what the web template looked like when displayed as a web page, you probably noticed the navigation bar on the left side of the screen. Publisher creates this navigation bar by default when you open the web template, but you aren't stuck with using it. Publisher makes it easy to create your own navigation bars.

To create a navigation bar, click the Navigation Bar icon. Publisher displays the dialog box shown in Figure 9.17, which enables you to choose the style of navigation bar that you want to create.

When you make your selection and click the Insert button, Publisher adds the navigation bar to the page. If you look at Figure 9.18, you can see that I have created a blank page so that I can show you what a new menu bar looks like. If you look at the document preview, though, you can see that Publisher has automatically added my new navigation bar to every page of the document.

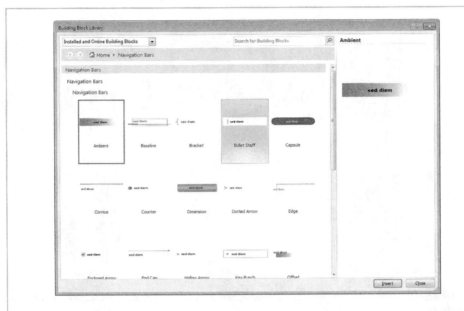

**Figure 9.17** *Pick the style of navigation bar that you want to create.*

**Figure 9.18** *You can preview a web page within a browser by clicking the Web Page Preview button.*

Just as Publisher enables you to control the general look and feel of the navigation bar, you can also control the individual menu items. To do so, right-click on the navigation bar and choose the Navigation Bar properties command from the shortcut menu. Publisher displays the Navigation Bar Properties dialog box shown in Figure 9.19.

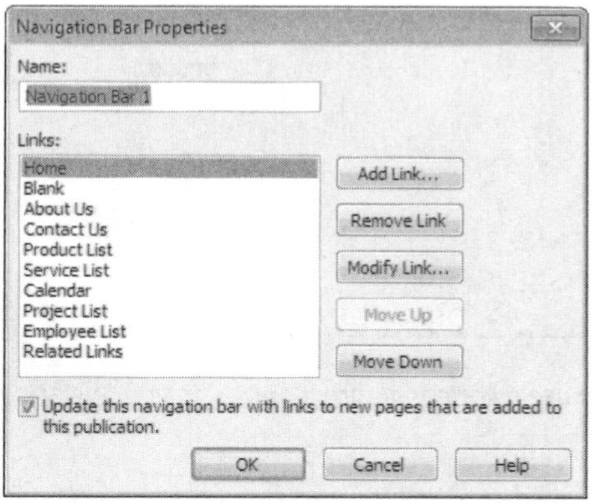

**Figure 9.19** *You can control the navigation bar's contents.*

The Navigation Bar Properties dialog box is pretty straightforward. If you want to change the order of the menu options, just select an option and then click either the Move Up or Move Down buttons to change the item's position on the navigation bar.

You also can add and remove items from the navigation bar by clicking the Add Link and Remove Link buttons. Keep in mind that when you use these buttons, you not only change your navigation bar, but also the document as a whole. For example, using the Add Link button adds an item to the navigation bar, but it also links that item to a new page within the Publisher document (unless you link the new menu item to an email address or a bookmark instead).

# Form Controls

The Form Controls icon enables you to add controls to your web page. Some of the controls you can add include option buttons, list boxes, check boxes, and text boxes. Figure 9.20 shows a document in which I have created a variety of form controls.

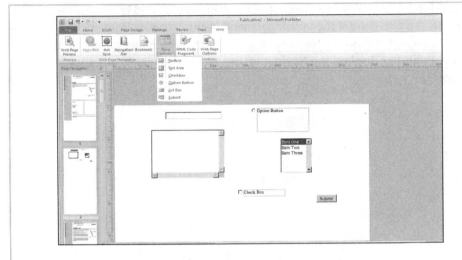

**Figure 9.20**   *You can use a variety of form controls in your web page.*

The main thing you need to know about form controls is that Publisher only enables you to create the controls themselves (and a submit button). It is up to you to build functionality around the form controls.

# HTML Code Fragment

When you create a website through Publisher, you are essentially creating an HTML document. The HTML Code Fragment option enables you to insert prewritten blocks of HTML code into your document. By doing so, you can create websites that are more elaborate than what Publisher is natively capable of creating.

The most important thing you need to know about the HTML Code Fragment option is that Publisher will not error-check the code you insert. It is therefore up to you to debug the code before adding it to your Publisher document.

# Web Page Options

The Web Page icons option enables you to add metadata to your web pages. Rather than manually coding meta tags on each page of your website, you can fill out the simple form shown in Figure 9.21. As you can see in the figure, you can create a page title, a description, and even some keywords for the search engine.

You also have the option of specifying a custom filename for each page. Although you don't have to provide a filename, it is a good idea if you expect to add on to the site in the future because descriptive filenames makes it easier to find the page you want to edit.

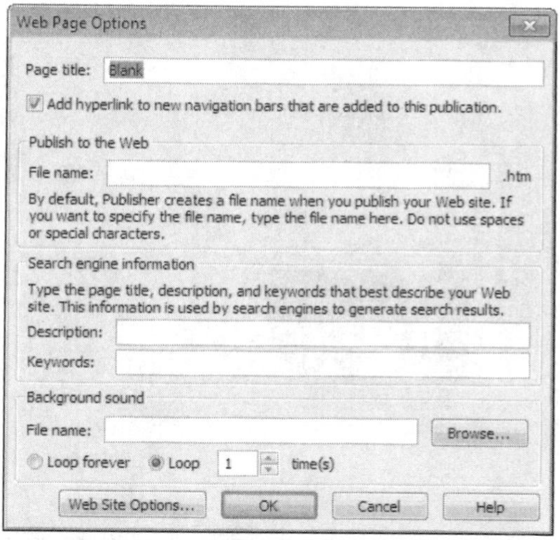

**Figure 9.21**  *The Web Page Options dialog box automates the creation of meta tags.*

 **LET ME TRY IT**

## Design Checking

In Chapter 7, "Finalizing Your Publisher Document," I showed you how you could use the Design Checker to check your publication for errors. Besides being able to check for general errors, the Design Checker also has the capability of treating a publication as a web page, and check it for web-specific errors. You can perform a web design check by following these steps:

1. Go to Publisher's File tab.

2. Click the Run Design Checker button.

3. When the Design Checker opens, deselect the Run General Design Checks check box.

4. Select the Run Web Site Checks check box, shown in Figure 9.22.

5. Correct any errors that are reported, and then click the Close Design Checker button.

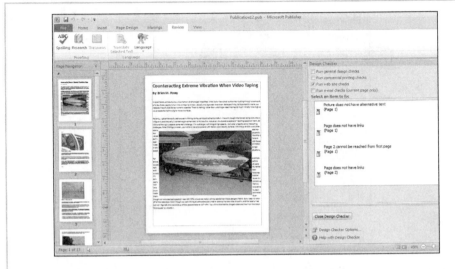

**Figure 9.22**    *The Design Checker includes a set of checks for websites.*

# Publishing Your Website

The last step in creating a website is to publish it. I realize that I have used the word "publish" a lot in this book, and that it takes on different meanings in different contexts. In this case, however, *publishing* refers to uploading your new website to the Internet so that it can be viewed by others.

Until you have created your first website, the concept of publishing probably seems a bit mysterious. I want to try to shed some light on the publishing process for you.

The one thing you absolutely need to have before you can publish a website is a host. A *host* is a server whose job it is to make your website accessible to the outside world. It links web server software, such as Microsoft's Internet Information Server (IIS), to a public (static) IP address.

Another thing that is usually required for the site is a domain name. Because I normally write about enterprise networking for a living, I am tempted to go into all the gory technical details involved in the anatomy of domain names, but in the interest of not boring you, I am going to refrain from doing so.

Instead, I will just say that for our purposes, the domain name can be thought of as the name that you enter into the web browser to get to the website. To be technically precise, the address you enter into a web browser to go to a site is known as a Uniform Resource Locator, or URL. A domain name makes up either a portion or all of the URL.

For example, the URL of my personal website is www.brienposey.com. The domain portion of the URL is brienposey.com.

## Acquiring a Domain Name

To get a domain name, you can go to www.register.com. This site enables you to check the availability of the domain name that you want to use, and lease your chosen domain name if it is available. It is worth noting, however, that many hosting companies (which I will talk about in a second) also lease domain names, and they are often less expensive than going through register.com.

## Choosing a Hosting Company

As I have explained, hosting a website requires a server, some specialized web server software, and a domain name. That being the case, most people (and even a lot of corporations) lack the budget, expertise, or desire to host their websites themselves. As such, it is common to outsource the hosting process to a hosting company.

A hosting company's job is to make your website available to the world. Generally speaking, you provide the domain name and the website, and the hosting company provides the server hardware, public IP address, and server software necessary to host your website.

Even though the hardware and software required for hosting a website can cost thousands of dollars, hosting companies can usually provide you with web hosting for 20 to 30 dollars a month (some are more expensive and some are less expensive). The hosting company can provide hosting services so inexpensively because they are not providing your site with a dedicated web server; instead, you are leasing a small percentage of a web server's resources. The server that is hosting your site may be hosting hundreds of other sites that are all isolated from each other.

There are countless different hosting companies in the world. Some of these companies will allow you to host your site for free, while others are fee based. The amount that you pay to host a website varies depending on the services that you need and the degree of professionalism that you want for your site.

Free hosting services, for example, don't usually provide any technical support. Furthermore, many of the free services cover their operating costs by attaching advertisements to the web pages they host. Additionally, you might not have the option of using your own domain name if you go with a free host.

There is also a big difference between hosting companies that do not provide their services for free. In fact, I pay about $14 per month to host one of my websites, whereas I pay $50 per month to host another website (I also have another site that I host on my own server instead of using a hosting company). The reason for the difference in price is that I am using two different hosting companies. One of the hosting companies provides basic hosting services, while the other provides premium hosting services.

You shouldn't choose a hosting company based on price alone. Instead, it is important to consider what is really important to you and then choose a host that can deliver those services. Here is a list of questions you should ask when choosing a hosting company:

- What programming languages do you support? (This makes a big difference in what capabilities you can build in to your site.)
- How much bandwidth am I allowed to use?
- Is there an overage fee for excessive bandwidth consumption?
- How many email accounts come with the hosting service?
- Can I register my own domain name?
- Do you provide any metrics for measuring site traffic?
- How often do you back up my site?
- What service-level agreements do you provide?
- Do you throttle bandwidth for visitors to my site?
- How much server space is my site allowed to consume?
- Do you attach advertisements to hosted sites?

## DNS Entries

When you sign up for a hosting account, the hosting company will have to create a DNS record for your site. As I mentioned earlier, every website is linked to a public IP address; even so, almost nobody enters a site's IP address into their web browser (even though you can). Instead, they enter the site's URL.

The DNS record is simply a table entry that contains a site's domain name and IP address. When someone enters a site's URL into their web browser, the web browser checks to see if it knows the IP address that goes with the domain portion of the URL. Assuming that the IP address is unknown, the web browser initiates a DNS query to look up the site's IP address.

I could probably write an entire book (or at least several chapters) on how DNS queries work. I won't bore you with all the details other than to tell you that not one single DNS server contains the IP addresses for every website in the entire world. Such a server would be completely bogged down by all the inbound name resolution requests, and would make an extremely tempting target for hackers. Instead, DNS is a distributed service.

Your hosting company provides a DNS server that is said to be authoritative for your domain. This DNS server is a part of an overall DNS hierarchy. As such, the other DNS servers must be made aware of the existence of the record for your website.

I tell you this because once your hosting provider creates the necessary DNS entry, it can take a day or two before other DNS servers in the hierarchy become aware of it. As such, you usually won't be able to upload your website right away. You will have to wait for the hosting company to configure your account and for the DNS propagation process to complete.

## Uploading Your Website

Earlier, I showed you how to save your web page in HTML format. The final piece of the puzzle involves copying the HTML files and any necessary support files from your computer to your hosting provider's server.

Your hosting company will provide you with a File Transfer Protocol (FTP) account and a set of instructions for uploading your website. Although Windows is natively capable of uploading web content via FTP, the process tends to be a lot easier if you have an FTP manager. I use an FTP manager called FTP Voyager (http://www.ftpvoyager.com/) for uploading updates to the websites that I own.

 **TELL ME MORE**   Media 9.4—Your Options for Web Development
*To listen to a free audio recording about web development, log on to*
***my.safaribooksonline.com/9780132182591/media.***

In this chapter, you learn all about merges and
bulk mailing techniques.

10

# Bulk Mailing Techniques

In Chapter 8, "Printing," I showed you some techniques for printing Microsoft Publisher documents. That chapter worked under the assumption that you were going to be printing multiple copies of each document, and that each copy was going to be identical. Although there is certainly nothing wrong with printing multiple copies of the same document, there is sometimes a better approach. What if you could incorporate business data into your Publisher document as a way of personalizing it or making the distribution process easier?

Incorporating business data into Publisher sounds complicated. After all, business data could mean anything, right? The process really isn't as daunting as it sounds, though, and you don't have to resort to using complex data-mining techniques (unless you want to).

One of the simpler forms of business data is contact information. Most organizations have a database or a spreadsheet they have used to compile the names, addresses, and phone numbers of their customers. Even if an organization doesn't maintain customer contact information, they undoubtedly have a list of employee contact information. Any of this information can be used to create personalized Publisher documents and to automate the document distribution process.

Of course, I realize that not all of you are reading this book with business in mind. Publisher can be an excellent outlet for creativity, so there are plenty of individuals who use Publisher for their own purposes. Even individuals can benefit from the techniques I am going to show you in this chapter. Whereas a business might use these techniques to produce customized marketing proposals or company newsletters, an individual might use the same techniques to produce party invitations.

## Mail Merge

Creating a mail merge is a process by which you can create a personalized document. In the document, field identifiers take the place of literal text. These field identifiers are linked to a data source, such as a list of names and addresses. The data from the data source replaces the field identifiers, resulting in personalized documents.

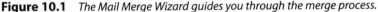

## LET ME TRY IT

# Creating a Mail Merge

I am going to be using an empty document in my mail merge demonstration. In the real world, you would almost always merge business data into a finished Publisher document. In this case, though, I am going to use a blank document just to keep my screen captures from becoming too cluttered. With that said, you can begin the process by following these steps:

1. Open Publisher and select a blank template.

2. Draw a large text box in the middle of the page.

3. Set the font size to something large enough that you can read it.

4. Select Publisher's Mailings tab.

5. Click the lower portion of the Mail Merge icon, and then choose the Step By Step Mail Merge Wizard option from the Mail Merge menu. When you do, the Mail Merge Wizard appears, as shown in Figure 10.1.

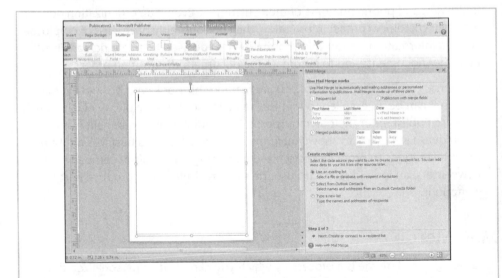

**Figure 10.1**   *The Mail Merge Wizard guides you through the merge process.*

As you look at Figure 10.1, you can see that there are three primary steps in the merge process: creating the recipient list, adding the merge fields to your document, and performing the actual merge.

# Creating the Recipient List

The first step in the mail merge process is to assemble the data you want to merge into your Publisher document. Before I show you how to do this, there are a couple of things that you need to know.

First, even though the technique of merging business data into a Publisher document is called a mail merge, you are not limited to merging address lists. You can include just about any type of data in your merge.

Second, Publisher gives you an extremely wide variety of options for importing the data that you want to merge. There are so many options, in fact, that I think this chapter would become really confusing if I tried to cover all of them (or even just the most commonly used options) right now.

That being the case, I am going to show you how to perform a mail merge using data that is stored in an Excel spreadsheet. After I walk you through the entire mail merge process, I will come back and revisit this topic. At that time, I will show you how to import data from some other sources.

With that said, I have created an Excel spreadsheet that contains a few friends' names along with some fake addresses and phone numbers (I think they would shoot me if I published their real contact information in a book).

Before I show you how to use this spreadsheet to perform a mail merge, take a look at my spreadsheet, which is shown in Figure 10.2. If you look in the lower portion of the figure, you will notice that the spreadsheet contains three separate tabs. Excel creates these tabs by default, even though only the first tab actually contains any data. When we actually import the data, it will be very important to know which tab the data actually exists on.

 **LET ME TRY IT**

# Importing Information

Now that you have seen my spreadsheet, let's go ahead and tell Publisher how we want to import the information. The steps I am about to show you are specific to my spreadsheet but can be easily adapted to any spreadsheet you might want to import. To create the list of data that is to be imported, complete these steps:

1. Click the Next: Create or Connect to a Recipient List link, located at the bottom of the wizard.

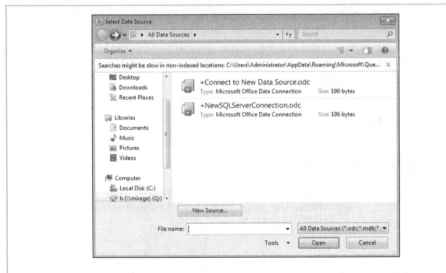

| | A | B | C | D | E | F | G | H | I |
|---|---|---|---|---|---|---|---|---|---|
| 1 | Name | Address | City | State | Zip | Phone | | | |
| 2 | Troy Thompson | 2365 Any Street | Brooks | KY | | 40109 502-555-0795 | | | |
| 3 | Shamir Dasgupta | 09087 Some Street | Louisville | KY | | 40299 502-555-4037 | | | |
| 4 | Peter Bruzzese | 3456 Bogus Street | Orlando | FL | | 32801 863-555-1234 | | | |
| 5 | Barb Joy | 2345 Anonymous Road | Knoxville | TN | | 37901 615-555-2345 | | | |
| 6 | Darren Sumner | 1234 Bourbon Street | New Orleans | LA | | 70053 504-555-4179 | | | |

**Figure 10.2**   *Excel spreadsheets usually contain multiple tabs.*

2. You should see a screen similar to the one shown in Figure 10.3, asking you to select a data source. Rather than choosing any of the options shown on this screen, type the letter of the drive containing your spreadsheet into the File Name field, and press Enter. For example, if your spreadsheet is located in a folder named C:\Documents, you would enter C:.

> The dialog box might look different on your system than it does in the figure, because each version of Windows displays dialog boxes in a slightly different way.

**Figure 10.3**   *Enter the letter of the drive containing your spreadsheet, and then browse to the correct path.*

**3.** Browse to the folder containing your spreadsheet.

**4.** Select your spreadsheet, and click the Open button.

**5.** You will see a dialog box similar to the one shown in Figure 10.4, asking you to select a table. Recall that my spreadsheet contained three separate tabs. Each of these tabs is listed separately on this dialog box as Sheet1$, Sheet2$, and Sheet3$. To select the first tab, choose the Sheet1$ option.

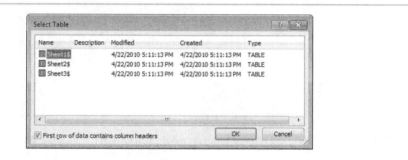

**Figure 10.4**  *Select the table in which the data is located.*

**6.** Verify that the First Row of Data Contains Column Headers check box is selected.

**7.** Click OK.

At this point, you should be looking at a dialog box similar to the one shown in Figure 10.5. This dialog box enables you to control which records are and aren't going to be included in your Publisher document once the merge is complete. Given the importance of this dialog box, I want to take a break from the step-by-step instructions and explain how it works.

As you look at Figure 10.5, the first thing you will probably notice is that the individual columns from my spreadsheet are being displayed. You will also notice that there is a header row that indicates the type of data that is in each column; for example, the Name column contains the names of the people whose contact information is included in the spreadsheet. Publisher is able to classify each column because the top row in my spreadsheet was a column header. You will also recall that in step 6, we actually select the check box that told Publisher to acknowledge the first row of data as a column header.

As I mentioned before, the whole purpose of the screen is to enable you to choose which records should be included in your mail merge. In this particular case, it would be really easy to choose because I am using such a short spreadsheet. If I wanted to omit any of the names from my mail merge, I could simply deselect the check box that goes along with the name that I want to leave out.

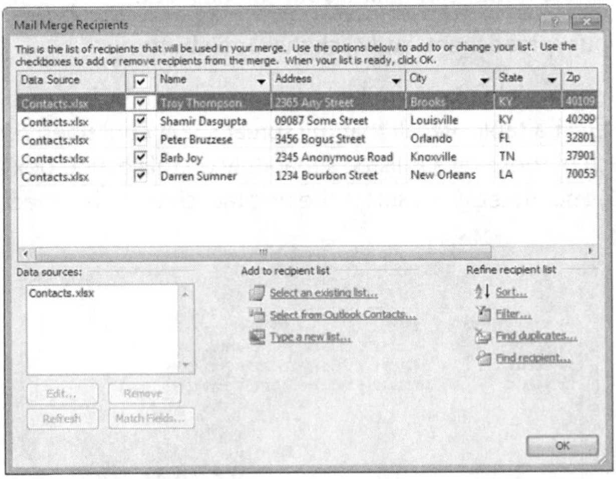

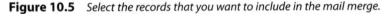

**Figure 10.5**  *Select the records that you want to include in the mail merge.*

In the real world, mail merges aren't always this easy. A spreadsheet filled with contact information can contain many thousands of records. Selecting or deselecting records individually just isn't practical when you're dealing with large data sets. Thankfully, Publisher gives you a few tools that you can use to make the process easier.

If you look underneath of the list of spreadsheet records, notice that there is a section titled Refine Recipient List. This section contains links that you can use to help you narrow down the list. For instance, you have the option of sorting the list or finding duplicate records. There is also a filter option that you can use to narrow down large data sets.

 **LET ME TRY IT**

## Filtering

If you refer to Figure 10.5, you will notice that two of the names on the list reside in Kentucky. Let's pretend that I was creating an invitation to an event that just happens to be in Kentucky, and that I want to invite only Kentucky residents. With such a short list, it would be easy to deselect the three people who live in other states. Just for kicks, though, let's create a filter that narrows down the list based on the state in which each person lives. To do so, follow these steps:

1. Click the Filter link.

2. Choose State from the Field drop down list.

3.  Set the Comparison option to Equal To.

4.  Enter KY in the Compare To field, as shown in Figure 10.6.

5.  Click OK.

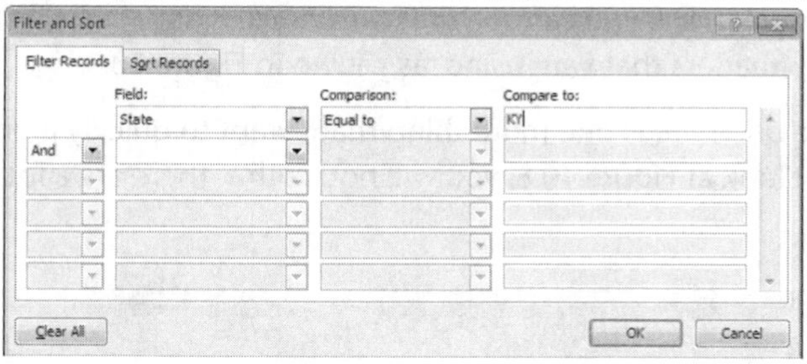

**Figure 10.6** *You can filter your data set.*

When you click OK, only those people who live in Kentucky remain on the list, as shown in Figure 10.7.

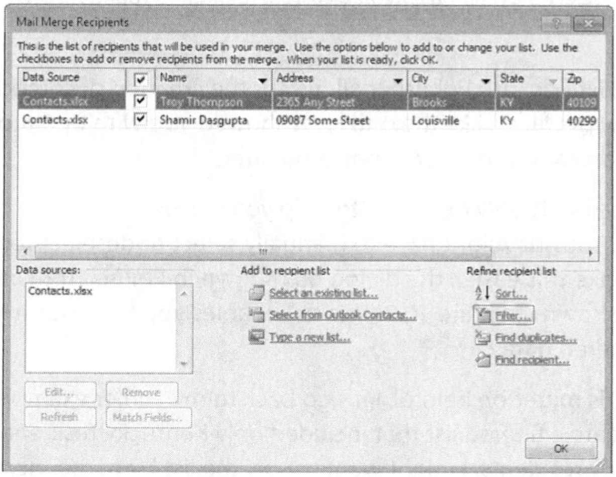

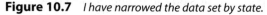

**Figure 10.7** *I have narrowed the data set by state.*

**SHOW ME**   Media 10.1—Filtering
*Access this video file through your registered Web edition at*
***my.safaribooksonline.com/9780132182591/media.***

At first, it might seem kind of convenient that Publisher allowed me to filter my data based on the state. However, the State filter isn't something that's built in to publisher. The available filters match the names of the headers used in my data set.

To show you what I mean, I am going to click the Filter link one more time, and then click the Clear All button to get rid of the filter. Now, if I click on the arrow on the Field dropdown list, you can see that the choices that are available are an exact match for the headers that I am using, as shown in Figure 10.8.

Before I move on, there is one more thing that I want to quickly mention about filtering. As you look at Figure 10.8, you will notice that there are a lot of empty rows.

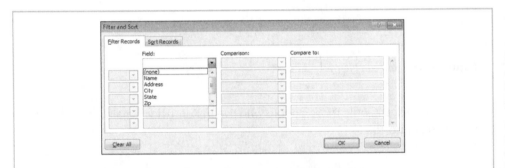

**Figure 10.8**   *Select the filtering criteria is custom tailored to your data set.*

These rows exist because Publisher allows for the creation of compound filters. By combining simple filters like the one I just showed you with operators such as And and Or, you can create some very powerful filters.

Of course, filtering is only designed to help you narrow down your data set prior to a mail merge. You still might have to manually select or deselect some individual records. To make this easier, the dialog box shown in Figure 10.8 contains a Sort Records tab, shown in Figure 10.9. This tab enables you to perform multilevel sorting on the filtered data.

To see how this might be helpful, let's go back to my earlier example in which I wanted to create a filtered list that included only Kentucky residents. If I had a long list of Kentucky residents, I might want to sort the list by name, city, or ZIP code. Because Publisher enables you to perform sorts on three different levels, it would be possible to sort the Kentucky residents by city, and then by ZIP code, and then alphabetize the names within each ZIP code. My point is that you can get very creative with filtering and sorting, and these powerful features can go a long way toward helping you narrow down your data set.

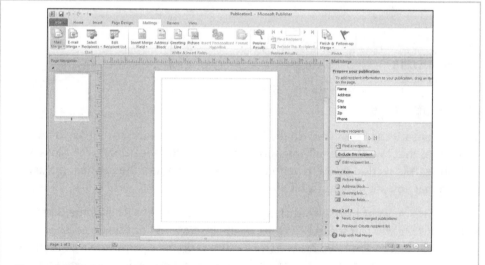

**Figure 10.9** *Publisher makes it easy to sort filtered data.*

# Adding Merge Fields to Your Document

Now that we have selected the records that we will be merging into our Publisher document, it is time to tell Publisher how those records should be displayed. At the present time, you should be looking at a screen similar to the one shown in Figure 10.10.

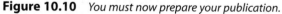

**Figure 10.10** *You must now prepare your publication.*

In Figure 10.10, notice that the Mail Merge section contains an area called Prepare Your Publication. This area lists each of the fields that we imported from the spreadsheet. To use these fields, all we have to do is click our text box to select it, and then double-click on the various fields to add them to the Publisher document.

Figure 10.11 shows what happens when you add the data fields to your Publisher document. As you can see in the figure, each field's name is listed between two

pairs of greater-than and less-than signs. It is worth noting that if you simply double-click on each available field, the fields will be crammed together in your document. The fields that you see within the document in the screen capture weren't
arranged that way by default—I took the time to organize them in a meaningful
way, just as you would do if you were creating a real mail merge document.

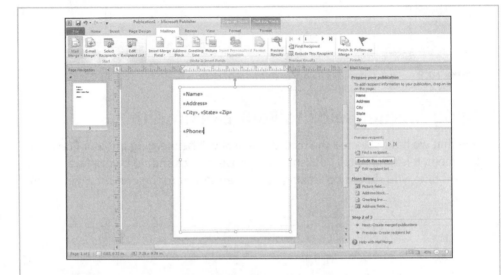

**Figure 10.11**    *Placeholders for the fields appear within your document.*

## More Options

Just beneath the list of fields in the Prepare Your Publication section are a few more
features that I want to briefly mention. The first of these features is the More Items
feature. This section contains various options that are designed to help make the
data that you are merging a bit more personable.

To show you what I am talking about, watch what happens if I click the Greeting
Line link. As you can see in Figure 10.12, the Insert Greeting Line dialog box automatically inserts the word Dear in front of the recipient's name and a comma after
it. The dropdown list that presently has someone's name in it allows you to choose
the format in which the name will be displayed. As you can see in Figure 10.13,
there are many different options. Finally, the dialog box also contains a generic
block of text (Dear Sir or Madam,) that will be inserted if Publisher is not able to
create the desired name format based on your data.

In case you are wondering, it is up to you match your data to the fields used by the
Greeting Line and similar functions. If you click the Match Fields button, shown in
Figure 10.13, you will be taken to the dialog box shown in Figure 10.14, which lets
you pick how you want your fields to be used.

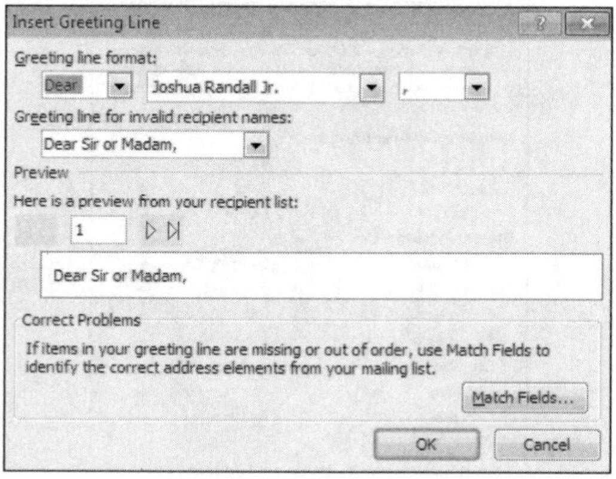

**Figure 10.12**    *The Insert Greeting Line dialog box makes it easy to create formal greetings.*

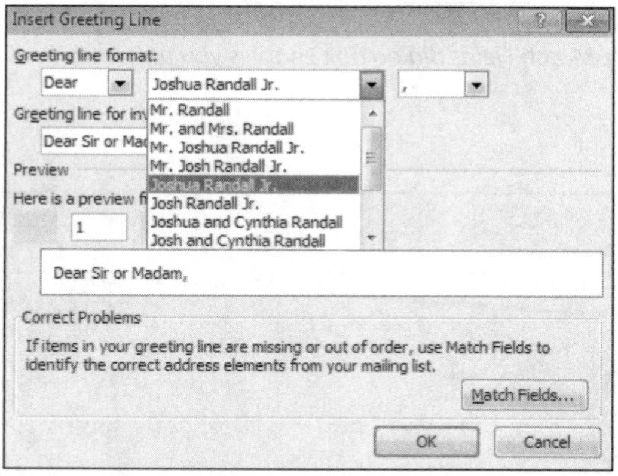

**Figure 10.13**    *Names can be displayed in numerous formats.*

Before I move on, I want to emphasize that the Greeting line function and the other functions found in the More Items section are completely optional. Publisher provides these functions as a way of making the mail merge process easier on you, but you do not have to use these functions unless you want to.

## Performing the Mail Merge

After all of our hard work, it is finally time to perform the actual mail merge. To do so, click the Next: Create Merged Publications link. As you can see in Figure 10.15, the resulting screen gives you three different choices for how the merge should progress.

**Match Fields**

In order to use special features, Mail Merge needs to know which fields in your recipient list match to the required fields. Use the drop-down list to select the appropriate recipient list field for each address field component

**Required for Greeting Line**

| | |
|---|---|
| First Name | (not matched) |
| Last Name | Name |
| Suffix | (not matched) |

**Optional information**

| | |
|---|---|
| Unique Identifier | (not matched) |
| Courtesy Title | (not matched) |
| Middle Name | (not matched) |
| Nickname | (not matched) |
| Job Title | (not matched) |
| Company | (not matched) |
| Address 1 | Address |
| Address 2 | (not matched) |

Use the drop-down lists to choose the field from your database that corresponds to the address information Mail Merge expects (listed on the left.)

☐ Remember this matching for this set of data sources on this computer

[ OK ]  [ Cancel ]

**Figure 10.14** *The Match Fields dialog box enables you to control how your data fields should be used by Publisher.*

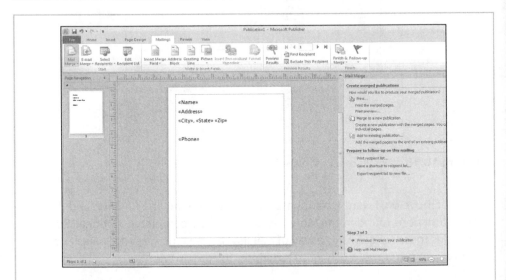

**Figure 10.15** *You have three different options for creating the merged publication.*

The first option is to print the publication. Choosing this option causes Publisher to display a preview of the merged document, as shown in Figure 10.16. As you can see in the figure, you can print the document by clicking the Print button.

**Figure 10.16**   *The Print option makes it easy to print your merged document.*

The second option is Merge to a New Publication. When you choose this option, Publisher creates a brand-new document and places each merged record on a separate page. The advantage to using this option is that after the merge process completes, you can save the new document so that you can use it repeatedly.

The last option is to add the merged data to an existing publication. This option is similar to the previous option but with one big difference. Rather than a new document being created, the pages containing your document with the merged data are appended to the end of another document.

**SHOW ME**   **Media 10.2—A Basic Mail Merge**
*Access this video file through your registered Web edition at*
*my.safaribooksonline.com/9780132182591/media.*

## Alternative Data Sources

Earlier I mentioned that Publisher was capable of importing mail merge data from a number of different data sources. Some of the data sources that Publisher supports include Microsoft Access, SQL Server, Outlook, and Oracle. Because this book focuses on Microsoft Office, I want to show you how to perform a mail merge using Microsoft Access and Outlook.

For the most part, the mail merge procedure is identical regardless of the data source that you choose to use. That being the case, I'm not going to bore you by repeating the entire procedure again. I am only going to show you those portions of the process that are different from what I have already gone through.

 **LET ME TRY IT**

## Microsoft Access

Reading data from a Microsoft Access database really isn't that much different from extracting data from an Excel spreadsheet. Begin the process by launching the Mail Merge Wizard. When you get to the screen that asks you to select a data source, follow these steps:

1. Type the letter of the drive containing your spreadsheet into the File Name field, and press Enter. For example, if your spreadsheet is located in a folder named C:\Documents, you would enter C:.

2. Browse to the folder containing your Access database.

3. Select the database, and click the Open button.

4. Verify that Publisher displays the database's contents in a legible manner, as shown in Figure 10.17.

5. Click OK.

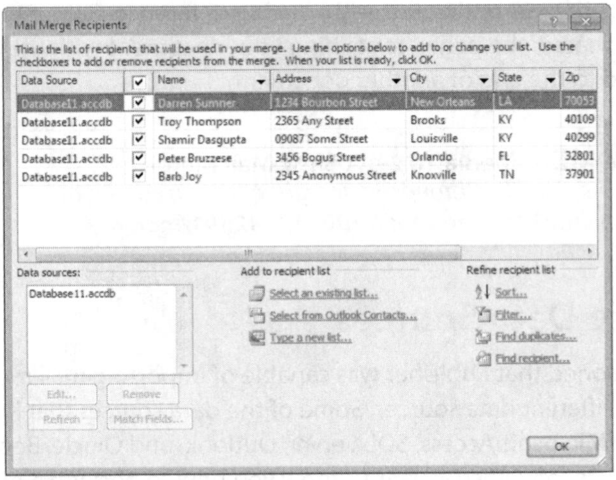

**Figure 10.17** *Verify that the database records are displayed correctly.*

**LET ME TRY IT**

## Working with Microsoft Outlook

You can include Microsoft Outlook contacts in a mail merge, but the procedure for doing so works quite a bit differently from what you used to import Excel and Access data. To import Outlook contacts, follow these steps:

1. Go to Publisher's Mailings tab.

2. Click on the down arrow on the Select Recipients icon.

3. Choose the Select from Outlook Contacts option, shown in Figure 10.18.

**Figure 10.18**   *Choose the Select from Outlook Contacts option.*

4. When prompted, select the Outlook data file that you want to pull the contacts from, as shown in Figure 10.19.

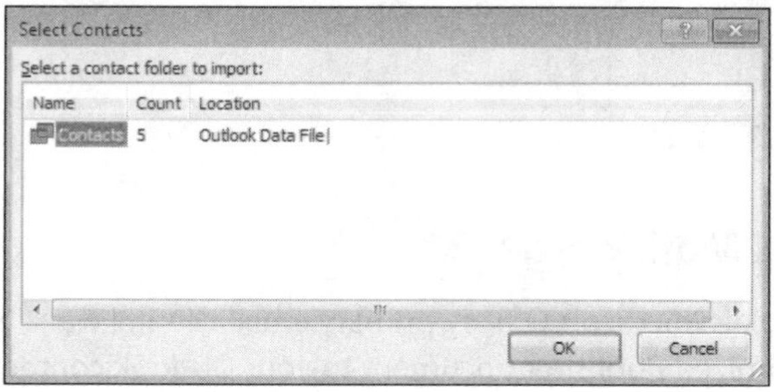

**Figure 10.19**   *Choose the Outlook data file that you want to use.*

5. Click OK.

6. Click the down arrow on the Mail Merge icon.

7. Choose the Step By Step Mail Merge Wizard option.

You can now begin including the various fields in your Publisher document. If you look at Figure 10.19, notice that the field names are different than they were when we were using Excel and Access as a data source. This is because Excel spreadsheets and Access databases contain user-defined fields. Outlook contacts, on the other hand, use a ridged set of predefined fields. It is also worth noting that because the fields are predefined, not every field will end up containing data. For example, in the screen capture shown in Figure 10.20, Publisher allows me to use the Company and Department fields, even though I have never populated those fields.

## Email Merge

Although I certainly don't condone spamming, there is a way to use Microsoft Publisher 2010 to send personalized email messages in bulk. The technique that I am about to show you is known as an Email Merge. As is the case with a regular mail merge, you can use a variety of different data sources, such as spreadsheets, databases, or Outlook contacts.

As you may recall, Publisher contains a Design Checker that you can use to finalize a document. The Design Checker offers a Run Email Checks option that you can use to prepare your document for distribution. This portion of the design checker primarily looks for the use of non-Web Ready fonts, which will have to be converted to a graphical image before the document can be sent. You can access the Design Checker by choosing the Info option from Publisher's File menu, and then clicking the Run Design Checker icon.

 **LET ME TRY IT**

## Performing a Mail Merge

Because Outlook is Microsoft Office's primary email client, I want to show you how to send a customized Publisher document to your Outlook contacts. In doing so, I am assuming that you have created some Outlook contacts and that Outlook is connected to an email account.

To perform an email merge, follow these steps:

1. Create a text box within your Publisher document.

2. Go to Publisher's Mailings tab.

3. Click the down arrow on the E-Mail Merge icon.

4. Choose the Step by Step E-Mail Merge Wizard option from the E-Mail Merge menu.

5. When the E-Mail Merge Wizard opens, choose the Select from Outlook Contacts option.

6. Click the Next: Create or Connect to a Recipient List link.

7. Choose the contact folder that you want to import, and click OK.

8. On the following screen, select the recipients that you want to include in the mail merge.

9. Prepare your publication by double-clicking on the fields that you want to include in the document, and then arranging them accordingly.

10. Click the Next: Create Merged Publications link.

11. On the following screen, click the E-Mail Preview link to see a preview of what the finished document will look like. When you are done, close the preview window.

12. Click the Send E-Mail link.

13. Verify that the To field contains the words Email Address, as shown in Figure 10.20.

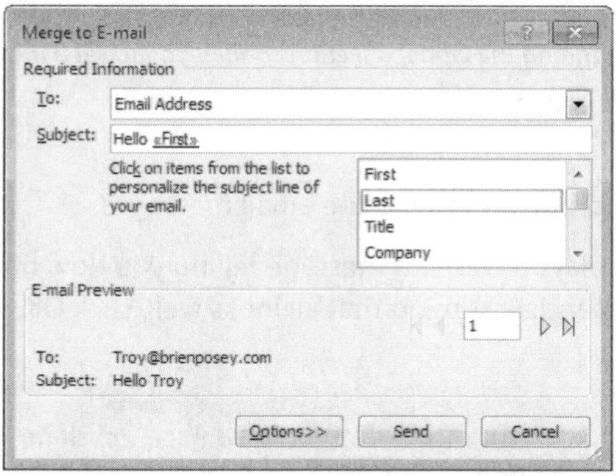

**Figure 10.20**    *You can customize the subject line to include personal information.*

14. Type the desired message subject line. You can personalize the subject line by including Outlook fields from the list beneath the subject line. The

figure shows an example of the recipient's first name being included in the subject line.

15. Click the Options button.

16. You may now specify a CC or BCC recipient, set the message's priority, or include an attachment, as shown in Figure 10.21.

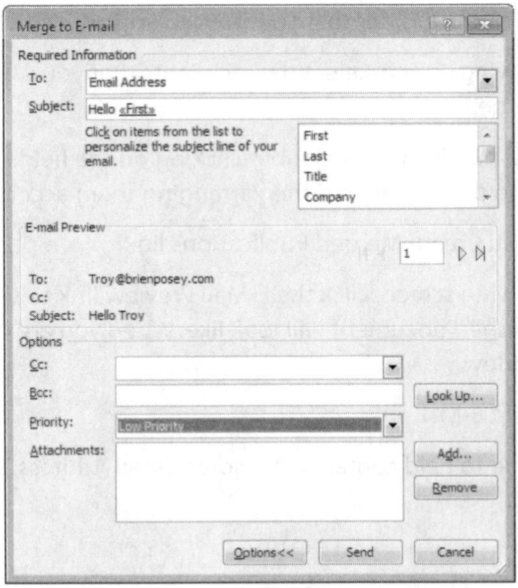

**Figure 10.21** *Expanding the Options section enables you to set a message's priority or include attachments.*

17. Click the Send button to send the email messages.

18. Publisher displays a warning message telling you how many messages you are about to send. Assuming that all looks well, click OK.

Publisher will allow you to send as many customized email messages as you like. Before you decide to do any mass mailings, though, keep in mind that even though Publisher won't stop you from sending out a billion email messages, your Internet Service Provider (ISP) probably will. If you don't have any documents to open, click the Documents stack icon in the Dock, and then click the icon for the file named About Stacks.pdf. The document opens in the application called Preview.

Most ISPs don't want to risk being blacklisted for allowing their IP addresses to be used for sending spam. As such, if an ISP detects a large amount of SMTP traffic (network geek speak for email messages) coming from one of their customers, they will probably block the traffic midstream.

To give you a more concrete example, I used to send out technology-related newsletters by email. At its peak, my newsletter had more than 30,000 subscribers. Unfortunately, though, my ISP started putting a stop to mail blasts after the first 20 messages.

 **SHOW ME**    Media 10.3—E-mail Merge
*Access this video file through your registered Web edition at*
**my.safaribooksonline.com/9780132182591/media**.

# The Recipient Experience

Right now, you might be wondering what a Publisher document looks like to the recipients when the document is sent by email. The answer is that it really just depends on what type of mail client the recipient is using. If the recipient is using Outlook 2010, the email message looks just like the original Publisher document. Of course, not everyone in the world uses Outlook 2010, so I recommend experimenting with various types of mail clients before you put a lot of work into a document. That way, you can get a feel for what your message might look like to those who receive it.

# Snail Mail

Back in Chapter 7, "Finalizing Your Publisher Document," I showed you how to include your business information in Publisher's metadata. I want to wrap up things by showing you how you can use your business information to your advantage in a mail merge document.

In many cases, if you are creating customized mail merge documents, you will be mailing those documents to the recipients. As you may recall, Publisher provides numerous document templates that you can use to expedite the creation of various types of documents. Among these templates are envelope templates and label templates.

## LET ME TRY IT

# Printing Custom Envelopes

With that in mind, let's take a look at how to print customized envelopes to go along with our customized Publisher document:

1.  Create a new Publisher document based on the Envelopes template. You can see an example of such a template in Figure 10.22. The actual layout might vary a bit depending on which template you choose.

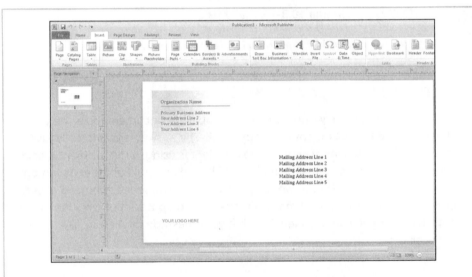

**Figure 10.22**  *Publisher enables you to create personalized envelopes.*

2.  Click the Organization Name. When you do, Publisher enables you to click an icon that displays a dropdown menu, as shown in Figure 10.23.

3.  Choose the Update from Business Information Set option from the menu. When you do, the text that says Organization Name will be replaced by the name of your business.

4.  Click on the return address, and then click the resulting icon to access the dropdown menu.

5.  Choose the Update from Business Information Set option. Publisher should now display your business's address.

6.  If you have added your business logo to Publisher's business information, you can click the Your Logo Here text. Upon doing so, Publisher displays the

now-familiar icon, which you can click to access the dropdown menu. Choose the Update from Business Information Set option, and your logo will be added to the envelope, as shown in Figure 10.24. Incidentally, the address shown in the figure is not my real address.

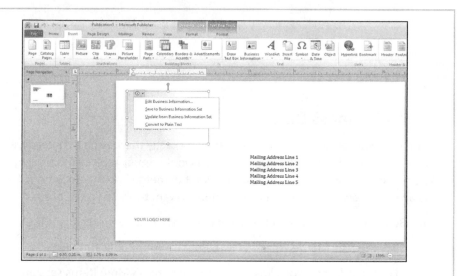

**Figure 10.23** *The dropdown menu enables you to populate your document with business information.*

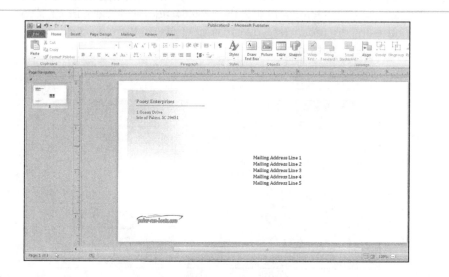

**Figure 10.24** *The envelope now contains our business information.*

Although you can insert business information into a document using the method I just showed you, this isn't the only way to get business information into your document. Publisher's Insert tab contains a Business Information icon. You can use this icon's dropdown menu to insert various pieces of business information into your document without having to retype it each time.

## LET ME TRY IT

## Merging Business Data

From here, you could perform a mail merge in exactly the way I have already shown you. If you wanted to use this approach, you would simply replace the Mailing Address Line text with the fields that you want to merge into the document. Because you already know about this method, though, I want to show you a shortcut:

1. Begin the mail merge in the usual way, and create your recipient list.

2. Click the Mail Merge Wizard's Next: Prepare Your Publication Link.

3. Click the Address Block link, found in the wizard's More Items section.

4. Use the Insert Address Block dialog box shown in Figure 10.25 to format the recipient's name. You should also verify that the Insert Postal Address check box is selected and that the preview address looks correct. If you notice any discrepancies, you can correct the problem by clicking the Match Fields button.

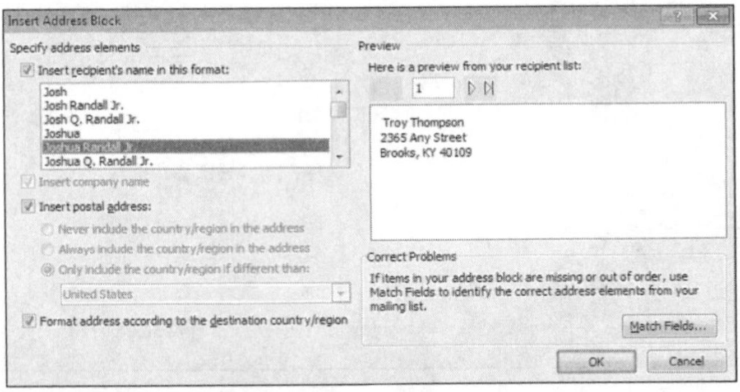

**Figure 10.25**  *Use the Insert Address Block dialog box to format the recipient's address.*

5. Click OK.

6. Publisher creates a new text box containing the phrase <<Address Block>>. Select this text, and press Ctrl+C to copy it to the clipboard.

7. Delete the new text box.

8. Select the text box containing the Mailing Address Line text.

9. Delete all the text from the text box, but do not delete the text box itself.

10. Press Ctrl+V to paste the address block into the text box, as shown in Figure 10.26.

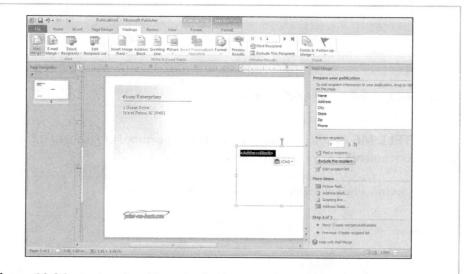

**Figure 10.26**   *Replace the address placeholder text with <<Address Block>>.*

11. Click the Next: Create Merged Publications link and complete the mail merge process.

Figure 10.27 shows the results of the merge process. As you can see, each page of the document contains a separate customized envelope.

Although the idea of printing personalized envelopes might seem a little odd, it works better than you might think. Back in the mid-1990s, a charity that I was volunteering for asked me to assist in a mass mailing. At the time, I was working a lot of hours and was also still in college. I didn't have time to address all those envelopes by hand. I knew that Microsoft Word could print personalized envelopes, but I wasn't sure about the actual printing. As it turned out, though, my printer had no trouble printing a stack of envelopes. All I had to do was adjust the paper tray to fit the size of the envelopes that I was printing, and Word did the rest.

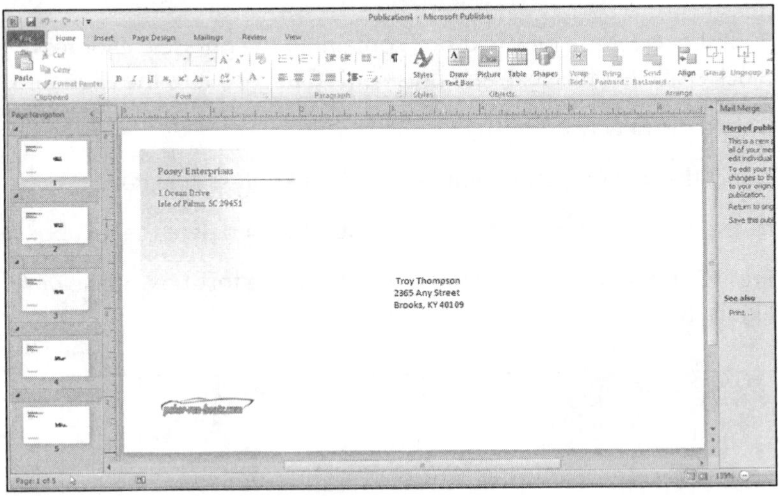

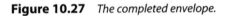

**Figure 10.27**   *The completed envelope.*

**TELL ME MORE**     Media 10.4—The Importance of Reviewing Your
Documents Before Merging Business Data

*To listen to a free audio recording about reviewing your documents, log on to*
*my.safaribooksonline.com/9780132182591/media.*

# index

## Numbers

3-D effects
  shapes, adding, 75
  Word art, creating,
    104-105

## A

Access, mail merges, 246-247

aligning text, 134

alignments, table cells,
  148-150

alternative document types,
  47-49

alternative text, web pages,
  212-214

art. *See* clip art; graphics

## B

backgrounds
  pages, changing, 40
  shapes, pushing to, 77-79

backstage view, 18-19

bookmarks, web pages,
  217-218

borders
  art, 144
  images, wrapping around,
    174-175
  tables, 143-145

Brochure template, 42-41

building blocks, creating,
  105-107

built-in guides, 27

bulk mailing. *See* mail merges

business data, merging,
  254-256

## C

calendars
  creating, 85-88
  photographs, replacing,
    86-88

captions, 63-70
  color, changing, 64-66
  gradients, 66-68
  inserting, 63-64
  patterns, 68
  photographs, 68-70
  textures, 67-68
  tint, 70

cells, tables
  alignments, 148-150
  margins, 148-150
  merging split, 153-155

charts (Excel)
  creating, 161-165
  designing, 162-163
  displaying, 163
  tables, importing to,
    160-165
  text, controlling within,
    164-165

clean installations, Office
  2010, 13-14

clear type, enabling, 56-57

clip art, 71-72
  copyright issues, 73
  key word searches, 73

CMYK color model, printing,
  195

CoCo (Radio Shack TRS-80
  Color Computer), 5-6

color effects, Word art, 100

color models, printing,
  190, 193-201

color schemes, 92-95

coloring
  shapes, 76-77
  Word art, 100-103

colors, captions, changing,
  64-66

columns
  tables
    *deleting, 153*
    *inserting, 152*
  text, 134-135

commercial printing. *See*
  professional printing

compact fonts, 169-170

costs, professional printing,
  191
  saving, 204-206

custom color schemes,
  creating, 95

custom envelopes, printing,
  252-254

custom margins, 23-24

Custom tab, offset printing,
  200

custom templates, creating,
  45-47

## D

data sources, mail merges,
  245-246

deadlines, professional
  printing, 205

deleting
  columns, tables, 153
  rows, tables, 153

Design Checker,
  181-185, 227-228
  accessing, 181

design elements, relocating,
  175

designing
Excel charts, 162-163
tables, 151
desktop publishing software,
early forms of, 6-7
diagonals, tables, 153-154
dictation software, proofreading documents, 168
directing, text, 133
DirectX Diagnostic Tool,
hardware verification, 11-12
displaying
documents, 18
Excel charts, 163
Excel spreadsheets as
icons, 160
DNS entries, websites,
230-231
documents, 167
alternative document
types, 47-49
calendars, creating, 86-88
color schemes, 94
creating, 21-22, 49-50
templates, 21
display, 18
finalizing, Design Checker,
181-185
fonts, compact fonts,
169-170
greeting cards, creating,
92
grid guides, 25-27
HTML documents,
217-218
alternative text,
212-214
bookmarks, 217
creating, 215-217
hyperlinks, 219
parts, 210-212
previewing, 221-222
publishing, 207-210
web templates, 220-221
margins, 22-24
custom margins, 23-24
merge fields, adding to,
241-245
metadata, 177-179

multipage documents,
109-110
adding images to,
120-124
formatting text boxes,
132-137
importing Word
documents, 118-125
master pages, 113-118
text boxes, 110-113
opening, 50
page backgrounds,
changing, 40
page orientation, 37-38
changing, 37-38
pages, sizes, 38-39
postcards, creating, 90-91
printing, 187-190
color models,
190, 193-201
duplex printing, 190
offset printing, 196-197
page layout, 189
page ranges, 189
paper size, 190
professional printing,
190-193
troubleshooting,
187-188
proofreading, 167-169
saving, 47-49
shapes, inserting, 74-75
spacing, adjusting,
169-175
subheads, adding, 174
tables
borders, 143-145
creating, 140
designing, 151
fill effects, 143
formats, 151
formatting, 141-150
importing Excel charts,
160-165
importing Excel
spreadsheets, 155-160
layout, 151-155
resizing, 141-143
rotating, 146-147
text wrapping, 147-148
templates, 40-47
Brochure template,
42-41
changing, 45

creating, 45-47
locally installed
templates, 43-44
web-based templates,
41
test printing, 175
text, 139-140
text boxes, spacing,
170-171
Word art, inserting, 96-98
domain names, acquiring,
229
drawings, 80-82
Drop Cap feature, 135-136
duplex printing, 190

## E

editing
hyperlinks, 207
master pages, 116
email links, creating, 216-217
email merges, 248-250
enlarging, rulers, 32
envelopes, printing, 252-254
Equation Editor, 82-83
equations, creating, 82-83
Excel charts
creating, 161-165
designing, 162-163
displaying, 163
tables, importing to,
160-165
text, controlling within,
164-165
Excel spreadsheets
creating, 155
displaying as icons, 160
linking, 159

## F

files. See also documents
PDF files, creating, 185
XPS files, creating, 185
fill effects, tables, 143
filtering, recipient lists,
238-240

fitting, text, 132-133

fonts, 54-63
  clear type, 56-57
  compact fonts, 169-170
  installing, 56-59
  pictures, inserting, 59
  previewing, 56-59
  purchasing, 54-56
  typography, 56

Form Controls icon (Web tab), 225-226

formats, tables, 151

formatting
  pictures, 60
  tables, 141-150
  text boxes, 110-111, 132-137

frames, overlapping, 171-172

## G

gradients, captions, 66-68

graphics
  captions, 63-70
  changing, 62-63
  clip art, 71-72
    copyright issues, 73
    key word searches, 73
  drawings, 80-82
  equations, 82-83
  formatting, 60
  multipage documents, adding to, 120-124
  shapes, 62-63, 74-77
    3-D effects, 75
    coloring, 76-77
    inserting, 74-75
  styles, 62-63
  text, inserting, 59
  transparency, 61
  Word art, 96-99, 105
  wrapping text around, 125-131

grayscale color model, printing, 194

greeting cards, creating, 92

grid guides, 25-27

grids, dividing pages into, 25-26

guides
  built-in, 27
  high-precision guides, 29-30
  ruler guides, 27-38
    enabling, 28-29
    multiple ruler guides, 30-32

## H

hardware, verifying, 11-12

hardware requirements, Publisher 2010, 8-12

high-precision guides, 29-30

hosting companies, choosing, 229-230

Hot Spot icon (Web tab), 222-223

HSL color model, printing, 195

HTML Code Fragment option (Web tab), 226

HTML documents
  alternative text, 212-214
  bookmarks, 217-218
  creating, 215-216
  email links, creating, 216-217
  hyperlinks
    changing appearance, 219-220
    editing, 207
  merge fields, adding to, 241-245
  parts, 210-212
  previewing, 221-222
  simple web pages, creating, 207-210
  web templates, 220-221

hyperlinks
  appearance, changing, 219-220
  editing, 219
  web pages, creating, 214-215

hyphenation, text, 134

## I

icons, Excel spreadsheets, displaying as, 160

image controls, 19-20

images. See also graphics
  borders, wrapping around, 174-175
  captions, 63-70
  changing, 62-63
  clip art, 71-72
    copyright issues, 73
    key word searches, 73
  formatting, 60
  multipage documents, adding to, 120-124
  shapes, 62-63
  styles, 62-63
  text, installing, 59
  transparency, 61
  wrapping text around, 125-131

importing
  Excel spreadsheets, tables, 155-160
  information, recipient lists, 236-238
  Word documents, 118-125

ink colors, professional printing, 205

inserting
  captions, 63-64
  clip art, 71-72
  shapes, 74-75

installation, Publisher 2010, 5

installing
  fonts, 56-59
  Office 2010, 12-16

irregularly shaped images, wrapping text around, 129-131

## L

layering, 77-79

layout
  tables, 151-155
  text boxes, 113

linking, text boxes, 111-112

lithography. *See* offset printing

locally installed templates, 43-44

long documents, 109-110
    images
        *adding to, 120-124*
        *wrapping text around, 125-131*
    master pages, 113-118
    text boxes, 110-113
        *formatting, 132-137*
    Word documents, importing, 118-125

## M

mail merges, 233
    creating, 233-243
    data sources, 245-248
    email merges, 248-250
    performing, 243-246
    recipient lists, creating, 235-240
    traditional mail, 250-256

margins, 22-24
    custom margins, 23-24
    table cells, 148-150

master pages
    applying, 115-116
    creating, 114-115
    editing, 116
    multipage documents, 113-118
    multiple master pages, 116-117

merge fields, documents, adding to, 241-245

merges (mail), 233
    creating, 233-243
    data sources, 245-248
    email merges, 248-250
    performing, 243-246
    recipient lists, creating, 235-240
    traditional mail, 250-256

merging split cells, tables, 153-155

metadata, 177-179

Microsoft Access, mail merges, 246-247

Microsoft Outlook, mail merges, 247-248

Microsoft Publisher 2010. *See* Publisher 2010

minimum requirements, Publisher 2010, 8-12

mistakes, professional printing, 192

moving, rulers, 33-35

multipage documents, 109-110
    images
        *adding to, 120-124*
        *wrapping text around, 125-131*
    master pages, 113-118
    text boxes, 110-113
        *formatting, 132-137*
    Word documents, importing, 118-125

multiple master pages, 116-117

multiple ruler guides, 30-32

## N

navigating, text boxes, 112

Navigation Bar icon (Web tab), 223-225

new features, Publisher 2010, 16-20

number styles, text, 137

## O

objects, building blocks, converting into, 107-108

Office 2007, upgrading from, 14

Office 2010
    installing, 12-16
    minimum requirements, 9
    uninstalling, 15-16
    upgrading to, 14

offset printing, 196-197
    color models, 197
    Custom tab, 200
    PANTONE tab, 200-201
    spot colors, 198-200
    Standard tab, 200

online publishing, 207
    simple web pages
        *creating, 207-210*
        *parts, 210-212*
    web pages
        *alternative text, 212-214*
        *bookmarks, 217-218*
        *creating, 215-216*
        *email links, 216-217*
        *hyperlinks, 214-220*
    websites, 228-231

opening, documents, 50

operating systems, requirements, 10

outer edges, shapes, coloring, 77

Outlook, mail merges, 247-248

overlapping, frames, 171-172

## P

packaging, professional printing, 202-204

page layout, printing, 189

page orientation, 37-38
    changing, 37-38

page ranges, printing documents, 189

pages
    backgrounds, changing, 40
    dividing into grids, 25-26
    master pages, 113-118
        *applying, 115-116*
        *creating, 114-115*
        *editing, 116*
        *multiple master pages, 116-117*
    sizes, changing, 38-39

Paintbrush, drawings, creating, 80-82

PANTONE tab, offset printing,
200-201

paper size, printing
documents, 190

paper stock, professional
printing, choosing, 204

patterns, captions, 68

PDF files, 18
creating, 185

photographs
calendars, replacing,
86-88
captions, 68-70

pictures. *See also* graphics;
photographs
captions, 63-70
*changing colors, 64-66*
*gradients, 66-68*
*inserting, 63-64*
*patterns, 68*
*photographs, 68-70*
*textures, 67-68*
changing, 62-63
clip art, 71-72
*copyright issues, 73*
*key word searches, 73*
formatting, 60
shapes, 62-63
styles, 62-63
text, inserting, 59
transparency, 61

postcards, creating, 90-91

predefined templates,
21, 40-47
Brochure template, 42-41
changing, 45
creating, 45-47
locally installed tem-
plates, 43-44
web-based templates, 41

previewing
fonts, 56-59
websites, 221-222

printers, commercial printing,
206

printing
documents,
187

*color models,*
*190, 193-201*
*duplex printing, 190*
*offset printing, 196-197*
*page layout, 189*
*page ranges, 189*
*paper size, 190*
*professional printing,*
*190-193*
*test printing, 175*
*troubleshooting,*
*187-188*
envelopes, 252-254
professional printing
*expectations, 201-204*
*saving, 204-206*

printing devices, commercial
printing, 206

professional printing,
190-193
costs, saving, 204-206
deadlines, 205
expectations, 201-204
file preparation, 205
ink colors, 205
packaging, 202-204
paper stock, choosing,
204
printers, 206
proofs, 204
quantity, 205

proofreading documents,
167-169

proofs, professional printing,
204

Publisher 2010, 1-2, 7-8
benefits, 1-2
documents
*display, 18*
*printing, 18*
image controls, 19-20
installing, 5
new features, 16-20
PDF files, 18
ribbon, 16-17
system requirements,
8-12
views, backstage, 18-19
Web mode, 20
websites, creating, 207

versus Word, 7
XPS files, 18

publishing (online), 207
simple web pages
*creating, 207-210*
*parts, 210-212*
web pages
*alternative text,*
*212-214*
*bookmarks, 217-218*
*creating, 215-216*
*email links, 216-217*
*hyperlinks,*
*214-220*
websites, 228-231

purchasing fonts, 54-56

# R

Radio Shack TRS-80 Color
Computer (CoCo), 5-6

recipient lists, mail merges
creating, 235-240
filtering, 238-240
importing information to,
236-238

resizing, tables, 141-143

RGB (red, green, blue) color
model, printing, 194

ribbon, 16-17

rotating, tables, 146-147

rows, tables
deleting, 153
inserting, 152

ruler guides, 27-38
enabling, 28-29
multiple ruler guides,
30-32

rulers
disabling, 32
enabling, 32
enlarging, 32
moving, 33-35
units of measurement,
changing, 33
zero mark, moving, 35-38

# S

saving
  documents, 47-49
  metadata, 178-179

shadow effects, Word art,
  creating, 103-104

shapes, 74-77
  3-D effects, adding, 75
  backgrounds, pushing to,
    77-79
  coloring, 76-77
  inserting, 74-75
  pictures, 62-63
  shifting, 105

Share option, HTML
  documents, publishing, 209

simple web pages, 207-210
  creating, 207-210

sizes, pages, 38-39

spacing
  documents, adjusting,
    169-175
  Word art, changing,
    99-100

spot colors, offset printing,
  198-200

spreadsheets (Excel)
  creating, 155
  displaying as icons, 160
  linking, 159
  tables, importing to,
    155-160

Standard tab, offset printing,
  200

stock, professional printing,
  choosing, 204

styles, pictures, 62-63

subheads, spacing, 174

switching, templates, 45

system requirements,
  Publisher 2010, 8-12

# T

tables, 139-140
  borders, 143-145

cells
  alignments, 148-150
  margins, 148-150
  merging split, 153-155
columns
  deleting, 153
  inserting, 152
creating, 140
designing, 151
diagonals, 153-154
Excel charts, importing to,
  160-165
Excel spreadsheets,
  importing to, 155-160
fill effects, 143
formats, 151
formatting, 141-150
layout, 151-155
resizing, 141-143
rotating, 146-147
rows
  deleting, 153
  inserting, 152
text wrapping, 147-148

templates, 21, 40-47
  Brochure template, 42-41
  changing, 45
  creating, 45-47
  locally installed templates,
    43-44
  web templates, 220-221
  web-based templates, 41

test printing, documents, 175

text
  aligning, 134
  columns, 134-135
  directing, 133
  Drop Cap feature, 135-136
  Excel charts, controlling
    within, 164-165
  fitting, 132-133
  fonts, 54-63
    clear type, 56-57
    inserting pictures, 59
    installing, 56-59
    previewing, 56-59
    purchasing, 54-56
    typography, 56
  hyphenation, 134
  images, wrapping around,
    125-131

number styles, 137
tables, wrapping around,
  147-148
text boxes, entering into,
  53-54
Word art, editing, 98-99
Word documents,
  importing from, 119-120

text boxes, 51-54
  creating, 52-53
  entering text into, 53-54
  formatting,
    110-111, 132-137
  layout, 113
  linking, 111-112
  multipage documents,
    110-113
  navigating, 112
  spacing, 170-171

textures, captions, 67-68

tight wrapping, wrapping
  text around images,
  129-132

tint, captions, 70

troubleshooting, printing,
  187-188

typography, 56

# U

uninstalling, Office 2010,
  15-16

units of measurement, rulers,
  changing, 33

upgrading, Office 2010, 14

uploading, websites, 231

# V

views, backstage, 18-19

visual elements, 51
  captions, 63-70
  clip art, 71-72
  color schemes, 92-95
  drawings, 80-82
  equations, 82-83
  fonts, 54-63
  layering, 77-79

pictures
  *formatting, 60*
  *transparency, 61*
shapes, 74-77
text boxes, 51-54
Word art, 96-105

# W

Web mode, 20

Web Page options (Web tab),
  226-227

web pages
  alternative text, 212-214
  bookmarks, 217-218
  creating, 215-216
  email links, creating,
    216-217
  hyperlinks
    *changing appearance,*
      *219-220*
    *creating, 214-215*
    *editing, 207*
  parts, 210-212
  previewing, 221-222
  simple web pages,
    creating, 207-210
  web templates, 220-221

Web tab, 222-223
  Form Controls icon,
    225-226
  Hot Spot icon, 222-223
  HTML Code Fragment
    option, 226
  Navigation Bar icon,
    223-225
  Web Page options,
    226-227

web templates, 220-221

websites
  creating, 207
  DNS entries, 230-231
  domain names, acquiring,
    229
  hosting companies,
    choosing, 229-230
  previewing, 221-222
  publishing, 228-231

simple web pages,
  creating, 207-210
uploading, 231

Word, versus Publisher, 7

Word art, 96-105
  3-D effects, creating,
    104-105
  color effects, 100
  coloring, 100-103
  inserting, 96-98
  shadow effects, creating,
    103-104
  shapes, shifting, 105
  spacing, changing, 99-100
  text, editing, 98-99

wrapping text around
  images, 125-131

# X

XPS files, 18
  creating, 185

# Z

zero mark, rulers, moving,
  35-38